SCIENCE
AT THE EXTREME

SCIENCE AT THE EXTREME

Scientists on the Cutting Edge of Discovery

PETER LANE TAYLOR

McGRAW-HILL

New York   San Francisco   Washington, D.C.   Auckland   Bogotá
Caracas   Lisbon   London   Madrid   Mexico City   Milan
Montreal   New Delhi   San Juan   Singapore
Sydney   Tokyo   Toronto

McGraw-Hill

*A Division of The **McGraw·Hill** Companies*

1 2 3 4 5 6 7 8 9 0   DOW/DOW   0 9 8 7 6 5 4 3 2 1 0

ISBN 0-07-135419-0

This book was set in Berkeley Oldstyle Book by North Market Street Graphics.
Printed and bound by R.R. Donnelley & Sons Company.

McGraw-Hill books are available at special quantity discounts to use as premiums and sales promotions, or for use in corporate training programs. For more information, please write to the Director of Special Sales, Professional Publishing, McGraw-Hill, Two Penn Plaza, New York, NY 10121-2298. Or contact your local bookstore.

To all those people who have risked their lives in the pursuit of something greater than themselves.

Ad astra per aspera. . . .
A rough road leads to the stars.

CONTENTS

FOREWORD *by Thomas E. Lovejoy, Smithsonian Institution*   ix

ACKNOWLEDGMENTS   xi

INTRODUCTION: The Next Frontier   1

EARTH: The Timeless World   7
The Comeback King   11
This Is Your Brain. . . . This Is Your Brain on Sulfur   37

AIR: The High Frontier   61
Are You My Mother?   65
Sitting on Top of the World   93
Bridge over Troubled Waters   119

FIRE: The Infernal Planet   147
Too Hot to Handle   151

WATER: Planet Water   175
One Small Step for Inner Space   179
It's All Fun and Games Until Someone Gets Munched   205
The Ice Man Cometh   231

SOURCES   259

FOREWORD

Some of my heroes when I was growing up were the modern-day versions of nineteenth-century naturalist explorers. The giant of them all, in my youthful view, was William Beebe of the New York Zoological Society, who actually lived for long stretches of time in the tropics at "Simla in Trinidad," and who also had descended deep into the ocean in a bathyscape.

There were also huge areas of the globe which were relatively unexplored. When I went to the Brazilian Amazon early in graduate school, there was but one road in all of Amazonia, and indigenous peoples were still being contacted for the first time. Inevitably, my heart was set on a life as a latter twentieth century explorer-scientist.

Since then, of course, it has become possible to travel to almost anywhere on the globe within 24 hours. Technology has brought us scuba and a vast array of other technologies, so that it is mostly true that there is no such thing as bad conditions, just bad equipment. One might conclude that romance and adventure have parted entirely from scientific investigation.

That is really not the case, for as long as there is human imagination, people will figure out ways in which scientific questions and adventure can coincide. *Science at the Extreme* is an account of some of the current blending of the two. Since one of the unfortunate trends concurrent with easier access to almost everywhere is the accelerating loss of plant and animal species which share the planet with us, sometimes this intersection involves the noble calling of conservation.

In this book you can vicariously accompany Peter Lane Taylor as he joins in the scientific quests of the current generation of explorer-scientists, the spiritual descendants of William Beebe. Tough, challenging, and adventurous as they all are, it is abundantly clear that this is not adventure for adventure's sake. This is adventure with a purpose, namely to advance the scientific understanding of our earth and its living things.

I was startled to discover how many of these examples I relate to in one way or the other. I was involved in the research to understand why peregrine falcons and ospreys were disappearing as well as in bringing back peregrines to New York City. I have floated during the middle of the night in Mamiraua in uneasy proximity to the black caiman. And I once went spelunking in search of an endangered daddy longlegs along the Stanislau River in northern California.

In contrast, however, what is much more interesting is that in almost every one of these examples of extreme or inaccessible environments, there is life. Some species or other has adapted to living in the sulfur caves, the canopy of the redwood forest, or the slopes of Mount Popocatépetl. This is truly a living planet, and the species that live at such extremes, whether surviving a poisonous sulfur cave or the physiological challenge of the peregrine's power dive at speeds approaching 200 miles an hour, illuminate the dimensions of life on earth.

So adventurers these scientists may be, but what drives them is the desire to understand what our living planet is all about. It is an ongoing saga. The men and women who find their William Beebe equivalents in this book will surely find their own way to combine adventure with science and conservation. What an exciting quest it is.

Thomas E. Lovejoy
Smithsonian Institution

ACKNOWLEDGMENTS

No book is a solo endeavor. Since this is no ordinary book, it is even less so. By its very nature, it has involved the help and commitment of hundreds of people worldwide. To some of them, I literally owe my life.

My deepest gratitude goes to the scientists themselves. For at least a month, through battering rainstorms and tent-bound blizzards, they folded me into their lives and tolerated my endless questions, requests, and choreographical needs. Without their enthusiasm and patience, these stories could never have been told.

I am equally indebted to my agent, Nicholas Smith, who in the process of helping to make this project a multifaceted reality, has played the role of a thousand men. I look forward to many more projects to come. My thanks also to his partner, Andrea Pedolsky.

At McGraw-Hill, I owe my sincerest gratitude to Amy Murphy and Griffin Hansbury, who were able to alchemize a coherent book from the masses of material and visions I brought them. Special thanks go also to Mary Glenn and Susan Barry for seeing the project's potential and putting it in the pipeline; to Roger Kasunic and Ede Driekurs for tolerating my impossibly anal photographic demands; and to Lynda Luppino, Claudia Riemer Boutote, Karen Auerbach, Jeannine Brinkman, Michelle Reed, and Jane Palmieri.

And two other people, in particular, deserve special thanks. First is Rand Knight, for his advice, encouragement, and endless reviews of the early manuscripts. This book would not have come out the same without his efforts. Second is David Middleton, who made me realize that the extreme science concept would make a great book in the first place.

For their help and advice in the field and during my training for this project, I owe a world of thanks—and my life—to literally hundreds of people: on Gorner glacier, the members of the *La Venta* exploring team, specifically Pasquale Suriano, Paulo Petrignani, Riccardo "Loco" Pozzo, Tullio Bernabei, Giuseppe Giovine, Giusiano Mauro, Giuseppe "Cagiu" Casagrande, Chiara Silvestro, and Tono de Vivo; in Prairie Creek

Redwoods State Park, Billy Ellyson, Mark Bailey, Brett Lovelace, Anthony Ambrose, and Jess Parker; in Mamiraua, Barbara Da Silveira, Ronis's assistants, Joao and Raimundo, Joao Paulo Viana, Ana Rita Alvez, Luis Claudio Marigo, and Jose Marcio Correa Ayres; in South Africa, Theo Ferreira, Nicolas Christo Kruger, Stephanie Sieberhagen, Juan "Carcharias," and Hendrik and Anique Krugel for their hospitality; in the pursuit of the peregrines, Brian Walton, Janet Linthicum, Scott Francis, Dr. Craig Himmelwright, Mary Platter-Rieger, Jason Hassrick, Remona Zeno, Christopher Kuntzsch, Rick Sharpe, Stan Moore, David Gregoire, the Caltrans Paint crews, and Jeff Sipple; in Villa Luz, Holly Shugardt, Dave Lester, Jim Pisarowicz, Doug Soroka, Lynn Kleina, Penny Boston, Kathy Lavoie, Robbie Lavoie, Joe Levinson, Bob Addis, and Christa Hay; in the air with the trumpeters, Brooke Pennypacker, Kevin Richards, Dr. Bill Slayden, Bill Lishman, Joe Duff, Donielle Roninger, the staff management and directors of the Airlie Foundation and the International Academy for Preventive Medicine, and Stephanie Scolari and Michelle O'Malley—the "swan moms"; in Florida's underwater caves, Bill Mee, Todd Kincaid, Robert Carmicheal, Michael Wisenbaker, Becca Fry, Eric Baker, Christopher Werner, Steve Straatsma, Steve Auer, and Ken Sallot; and on Mexico's volcanoes, C.P.A. Alejandro Cevallos, C.P.A. Raul Lascano, C.P.A. Francisco Zarate, Antonio Ariza, Esteban Castro, Dr. Roberto Meli, Dr. Jaime Urrutia Fucuguachi, Dr. Enrique Cabral Cano, Sra. Teresa Guarneros, Lucio Cardenas Gonzalez, Lorenzo Ortiz Armas, Adalberto Diaz Vera, Ivan Rivko Hernandez, Efren Reyneso Rioja, Antonio Romo Rasgado, Marcos Luna Alinso, Paul Armabula Mendoza, and Dr. Ramon Alvárez Bejan.

For helping to make the entire project more manageable and more complete, and for getting balls rolling I never could have started on my own: Willard Whitson, Barry Lewis, Heather Schultz, and Patty Connolly at the Academy of Natural Sciences; Amy Bucher, Whitney Wood, Larry Engel, and Steve Engel at Engel Brothers Media; Katie Arnold at *Outside* magazine; Milbry Polk; Mary Tiegreen; Philip Engelhardt; Lisa Sonne; PhotoCraft Laboratories, specifically Jim Sincock, John Botkin, and Bo Hildebrand; Frita Bright at Bright-Cooke Travel for her many minor miracles; Frank Garber at the Chestnut Hill Camera Shop; Jenny Lawrence; Jim Zug; David Taylor; Matt Taylor; Porter Fox; Reed Noss; Jim Butler; Rosamund Kidman Cox; Jim Seymore; Nick Paumgarten; Galen Rowell; Sylvia Earle; J. Noble Wilford; Joel Helioua; Rob Sheppard; Jim Motavalli; Paul Hanle; Jerry Franklin; Steve Trombulak; George Schaller; John Nuhn; Jim Merritt; Nell Hupman; Chris Howes; David Woo; Peter Longstreth; Alberto Ibarguen; Amanda Hesser; Bob Richards; Bob Van Pelt; Deborah Mekeel; Dave Andrews; Matt Ward; Brian Rothenberg; Kathy Conforti; Jared Tobman; Eliza Booth; John Alderman; Stanley Williams; John Thorbjarnarson; Eric Davis; Phil Benoit; Maryalice

Yakutchik; Kate Milliken; Chuck Thompson; Greg Hanscom; John Elder; Peter Klimley; Peter K. Burian; Stephen Pyne; Lynn Simarski; Gary Fallesen; Kent Vliet; Bob Peck; Jim Luhr; John Ewert; Rick Watson; Wayne Lynch; Gary Halpern; Patricia Corry; Marina Cappabianca; Chris Harris and David Sykes at Graham Harris; Alex Paine and Joe Conte at Websight Design; and Ted Miller and ENMET Corporation.

Special thanks, too, to the many scientists who tolerated my endless interrogations while I found the right mix for this book, especially Gary Alt, Alun Hubbard, Duncan MacRae, Martin Jeffries, Charles Corfield, Tom Sisson, Meg Lowman, Jean Philipe Babli, Gerry Kooyman, Howard Quigley, Kent Klegg, Mike Kearsley, Gary McCracken, Jonathan Gordon, Dave Garsalon, Teb Hobson, and Alan Rabinowitz. In one way or another, all of their stories deserve to be included here.

And finally, my eternal appreciation to my family, all of whom have tolerated my transience and recklessness with unspeakable patience. They helped to nourish this project to the very end. For their hospitality during my most transient months, I also owe my thanks (and massive bills for back rent) to Theo, Isabelle, Alix, Cynthia, and Elouise Armour, and my grandmother, Mrs. Norman Armour.

Introduction:
The Next Frontier

*Any fool can put his hide on the line and throw his life away in the
process. The idea is to be able to put your hide on the line—and then
have the moxie, the reflexes, the talent, and the experience to pull it
back in at the last yawning moment—and then to be able to go out
again the next day and do it all over again—and in its best
expression, to be able to do it in some higher cause, in some
calling that means something.*
—Tom Wolfe

We all have stereotypes of scientists. For many of us, they are the very embodiment of smug academia; for others, like a knowledgeable friend of mine, science in all of its manifestations "is nothing but counting." Nothing, however, could be farther from the truth.

On the far reaches of the science frontier, there is a little-known school of scientific inquiry that breaks all the rules and continuously redefines the way we view the search for scientific truth. The scientists themselves don't wear lab coats, publish prolifically, or hover over test tubes and formulas. When you see them, if ever, they're unkempt, only in town until the weekend, strung out from coffee and jet lag, and cloaked under heavy cover in Levi's, polyester fleece, and organic cotton T-shirts. Like most scientists at heart, they are brutally candid, concerned, and engaging.

What most discernibly sets these researchers apart from their scientific peers is what they do in the field. They hang from 500-foot suspension bridges, climb to the tops of the world's tallest trees, and crawl through cave shafts into the bowels of the earth itself. They swim with great white sharks, wade with crocodilians, rappel into active volcanoes, and scuba dive inside creaking, glacial crevasses. Their "labs" are in places most of us have never heard of, and they work with little-understood subjects in

*Great deeds are
usually wrought at
great risk.*

—*Herodotus*

1

inaccessible habitats far from the comfortable islands of the scientific mainstream. They are the pioneers of humanity's newest generation of scientists and explorers and in one way or another, each is reshaping the way we look at the world. They are scientists at the extreme.

The same risk that defines high-alpine mountaineering and solo ocean sailing reflects, in part, the very essence of extreme science: if something goes wrong, you die. But unlike its purely recreational cousins, extreme science is not about public grandstanding or the headlining adrenaline hunt that has come to embody the current ethos of finding the next frontier. Extreme science is adventure with a purpose, and despite the sensational connotations, it's as much about birds and epiphytic flowers as it is about bears and drooling fangs. Stripped down, science at the extreme is fueled by the passion for scientific intimacy, and the unyielding drive to understand not simply the *whats* of evolution but the *wheres, hows,* and *whys* as well. Extreme science is about getting closer, getting involved, and regardless of the risks, getting on-site when nothing other than firsthand observation will do. Extreme scientists don't risk their lives for tenure; they risk their lives because there's no other way to get the data.

What elevates extreme science above ordinary, extreme adventure is not simply selflessness, however. On a deeper level, today's extreme scientists walk in the footsteps of humanity's great naturalist explorers, like Charles Darwin, Sir Ernest Shackleton, Meriwether Lewis and William Clark, and John Wesley Powell. In their respective times, all of these men mounted similar endeavors of precedent human exploration which were every bit as dangerous—and every bit as scientific—as diving with great white sharks today. Like modern extreme scientists, they were fueled by the knowledge that humans are uniquely capable of something greater than just survival; that if they push far enough and gamble big enough, they can change their lives. These were the first extreme scientists. What has changed today to make extreme science seem so sensational is the context of exploration itself.

Human civilization is currently in the throes of a resurgent Adventure Age. With real, physical frontiers rapidly shrinking and the Cadillac-ride into the new millennium utterly too safe, many people feel unchallenged by life on a deep, Darwinian level. As a result, courting adventure has recently become one of the hottest extracurricular recreations on the planet. Ironically, what most of these people desire is simply to feel mortal again. They yearn to feel changed, to experience the enduring rites of frontier passage which safe society has denied them, and to realize their full human potential in the pursuit of something bigger. Flushing with myriad chemicals, hormones, and neurotransmitters when stimulated, our body systems are designed to achieve peak perfor-

If you have the desire for knowledge and the power to give it physical presence go out and explore. . . . Some will tell you that you are mad, and nearly all will say "what is the use?" If you march your winter journeys, (however) you will have your reward, so long as all you want is a penguin's egg.

Apsley Cherry-Gerrard

The Worst Journey in the World

We create technologies and make discoveries, but in order to do that, we have to push beyond the set of rules governing us at that time.

—Frank Farley

mance as perceived risk increases. Remove the external threats, however—as modern civilization has so effectively done—and those systems inevitably go off-line. Today, people complain of feeling "soft," desensitized, and driven more by social and cultural mimicry than innate, personal experimentation. In response, many have finally lashed out as any true *Homo sapiens* would—by fighting fires, driving Indy cars, scuba diving at night, and leaping from airplanes, in short, by making danger a way of life again.

Courtesy of the Adventure Age, that heart-slamming run for our lives is now available in prepackaged form and, for better or worse, life-threatening adventure today is a chic, global fad. There are now adventure Olympics, adventure vacations, adventure channels, adventure magazines, adventure towns, and adventure schools. The good news is that the current "experiment or die" adventure renaissance has reawakened the Lewis and Clark chromosome in even the most sedentary eddy of the human gene pool. The bad news is that adventure today is less a chisel of human destiny and humanitarian progress and more a kind of modern, existential Prozac. When the human story is told centuries hence, our time will be remembered as the first in the history of our species that *Homo sapiens* used his cerebral capacity and technological wizardry to minimize risk with one hand and maximize it with the other. It will be remembered for skydiving, free-basing, day trading, and an unprecedented collective willingness to flaunt the prosperity of the Industrial Revolution and reasonable world peace to play chicken with evolution again.

Sadly, it will also be remembered as a time when vast segments of humanity showed more willingness to die for its own selfish gratification than for the people, places, and species that actually needed a martyr. While at the same time ignoring those who risk their lives every day to feed their children and save others—like wildland firefighters and police rescue divers—society has recently made unlikely heroes of cavalier adventurers willing to throw themselves in front of the metaphorical bus. Until the dawning of the Adventure Age, adventure always had a purpose; the danger and lack of control—the *adventura*, as it is known in Latin—were incidental to the task. These days, however, the situation is exactly the opposite: the purpose of adventure has become danger itself.

Not surprisingly, it is this fact which illustrates most clearly the difference between extreme science and extreme adventure in the first place: when risking one's life for science and exploration, danger is minimized in order to maximize the probability of achieving one's goals, not the other way around. Extreme scientists are not on the edge to see how high or far they can go, but rather to document what they see along the way, and most important, to get extreme long enough, regularly enough, to draw some scien-

Life is either a daring adventure or nothing at all.

—Helen Keller

tifically defensible conclusions in the process. To characterize extreme researchers as adrenaline junkies on a scientifically justified free-fall establishes an entirely different and equally inaccurate scientific stereotype, one that is filled with John Wayne heroics and against-the-clock game savers instead of ivory academic towers.

Yet, for many species and habitats extreme scientists *are* heroes. By providing information where only footprints and conjecture existed before, they are inevitably the frontline advocates for whatever they study. They have given the frontier a name we can talk about and, in many cases, a face we can love. They have also given the conservation movement defensible ammunition. Collectively, extreme scientific research from hundreds of scientists around the world provides the adhesion for today's information-based conservation initiatives. The data initiate action, provide proof, hold management strategies together, and represent the informed voice of science to an often skeptical public. No one will save what they don't understand, and so without such extreme, scientific access, there can never be truly informed conservation advocacy.

The great contribution of today's extreme scientists is deeper than just species and salvation however. It is also psychological. Through their discoveries, they have shown that the world's frontiers are as wide open now at the beginning of the third millennium as they were four centuries ago; they have simply changed shape. By exploring with both the mind and the body and continually finding *terra incognita,* they have demonstrated that the great unknowns are no longer just geographic—"out there" on top of mountains we haven't climbed and across oceans we haven't sailed—they are also "in here," in consilient relationships and dynamics uniting the natural world that we don't yet understand. Just before I began this book, a friend attempted to convince me that the great age of discovery was over, that it had been cut short before my generation was even given a chance to contribute to it. Thankfully, he was wrong. Over the past two years, each of the scientists contributing to this volume has taught me that the frontier continues to thrive in the private lives of crocodiles and the Sistine artistry of the forest canopy, and slams with a clear, liquid pulse through the hearts of the world's glaciers. It thrives where it has always thrived: wherever there is wonder, wildness, uncertainty, and danger—and more often than not, wherever humanity is not yet omnipresent.

Ultimately, the most common question I was asked by family members and friends while doing the field work for this book—and consequently risking my own life—centered around extreme science's most captivating aspect in the first place: death. Why, they asked incredulously, would anyone risk his life for science or original exploration? And what's so important about prey remains and cave passage in the first place?

Having watched the full moon rise from the top of one of the world's tallest trees, circulated inside a glacier, and helped a clutch of endangered crocodilians break from their eggs into the world, I can say that I now know in part what drives extreme scientists to make danger a part of their lives. It's what they get in return beyond the numbers—a kind of magic that can't be counted and modeled. It's the way the human spirit is lifted up in the immediate presence of nature's miracles, as if the ancient chromosomes for discovery were literally coming out of remission. After just brief sojourns in their worlds, I find it unfathomable now that someone wouldn't risk life itself to feel the same way. Extreme science is so much more than an adventure. It's a state of mind and a way of life.

To the same extent that extreme science affirms life, however, it also takes it away, and no book celebrating the contributions of today's cutting edge scientists should fail to recognize those who died in the name of science and exploration. It is because of pioneers like Dian Fossey, George Mallory, Amelia Earhart, Ted Parker of Conservation International, and French volcanologists Maurice and Kattia Krafft that we continue to push the limits of science and exploration today. They remind us not only of what is at stake, but also, as Sir Francis Bacon put it, that "he that dies in an earnest pursuit is like one that is wounded in hot blood, who for the time scarce feels the hurt." In their enduring immortality, they remind us that there is nothing more admirable—or more human—than dying for a higher cause.

It is with the memory of these people in mind that the extreme scientists in this book carry the passion for discovery forward into the new millennium. Their successes continue to reinforce that there are no barriers to knowledge, and their commitment to scientific inquiry sets the bar for all to follow at a time when going farther for better data is more important than ever to sound science and effective conservation.

We are not here merely to make a living. We are here to enrich the world, and we impoverish ourselves if we forget this errand.

—*Woodrow Wilson*

EARTH
The Timeless World

There is little point in setting out for a place one is certain to reach.
—H. W. Tillman

North Cascades National Park, Washington.

Planet earth today is no longer the open door it once was. Many of the most prized geographic frontiers are now largely known and explored, and science continues to dissect nature's most inscrutable mysteries at a dizzying rate. With global population now on to the next threshold of 7 billion people, humans have become more ubiquitous worldwide than water itself, staking their claim to flood plains, fault zones, and rainless moonscapes devoid of virtually any living thing. We've summited the planet's highest peaks, run its major rivers, reached both the north and south poles, and dropped over a thousand meters beneath the surface of the earth itself. In fact, it's almost impossible these days to find a place on the planet where *Homo sapiens* hasn't been, and where the signs of civilization don't yet exist.

Whether such ubiquity is right, wrong, or natural isn't the critical issue, however. The greater challenge for generations ahead is learning to cope with what we've lost in the process—aesthetically, ecologically, and emotionally. On the heels of the same "expeditions of discovery" that opened the planet's remote geographic frontiers in the eighteenth and nineteenth centuries, mass environmental destruction has followed at the hands of an ever-expanding human population. Old-growth forests have been ravaged, wildlife and native plants have been decimated, rivers have been dammed, coastlines have been rearranged, and the crust of the earth itself has literally been turned inside out. Yet the ultimate price of human omnipotence isn't simply the loss of vital natural resources or the extinction of species. There is a deeper dispossession at stake, of something that cannot be measured and quantified by science. For the first time in human history, there's no more room to run. The great age of geographic exploration on earth is effectively over, and we must now necessarily ask ourselves: Where to next? Are there still opportunities here to be challenged and to grow? And perhaps most important, what is the role of science and exploration in a world in which terrestrial frontiers increasingly cease to exist and the essential facts of life on earth are no longer matters of mystery and speculation?

Contrary to what the physical evidence might suggest, however, reports of the death of the frontier have been greatly exaggerated. Earth's wild and unstudied extremes still abound in places we've never looked and in forms we're just beginning to imagine. They are simply harder to find and more difficult to understand. For expeditions as recent as a century or two ago, such as those mounted by Lewis and Clark across North America and John Wesley Powell down the Colorado River, original science was often just a matter of showing up and making physical observations. Although, given the time and the place, such a proposition in itself was often a matter of life and death, the basic questions in general were more obvious and taxonomic, like "what is that?" and "can we get there from here?"

Today, expeditions of original discovery must involve much more than willing, go-west curiosity. Earth's lasting physical frontiers remain untrammeled for a single reason: Ensconced behind impenetrable geography, deadly weather, and perennial armed conflict, they kill. Thus, due to the very nature of where and in what form the terrestrial frontier still endures, today's field specialists must climb higher, push farther, and stay longer, with better technology than ever before. Yet, where these last terrestrial refuges exist, they harbor untold secrets about global geography and represent the last strongholds of some of the world's most enigmatic predators, such as the anaconda and the snow leopard. Take as a hopeful example the recent experience of Canadian Forest Service biologist Karsten Heuer. On a 2000-mile Lewis and Clark–style survey trek along the length of the northern Rockies, from Yellowstone National Park to Watson Lake in Canada's Yukon Territory, Heuer crossed 92 mountain passes on foot and survived 11 face-to-face run-ins with grizzly bears, but he encountered only 8 major highways. Heuer also found evidence almost daily of wolves, elk, wolverines, mountain goats, dall sheep, and mountain lions.

As the work of scientists like Heuer demonstrate, cutting-edge exploration today is still, in part, a geographic proposition. Yet, the growth of human knowledge and technology in the past century has broadened the scope of the questions science is capable of asking, and in today's shrinking physical world, that presents another kind of frontier, one that is as much a journey of the mind as it is an expedition of the body. In many instances, cutting-edge scientific discovery today is much less a process of observation than about a change in perspective, based on the unification of once disparate scientific disciplines, which eminent Harvard biologist Edward O. Wilson has so suitably termed *consilience*. Instead of seeking out new physical frontiers, the goal of consilience is to transcend the accepted and often mutually exclusive boundaries of scientific thought, and look deeper into the places we already know. It is here, Wilson insists, that the most original discoveries about biology, ecology, and the mechanics of life itself will inevitably occur.

For those scientists embracing today's new frontier, planet earth is still a wide-open door. In the great tradition of history's earliest explorers, they are driven by the firm belief that frontiers and mysteries don't disappear; people just get lazy and accept the world as it is given to them. A world without enigmas, like crocodiles and sulfur caves, however, is much worse than a world that has simply lost its rare predators and habitats. It's a world devoid of curiosity, a place where no one wants to look around the next corner because we already know what's there. This, tragically, would be a world without the need for science.

The Comeback King

Deep in the rain forest of the Brazilian Amazon, there are enduring myths about every animal. Part fact, part fiction, they have been passed down from generation to generation for so long that they are now cultural truths, animating life in this remote equatorial region with slithering thieves, winged saviors, and pitiless, predatory villains. In a place called Mamiraua, the villain's name is *Melanosuchus niger*: the black caiman.

"The legend of *Melanosuchus* is very short," Brazilian crocodilian biologist Ronis Da Silveira tells me, gesturing out from our small skiff into a raucous, rain forest night. "They kill."

In the folklore of the Amazon, the black caiman is Conrad's "heart of darkness" defined. Carnivorous, cold-blooded, and largely nocturnal, the species symbolizes everything about the jungle which lurks, menaces, deceives, and kills. Owing, in part, to this very paranoia, the black caiman remains extinct throughout most of its historic range. The exception, Ronis points out, is here in Mamiraua.

Idling slowly just upriver from the small, floating houseboat Ronis has called home for the past two years, we part a sea of planktonic constellations. Illuminated in our headlamps, they are shining *Melanosuchus* eyes, drifting two-by-two into the distance. In the tall grass on shore, the smallest of them cluster into imploding nebulas. Farther out in the open of Lake Mamiraua, the largest ones burn lonesome and red like distant planets.

"Those," Ronis whispers, training his light on a large pair of eyes 50 feet off the bow, "are the monsters, the true kings of the jungle."

Ronis Da Silveira's floating house on Lake Mamiraua.

Facing page:
The rain forest of Mamiraua is submerged for five months every year by up to 30 feet of seasonal meltwater from the Andes.

11

The ancient eye of an adult black caiman.

He pauses briefly and scrutinizes a slow, silent wake in front of us. "A big male," he says quietly. "You see, it is as if the eyes are lit from within."

Up ahead, what appears to be an airplane wreck slowly materializes into the head of a massive adult black caiman, floating free in the darkness as if decapitated. The caiman cruises parallel to our skiff with an aloof, predatory certainty, encrusted with algae and mud as if he'd just risen from evolution's primordial soup. Black swatches of war paint streak vertically down both sides of his maw. Out from underneath the lips, he bares three feet of long, conical teeth in a permanent, patronizing smirk.

"This one," Ronis whispers over his shoulder. "We'll take this one." Ronis's assistant Joao cuts the engine and sets the skiff on a slow collision course with the caiman. Tip to tail, he is as long as our own 12-foot water line. Ronis whispers briefly into his microcassette recorder, noting the animal's distinguishing marks, sex, and size, then turns and gives me four pieces of advice. Don't talk unless you have to scream. Keep your hands inside. Watch the tail. And whatever happens, don't tip the skiff. Already overloaded by a hundred pounds, we are floating only eight inches above the water.

"Whenever we go for the 'Big One,' " Ronis adds, "there can be no mistakes." He then turns to Joao and gives him a reassuring thumbs-up. "Joao is still terrified. He thinks I'm trying to capture the devil."

Ronis balances on the bow to slip his noose around the neck of a diving black caiman.

Cloaked in a black sweatsuit, shin pads, cycling gloves, and a construction helmet, Ronis creeps to the bow and steps onto the gunwales, balancing barefoot with the poise of an indigenous hunter. In his right hand, cocked high above his ear, he holds an 8-foot bamboo pole with a wire noose on the end; in his left hand hangs a 10-foot leader of nylon rope. Wedged between the front and middle thwarts, Ronis's second assistant, Raimundo, cradles an additional hundred feet of rope backing should the caiman decide to run. For the first time since I arrived in Mamiraua, the rain forest is eerily quiet, as if waiting for the coming anarchy. From behind a drumskin of stratus clouds, a gibbous moon bathes us all in a ghostly spotlight.

Finally, the skiff glides to a stop within arms-reach of the caiman—so close we can see clearly the membrane of his ear and the pupils of his ancient yellow eyes. Just beneath the water, he wears an immutable sneer, as if hiding some devious plot. Almost 15 feet behind his massive head, the tip of his tail swirls under the surface like a different animal. For an instant, there is a prickly electricity in the air, and it's unclear just who's stalking who. Then suddenly, as quickly as he appeared, the caiman rolls his eye, smiles at Ronis as if to say, "Sorry, chump," and founders out of sight.

"You see," Ronis explains, turning and grinning with reverent satisfaction, "they are like *fantasmas*—ghosts." He motions for Joao to motor upstream and readjusts his noose. "That one wasn't big enough anyway. Tonight, I want the king of the lake."

Taxonomically, *Melanosuchus niger* is the largest of five caiman species belonging to the crocodilian subfamily *Alligatorinae* and one of three caiman indigenous to the Amazon itself. In Brazil, it goes by many names: *jacaré acu, caiman negro, cocodrilo,* and Ronis's favorite, *El Grande*—the Big One. Reaching lengths up to 20 feet, the black caiman is both the largest predator in the Amazon and the largest crocodilian in the western hemisphere. Having once been eradicated from approximately 99 percent of its original range throughout equatorial South America, it is also rebounding from the brink of extinction, which is exactly why Ronis is here. Part of his job is to help nurse the species back for good.

Descended from the now-extinct, 40-foot terror crocodile (genus *Deinosuchus*), adult *Melanosuchus* are every bit the monsters people imagine. Lacking any real predators except man, they can eat virtually anything, live for a century, and lay claim to just about any beach they please. With their 4-foot hydraulic jaws, they could tear a buffalo in two and crumple a scientist's skiff like a soda can. *M. niger* also happens to be one of a dozen or so species on earth capable of taking down *Homo sapiens,* which, from a purely empirical point of view, is something Ronis would love to see.

"It would be so quick and so certain," he imagines, emphasizing the biological

Mamiraua's "children of the manatee."

nature of his speculations. "Out from under the floating mats [of vegetation] like lightning. Can you hear the sounds? The bones breaking, flesh ripping. It's fantastic."

Using a local *Cabocio* fisherman as his example, Ronis goes on to explain how, like all crocodilians, black caiman don't chew their prey into discrete bite-sized pieces. Instead, they knock it back virtually whole, like a shot of tequila—arms, legs, lines, and all. Given such imaginative scenarios, it's no wonder black caiman have long suffered from ill-repute. Even today, their presence in proximity to Mamiraua communities is still considered much more of a menace than a miracle. In reality, Ronis insists, *Melanosuchus* have no taste for human flesh. They are *tranquilos*—tranquil. When predation attacks do occur, they happen in the same way we might try curried beetles if they came by on a cocktail tray—more out of curiosity than bloodsucking voracity.

"These 'attacks' they all speak of; they are not attacks," Ronis argues. "They are defenses against us. How can people be afraid of a species that is almost gone because of us?" He then pauses briefly, as if reconsidering his thought. "Of course, if they want, they can destroy you."

Whatever the motivating factor for an attack, public outcry is invariably the same. Why, the villagers ask him, do you want to protect and propagate a killer? Is this the greater good of science and conservation in Mamiraua?

Science, however, is only beginning to understand the dynamic ecological value of *Melanosuchus niger,* and what researchers have documented thus far amounts to little more than biological sightseeing. As with many of the world's 23 crocodilians, the black caiman's more secretive habits are virtually unstudied in the wild. No one really knows how many are still out there now, where they go when the forests of Mamiraua flood each November, or to what extent they utilize Mamiraua's diversity of habitats over a given year. Most curiously of all, no one can say for sure how, after a century of wholesale meat slaughter, skin hunting, and systematic, phobic eradication, the species has managed to survive at all.

"All we know for sure," Ronis says, "is that they have been here much longer than us, so whatever the reason they have survived, it is a good one." Anecdotally, Ronis suspects the answer has been right here in front of us all along: the "great, green jungle."

Rain storms engulf Mamiraua virtually year-round, inundating the region with an average of almost 10 feet of rainfall per year.

Engulfing a major part of eight South American nations, the Amazon basin is the closest thing to infinity the human race will ever know on earth. So vast is the rain forest itself that one can fly east–west in some places for hundreds of miles without seeing so much as a road, and countless species still exist undiscovered by modern man. Ecologically, the basin's reach is planetary in scope. Its matrix of water, flora, and fauna helps regulate global nutrient cycles and affects climate change. The Amazon River itself holds up to one-fifth of the world's freshwater, pouring a sediment plume into the Atlantic Ocean that can be seen from space. In some places, the river is over 300 feet deep. At its mouth, it's 200 miles across, wider than the coastlines of neighboring French Guyana and Surinam. Biologically, the Amazon is so saturated with evolutionary miracles, it's more a state of mind than a state of nature.

"The brain is so tiny and so new," Ronis sighs, shining his spotlight into the nearby forest, "and the Amazon, it is so old and complex. We will never understand it completely."

Back inside the trees, the industry of Mamiraua's night shift rises like a full orchestra. No one species outplays another; the collective resonance is deep and complete. Only occasionally above the cacophony can we hear the struggles for life and the cries of something dying. Suddenly, Ronis faces the grassy shoreline and joins in. He

Prime caiman habitat on Lake Mamiraua.

inhales deeply, thumps his chest, and exhales forcefully in succession, *Bwaa, Bwaa, Bwaa.* Within seconds, his challenge is accepted by a male *Melanosuchus* just upstream, who calls back in mock imitation. Soon, a second reply comes from the other side of the river, then three more from behind. Ronis turns back to me and smiles.

"You see?" he whispers. "Surrounded by five monsters . . . only in Mamiraua."

Mamiraua proper—literally meaning "children of the manatee"—is a cake slice of rich, seasonally flooded forest locally called *varzea,* which extends 200 miles upstream from the confluence of the Japura and Solimoes (as the Amazon is known upriver from Manaus) rivers. Enriched every November by 30 feet of silt-laden *agua branca* (white water) from the eastern slope of the Andes and up to 10 feet of annual rainfall, it is one of the only places on earth that is both terrestrial and aquatic in a given year. During the four to six months of high water, rivers literally run canopy high, and the *varzea* becomes a sea unto itself. For aquatic and amphibious species like the black caiman, manatee, and freshwater turtles, the floods open vast areas of the jungle that are completely inaccessible during the dry season, and as scientists like Ronis are now discovering, represent the driving force behind many species' seasonal migrations between habitats. Even for those terrestrial species which must flee the floods, however, the annual inundations are an inevitable consequence of ecological plenty. For the very same hydrological reasons, Mamiraua is also one of the most diverse and productive bioregions in the world.

In addition to being one of the wettest places on earth, Mamiraua is also one of the wildest, comprising one part of the largest protected area in the Amazon—over 2 million contiguous hectares—and the largest remaining tract of flooded forest in the world. Four hundred miles equidistant from the Peruvian border to the west, and the Brazilian cities of Manaus to the east, Porto Velho to the south, and Boa Vista to the north, Mamiraua is also one of the places most distant from large-scale, human-induced disturbance in the hemisphere. From Ronis's houseboat, there isn't a paved highway for 380 miles in any direction, which from a scientific standpoint is precisely its value. With the exception of a few small reserves in Venezuela and Colombia, Mamiraua is the only place left in South America where monsters still lurk outside of the imagination, and where *Melanosuchus* populations remain sufficiently intact to conduct baseline distribution, abundance, and reproductive research. From a conservation point of view, Mamiraua is the perfect place for *M. niger* to hide out, fatten up, and regenerate.

"People think the gold is in Switzerland," says Ronis, "but in reality, it's here, in the Amazon and in Mamiraua. The gold we have now is the rain forest, and not just for the trees, the wildlife, and the fish—also for research."

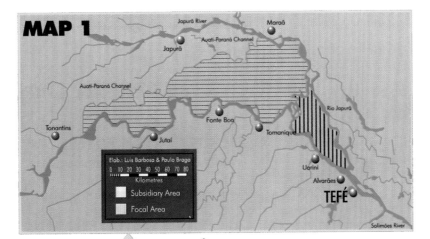

The Mamiraua Sustainable Development Reserve is a cake slice of seasonally flooded rain forest locally called *varzea*. Covering over 1 million hectares, the reserve is one of the largest protected areas in Brazil and the largest remaining tract of flooded forest in the world. (Courtesy of the Mamiraua Management Plan.)

Welcome to the world. Ronis assists a hatchling in breaking free from its egg.

For roughly 340 species of birds, 300 fish, 200 trees, and countless invertebrates, many of which are endemic to the *varzea,* Mamiraua is an ecological paradise. It is the only place for tens of kilometers in any direction where the uniform shield of the dry, "terra firma" rain forest is broken, offering species a rare matrix of six habitats to find their niche, including wet and dry forests, shrubby grasslands, and open sandy marshes.

"In the Brazilian Amazon," Ronis explains, "people say we have huge biodiversity. But in the *varzea,* we have both—we have diversity of habitat and life. This is what makes Mamiraua so special, so complex, and so abundant."

For the wide-ranging black caiman, the upshot is a pleasing abundance of diversified real estate, and as Ronis's initial population data seem to indicate, a predictable, temporal distribution throughout every inch of it. Rather than dividing the *varzea* up into permanent, individual fiefdoms as one might expect, Mamiraua's remaining *M. niger* seem to use each habitat at distinct times in their lives for different reasons.

Ironically, as little as five years ago the *varzea* here was a much emptier place. Drastically overfished and overharvested by commercial boats from as far away as Manaus, 400 miles downriver, the headwaters of Mamiraua lay mirror-still, virtually devoid of life. While apex megafauna like the panther (*Panthera onca*) and anaconda (*Eunectes murinus*) escaped the onslaught deep into the forest, the river otter (*Pteronura brasiliensis*) and tartaruga (*Podocnemis expansa*), one of the world's largest freshwater turtles, were hunted right into extinction. When I ask Mamiraua old-timers about what happened, they remember only the eerie silence, as if all the music had ended at once. They say it was the first sign they knew that something was very wrong. For *M. niger* specifically, Mamiraua was literally a war zone.

"When I got here, every lake stank of *jacaré acu,*" Ronis remembers, referring to the beginning of his Ph.D. work here. "Everywhere you looked, there were dead carcasses and caiman bodies left to rot without skins or meat. It was scary to see how quickly a place so rich and fertile could become so barren."

Ronis then points at himself, and then at me, "And all because of us—*Homo sapiens.*" He emphasizes the last two words in particular, making sure I understand the irony

Life's first seconds. With its umbilical cord still attached, a hatchling erupts from its egg and experiences the sensations of life for the first time.

of the name itself. *Sapiens*—wise—is the last adjective any wildlife biologist studying an endangered species like the black caiman would use to describe the human race.

Like many other exotic species, black caiman were not exterminated for survival or subsistence. They were killed by fashion. Between 1950 and 1965, over 7 million black caiman skins were exported from the state of Amazonas alone, a quantity so large, it's hard to imagine how widespread *M. niger* must once have been. These days, the total human take has tapered substantially, but hunting remains widespread. Instead of being harvested illegally for their leather, *Melanosuchus* meat is now pawned off in Colombia as low-grade catfish. Although the black caiman has been an officially protected species since 1967, an estimated 80 tons of meat are still exported from Mamiraua annually, a tonnage which, according to Ronis's data, translates into more than 5000 adult *Melanosuchus*. For certain renegade communities in the farthest reaches of the Mamiraua region, however, the illicit black market is the sole form of cash during the long and often unproductive dry season.

"The Mamiraua communities still think the caiman are a gift to them from God," Ronis explains, the frustration clearly evident in his voice, "and that no gift from God can ever run out, but they are wrong. They don't understand the damage they are doing. When they take eggs for cakes and kill the males for meat, they are taking away the future of *Melanosuchus*. Their children will grow up in a jungle without its king."

That this might actually happen was enough to persuade the Brazilian government in 1996 to designate Mamiraua as the world's first Sustainable Development Reserve and, in the process, to hand over more than a million hectares of the country's most productive land to the dubious hands of science and conservation. So far, however, much to the chagrin of the initial critics, Mamiraua's local brand of sustainable development seems to be working. Rooted in the sound foundations of scientific evidence and public governance, the reserve has succeeded by deftly avoiding the pitfalls of prepackaged, Gestapo conservation that have so often plagued sustainable development initiatives in other parts of the developing world.

"Many times before in Brazil," Ronis notes, reflecting the sentiments of many Mamiraua scientists, "the government removed people from areas of high biodiversity, good soil, good fish, and good meat for reasons of science and protection and relocated them to areas with nothing. What happens to the people then? It doesn't work. . . . All plans to protect biodiversity everywhere must be accepted and implemented by native residents. But until now—until Mamiraua—we never did it."

Thanks largely to the work of dedicated scientists like Ronis, Mamiraua has also produced defensible data and quantifiable results. With self-enforced, scientifically based conservation laws now in effect, the reserve's fish have come back to life. Deforested areas are regenerating, and previously extirpated species, like the manatee (*Trichechus inunguis*), pink river dolphin (*Inia geoffrensis*), and the indigenous white uacari monkey (*Cacajao calvus calvus*), are rebounding as if they now have something to prove. In the few years Ronis has worked with local *jacaré* populations specifically, he has witnessed nothing short of a biological miracle. For the first time in decades, Mamiraua's rivers, once dark, desolate back alleys into the jungle, are again glittering with eyeshine, "like the lights of Rio de Janeiro itself." As a scientist, the result for Ronis is a thriving *Melanosuchus* laboratory. In the last year alone, he has identified 43 new, active nests, and twice he has arrived on the scene for regular monitoring updates to find hatchlings breaking out of their eggs, something, to his knowledge, no other scientist on earth has ever seen.

Ironically, black caiman are now so widespread that Ronis's major concern is no longer extinction but rather an upsurge in attacks as the large subadult males start heading downstream looking for open territory. Like black bears in the eastern United States, the black caiman may very well be considered a "nuisance species" in the near future.

"Now that there is less hunting," Ronis warns, "the Big Ones aren't afraid of anything. So if someone in Tefe gets attacked, they will blame me. They will blame Mamiraua because we are protecting and increasing the population."

Tools of the trade. Ronis's assistant Joao uses radiotelemetry equipment to track radio-collared black caiman throughout their range and to identify the nest locations of females.

The Comeback King   23

While essential in protecting and propagating Mamiraua's population of black caiman, however, the reserve's success has done little to demystify the species' more secretive habits, such as reproduction and sociobiology.

"The more caiman I catch," Ronis admits, "the more I see, and the less I understand." He looks at me keenly behind his headlight, as if inviting me to stay an extra year to see for myself. "In the big picture, we still know nothing, absolutely nothing."

None of this, of course, is Ronis's fault. Ghosts like *M. niger* don't make easy study subjects. In the human world, success is about being first. For crocodilians, it's about patience, survival, and a kind of evolutionary endurance that can only be measured in millions of years. Like most reptiles, black caiman are capable of such determined sloth and anonymity that they can become part of the landscape for weeks at a time, literally sprouting seedlings from their backs. Most of the time, were it not for the reflective nictitating membrane over their eyes, no one would even know the black caiman were there. *M. niger* also happens to have the same basic habitat preferences as panthers, anacondas, malaria, and drug czars.

"To do anything in the Amazon is dangerous," Ronis explains with the utmost humility, "because death is everywhere, in so many forms, but you can never see it. No matter where you're working or what you're working with, you're always in contact with something that can kill you." To survive three years of Ph.D. research in the middle of it all, Ronis and his family have lived by five basic rules: Always check your boots for snakes. Don't walk in the tall grass at night. Don't follow fresh tracks unless you really want to find something. Don't assume anything is what it appears to be. And don't go swimming. Ever.

Black caiman are mound nesters, building an insulating pile of vegetation that will maintain nest temperature and humidity at precise levels.

In spite of the rules, Ronis's field research here in Mamiraua is as "hands-on" as science gets. Employing nocturnal surveys, radiotelemetry, and a long-term "mark and recapture" program, he's confirming such elemental questions as: How many black caiman are out there? What do the demographic pyramids actually look like? and most important from a conservation point of view, To what extent do individuals disperse among *varzea*'s different habitats throughout their lives for different tasks such as nesting, breeding, and feeding? By personally tracking the individual

The future of Mamiraua's black caiman population is literally in Ronis's hands.

movements of 28 radio-tagged specimens through the forest, for example, Ronis has not only been able to identify distinct, seasonal patterns of habitat use, but he has also tracked reproductively active females to their previously top-secret nesting ponds.

"If we didn't put on the radio tags," Ronis explains, "we never would have found [these lakes and] the nests because we never would have gone there. They are so far and so inaccessible."

What has made Ronis's research particularly noteworthy among scientists, however, is his mark and recapture program. By catching, manually tagging, and then recatching as many *Melanosuchus* as possible, Ronis has amassed the world's first database on the species' size and age class structures and generated GPS-based maps on the extent of age-based migrations throughout Mamiraua's habitat matrix. What's even more remarkable is the fact that he's done it using a technique as time-tested as good ole' boys and pickups, technically called "spotlight fixation." By "freezing" the caiman in the beam of a 12-volt powered, light like a deer in front of an oncoming car, Ronis has been able to get face-to-face with literally thousands of *M. niger* for capture and observation.

The risk for Ronis, of course, is that when something goes wrong, the results are almost always catastrophic. Although slothful by appearance, black caiman are capable of nuclear explosions of speed without warning. They can run faster than they can swim, and they can strike with the force of a runaway freight train with a flick of their half-ton tail. At any time during a typical capture night like tonight, they can also rip your arm off as easily as biting off a hunk of beef jerky. In a worst-case scenario, a captured caiman could sink its jaws into the bow, flip the boat like a pool toy, and systematically dismember everyone aboard.

"Human jaw compression is around 100 kilograms per centimeter," Ronis explains matter-of-factly, "and I could bite off your finger. *El Grande*'s compression is over 2000 kilograms. He could tear you in half."

So far, even after more than 2000 captures spanning eight years, no one's been munched in a serious way, but there have been many close calls. Twice, Ronis has been bitten on the forearm, and a dozen times, he's almost had his skiff upended.

"The last time I caught *El Grande* in February," Ronis admits, pointing to the extra large noose on the end of his pole, "I told my wife I'd never do this again, especially now that we have a baby. But we need to know how many of them are out here." Ronis then smiles mischievously.

"Now I tell her we only go for the juveniles."

The greater benefit of Ronis's mark and recapture research, though, is not simply to confirm the extent to which *M. niger* has returned. By correlating data on age-based dispersion with habitat characteristics like water temperature, depth, and proximity to the forest, Ronis has been able to make some educated guesses about why caiman go where they go in the first place—guesses which will eventually have major conservation implications.

"What seems to be most important to the caiman is the quality of habitat," Ronis postulates, "and this is a relatively new discovery." He gestures to the near shoreline, which alternates between broad beaches and tall grass prairie. Fifty feet back from the water, spotlighted in Ronis's floodlight, trees of all shapes and sizes crowd the riverbank for the sunny, front-row position. Some twist upwards like snakes being coaxed from the earth; others buttress the edge of the forest in great Ionic columns. Thirty feet up on the trunks themselves, like sedimentary strata in exposed bedrock, white bathtub rings mark the exact points of previous high water.

"This kind of dynamic habitat use is the most important thing to understand for management," Ronis continues. "For example, here in [Lake] Mamiraua live the juveniles and large subadult males, but no breeding females. They are back in the small hidden lakes. So if we say, 'Protect the caiman here in Mamiraua,' and let the people hunt there . . . ," he pauses and draws his hand slowly across his throat like a knife, "adios—the population is gone."

Ronis is also amassing the first data ever on *Melanosuchus* reproduction. As with similarly invasive research on other large predators, however, what he now knows—that over 600 nests exist in the reserve's focal area, that single nesting ponds can be shared by up to 17 females, and that nest predation by jaguars and Tegu lizards is as high as 70 percent—is grossly overshadowed by what he doesn't. Despite three years of stalking six radio-tagged females, monitoring 80 remote nests on a weekly basis, and getting charged four times by particularly angry mothers in the process, Ronis has yet to determine such basic reproductive traits as where, when, and how copulation occurs, whether females nest every year in the same place, and even the exact duration of egg incubation. In general, so secretive are the nesting habits of crocodilians that few scientists have ever really seen one build its nest in the wild.

With respect to conservation of the species, however, one major conclusion has emerged: Were it not for the seasonal nesting ponds hidden in the most remote regions of the reserve, *M. niger* would have disappeared long ago with the otter and tartaruga. Ronis calls the ponds "*refugios*," or refuges, and credits them with harboring the last reproductively active females in safety during the worst years of hunting—like cathedrals in a bloody coup. Even now, Ronis theorizes that for every male *Melanosuchus* sunbathing in plain view on an open beach—and ultimately getting axed in the skull by a local poacher—there are a dozen Amazon queens sequestered deep within the *varzea* prepared to carry the species onward as they have for decades.

In tune with Mamiraua's precepts of sustainable development, Ronis's research is also about people. Using analyses of hunting trends among the reserve's 43 primary communities, Ronis is determining to what extent the regenerating black caiman population might be legally harvested by locals in a controlled market environment. The goal, he explains, is not only to eliminate an illegal and inefficient black market for caiman meat but also to create sustainable economic incentives for locals less inspired by arguments about genetic diversity.

"It is very difficult when you go to talk to locals and say biodiversity is important; we must protect," Ronis explains, "when they don't have food, clothes, money to take care of their teeth, and help against disease." He gestures to Joao, who smiles broadly with the endearing toothlessness of an old sage.

"In Mamiraua," he continues "we must always think in terms of society, economics, and people. Caiman are a threatened species, yes, but they are also local resources. We have many people here, and many families who have many problems. It is good to save a species and save the forest, but if we do it without involving the people, we will lose *Homo sapiens*. Do you want to be the one to tell them they can't eat or feed their children?"

Not surprisingly, Mamiraua's inclusive strategy has reaped immediate benefits. Not only have researchers shown that the protection of biodiversity—and even the black caiman—can have intrinsic value for everyone, but among the majority of Mamiraua communities, basic quality of life indices are also fast on the rise. Disease and infant mortality are plummeting, while literacy, median income, and life expectancy have climbed steadily. Residents have learned that scientific research and species protection are not the enemies of community and development. To its early credit, Mamiraua Sustainable Development Reserve has been so successful in balancing the needs of humanity and ecology that it is now referred to in regional conservation circles as simply "the model."

It's already well past one in the morning, more than two hours since we left Ronis's houseboat. Our espresso is gone and the air begins to hang with a sleepy humidity. For everyone except Ronis, fatigue is creeping on, which can easily precipitate a fatal lapse of concentration. Ronis leans back casually against the gunwale, motions for Joao to motor upstream another kilometer, and rumbles through a box of pliers, metal tags, and knives for a larger noose. The clouds overhead drift apart in celestial icebergs, backlit by a bright, white moon. "Not a good omen for catching the 'Big One,'" Ronis quips. "They will see us coming."

Facing page:
The battle between kings. Capturing *El Grande* is an all-night, high-stakes affair requiring a minimum of three people and four hours.

Despite their lethargic appearance, black caiman are capable of explosive speed.

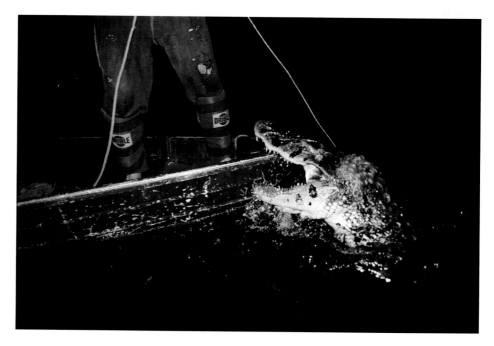

Black caiman will occasionally strike at the skiff itself when they are brought alongside.

Suddenly, the boat rocks hard from an unseen wake. Ronis aims his spotlight off the bow where a dark ghost ship appears to plow through the water. "Another monster male," he whispers. Joao and Raimundo train their headlamps out into the darkness for a better look. Then Ronis stops and looks harder. "That's him," he says excitedly, "the king of the lake!" Joao turns the skiff gently and cuts the engine. As we glide closer, Ronis turns to me and smiles nervously. "These are the ancient ones." Scientifically, they represent the outer edge of Ronis's three-year sample group—the statistical scatter plots that shouldn't really exist anymore, but they do.

Drifting within a boat length, Ronis estimates the caiman's size at 14 feet. Behind his eyes, the caiman's neck piles up into a leathered mountain range, unfolding down the length of his back in a fierce, faulted topography. Dragging over 10 feet behind the head itself, his tail slithers just under the surface of the water like an anaconda. Unfazed, the caiman shadows the skiff as we idle out into the center of the lake. He fixes intently on our headlamps and scans us with his deep yellow eyes. Finally, Ronis moves to the bow. He stands, balances carefully, and dips his noose into the water just in front of the caiman's snout.

Suddenly the caiman folds his head like a stiletto blade and dives to the bottom. The noose is firmly around his neck. Ronis squats deeply into his thighs as if waiting to be hit broadside and lets the rope hiss through his gloves. Joao has already started the engine and kicks it into forward to reduce the strain. In seconds, the caiman hits the bottom 40 feet away. The skiff rocks violently once, then stabilizes as if anchored. *El Grande* rests and ponders his options.

"This is a true monster," Ronis says finally, already breathing hard. He drops to the floor, props his feet underneath the gunwales of the bow, and locks his legs. Behind him, between the middle thwarts, Raimundo does the same. Joao revs the engine to slack the scope of the rope and they pull in simultaneously as if in a tug-of-war. Suddenly, the caiman decides to run again. He rises to the surface, eyeballs Ronis with the species' trademark "wait-till-I-get-my-hands-on-you" sneer, then dives in the opposite direction. At the bottom, he circles back twice on the rope in an attempt to sever it on his own armored plating, but Ronis and Raimundo keep the slack tight. Unsuccessful, the caiman finally makes for the shelter of a fallen tree 50 feet away, pulling the skiff through the water like a barge. Joao kicks the engine in reverse and stops him cold.

Within 20 minutes, the black caiman's nuclear fuel is spent. Just five feet away from the boat, he rolls from his back to his stomach, like a massive driftwood log. When his head clears the water for the first time, he turns toward Ronis, opens his jaws wide, and

The true king of the jungle. The largest black caiman can weigh up to 700 pounds and measure over 14 feet in length.

Final tallies: 3.86 meters in length and 742 pounds.

releases a deep hiss, as if some abysmal gas were soon to follow. Then, with a quick flick of his powerful tail, he lunges and clamps his teeth deep into the thin skiff's aluminum veneer. Ronis leaps back but keeps the rope tight. The caiman holds the bow briefly, shakes it like a chew toy, then releases his grip. As he rolls again onto his back for the last time, his eyes speak a wordless, submissive rage.

"Four meters," Ronis says between deep exhalations, "maybe more. Male. This is definitely the king of the lake." He pauses and takes in the caiman's full length and girth. He is as long as the skiff, but thicker. "We are very lucky."

Pulling the caiman along next to us, Ronis nods to Raimundo, who slips a stabilizing noose around his thick, leathery neck. Ronis then hands his rope to Joao and reaches into a toolbox for a ball of packing string. He makes a loop, drops it casually over the caiman's massive jaw, and ties it shut like a Christmas present. "They can bite you in half coming down," Ronis explains, "but they can barely open up against the weight of their own head." For good measure, Ronis finishes the job with a dozen wraps of duct tape. Within minutes, the caiman is carefully immobilized in double nooses and leg knots and is ready to be taken to shore.

Once in the grass, the caiman's true beauty and immensity become apparent. On top, his skin is reinforced with hard, pewter plates; underneath, he is shingled with white porcelain tiles polished smooth by the river bottom. His tail is as thick and heavy as an old-growth tree. In relation to the rest of the body, the front and hind legs appear grossly out of proportion, as if God had no intentions for the caiman to run.

"He is a beautiful animal, no?" Ronis says, stroking the underbelly. "And to think we almost lost them. They are like your buffalo—so big, so close to extinction. But I will not permit this."

Joao pulls out a clipboard and notes the extrinsic environmental conditions of the capture site—water and air temperature, depth, bottom substrate, and a brief habitat description—then fixes the coordinates of the area on a GPS. Ronis squats over the caiman and pulls from his toolbox a tape, a knife, and a V-shaped aluminum tag to begin his battery of measurements. Raimundo and I brace the mighty tail between our legs. Beneath us, *El Grande* lies tied and gagged like a kidnapped victim—a conquered king.

After a final weigh-in over a nearby tree, we take the tallies from the evening: Total length: 3.86 meters—over 12 feet; Overall weight: 742 pounds; Capture time: 39 minutes; Collateral damage or deaths: none.

By the time the caiman is back in the water, tagged and registered as the one-hundredth large, adult *Melanosuchus* in Ronis's sample group, it's three o'clock in the morning. Joao starts up the engine without speaking and points the skiff for home.

Ronis's floating house is an oasis of humanity amid the endless isolation of the Brazilian *varzea*.

Raimundo is already asleep against the back thwart. As we ride up through the darkness, the glittering eyes of juvenile *Melanosuchus* part before us in a stream of runway lights, drifting away into the distance until they mix with the stars on the horizon. A kilometer down river, the only sign of humanity is the warm, lighthouse glow of Ronis's floating home.

Back in Ronis's kitchen, we take one last coffee before bed and rehash the evening. Ronis cradles his daughter Bruna on his knee. A massive *Melanosuchus* skull, confiscated from a hunter years ago, peers out from the top of a freezer in the corner, making eye contact with everyone in the room. The largest incisors, hollow on the inside, are four inches long, bright white, and still sharp. Ronis estimates the age of the skull at 80 to 100 years and believes there are black caiman out there in Mamiraua right now that are larger still—monsters so sly and secretive no human has ever seen them. The skull is smiling, as if it knows the punch line to some evolutionary joke we'll never understand.

"You know what I want most?" Ronis says finally. "I also want to live a hundred years and see the next generation of humans and black caiman. I want to see the size of the population, the size of the monsters, and the beauty of the Amazon *varzea* when everything else in Europe and America is gone." He pauses, nods at the skull, and gives Bruna a flip into the air off his knee. "I want to see how humans and caiman finally learn how to get along . . . because *El Grande* is back."

This Is Your Brain. . . . This Is Your Brain on Sulfur

The karst kingdom. High mountains, thick limestone bedrock, and active hydrology in the mountains of Tabasco and Chiapas create prime conditions for the formation of caves.

The Other Buzzing Passage is deep underground and as dark as a coffin. Over a half-mile from the last breath of fresh air, it's a place so tight, so toxic, so inhuman, it's hard to find a logical reason to be there—which, given my circumstances, is exactly what I'm trying to do.

I'm pinned on my belly in an underground river beneath 70 to 90 feet of solid limestone bedrock. My feet and legs are soaking in a gruel-like acid mud. Through my rusting respirator, near-lethal concentrations of hydrogen sulfide (H_2S) burn into my lungs with the vile stench of raw sewage. Lost and alone, I hyperventilate against the resistance of my gas mask and try to bury the upwellings of panic.

Suddenly, the far wall of crystallized gypsum begins to glow. Each tiny prism catches a distant flame and ignites from within like an oil lamp. The light grows steadily from rust to orange, then finally to a blinding yellow.

"Is Villa Luz incredible or what!"

Louise Hose pokes her head around the corner and crawls toward me through the darkness and mud. Her words echo down the passage like so many soaring angels, and her carbide headlight illuminates the walls in a tormented netherworld of tones, chromes, and sparkling crystal refractions. For a fleeting moment, the cave ceases to be the planet's purest source of evil.

"You should see what's in there!" she exclaims. "There's a deep spring I never noticed before. And the folia and biovermiculations! Want to go back in?"

"Uh . . . no thanks," I stammer. "There's so much to see right here."

Facing page:
Dawn light smolders over the restored colonial village of Tapijulapa, in south-central Tabasco, Mexico.

37

"Couldn't find your way out, huh?" Louise snickers. "Looks like Villa Luz is getting to you."

Villa Luz, known officially in Southern Mexico as Cueva de las Sardinas, is the most biorich of a dozen known sulfur caves on earth—a rare underworld so biologically active, it's more animal than mineral. Few other global environments, in fact, offer a comparable phantasmagoria of bacteria, slimes, and slithering microbial unknowns—which is exactly why Louise is here. Louise is one of a handful of speleologists on the planet with the technical skills, scientific expertise, and undiluted audacity to drop inside and figure out what's really going on.

Villa Luz is also deadly. The sulfuric acid (H_2SO_4) on the cave walls can bring flesh to a boil. With pH levels rivaling battery acid, the cave muds and sediments can inflict third-degree skin burns on contact. In some rooms, carbon monoxide (CO) levels rev so high, it's the equivalent of running a NASCAR race in a toolshed. In others, oxygen (O_2) concentrations are lower than at the summit of Mount Everest, threatening cavers with anemic blood, bloated brain tissue, and even death from a dangerous cardiovascular condition called *hypoxia*. Although currently unsubstantiated, Louise also suspects that volcanic trace gases like sulfur dioxide (SO_2) and hydrogen fluoride (HF) may lurk in the cave's farthest rooms, threatening cavers with an even more mysterious miasma.

"Snottites," named for their obvious mucouslike appearance, drip from the high ceilings in Snot Heaven, one of the cave's largest and most toxic rooms.

Of greatest concern to explorers, however, are the cave's high concentrations of hydrogen sulfide (H_2S), which can exceed 150 parts per million (ppm). According to recent data, exposure to H_2S concentrations above just 10 ppm for any period of time is a "significant health hazard." General symptoms of H_2S poisoning run the gamut from skin discoloration to death. Some effects are external, like rashes, welts, and boils. Others are unnervingly internal, like nausea, loss of balance and dexterity, bronchial inflammation, and deteriorating short-term memory. By taking the place of calcium and potassium in the brain's nerve cells, H_2S penetrates to the core of the body's neurological systems and affects vital autonomic functions just when they're needed most, such as chest deep in a crawl space two kilometers back in a cave. Researchers from last year's expedition vividly recall instances of such cerebral congestion that they couldn't find their way out of Villa Luz just 50 feet from the entrance.

"H_2S is one of nature's most dangerous gases," Louise admits. "We just have no idea what we're dealing with. The effects of hydrogen sulfide also aren't just due to the concentrations you breathe. It's also how *long* you breathe it and how much you absorb through your skin. In Villa Luz, you're literally being soaked with H_2S inside and out. We also don't know anything about the long-term consequences of cumulative exposure. We know the short-term effects are immediately hazardous. But what happens weeks later, months later? What are we carrying around in our brains, internal organs, and other tissues?"

Given hydrogen sulfide's obvious toxicity, the Environmental Protection Agency (EPA) and the Occupational Safety and Hazards Agency (OSHA) have come down crystal clear on industrial H_2S protocols: *No Tolerance*. In the unfortunate instances when direct exposure must occur, personal self-contained breathing equipment is considered mandatory. For Louise and her team, such extensive safeguards are rarely employed, for both logistical and financial reasons. Instead, they rely on the cheapest life support available: a four-gas monitor, Tyvek chemical suits for the most toxic passages, and over-the-counter chemical respirators guaranteed for "evacuation only." Not surprisingly, Louise worries about a survival scenario. Should a spike of carbon dioxide, hydrogen fluoride, or sulfur dioxide occur in a tight back passage, the consequences might very well involve a body bag.

"The good news," she jokes, when we talk about the dangers, "is that no one's keeled over yet. The bad news is that we don't know why." Ultimately, rather than trust suspect safety equipment on an uncertain frontier, Louise and her team rely on the one thing every caver believes in: experience. Safety equipment is designed to get you out of a possibly fatal jam. Experience keeps you from getting into one in the first place.

Louise edges along a catwalk to bypass one of the cave's longest and deepest sulfur pools.

For every way that Villa Luz endangers the life of *Homo sapiens,* however, it nurtures a subsurface biological community that exists nowhere else on earth. Villa Luz is one of the only caves with hanging microbial veils, colonial "snottites," and gill-to-gill concentrations of the troglophylic (cave-adapted) fish, *Poecilia mexicana.* It is the only cave with "copious" energy inputs, "abundant" biota, and a "robust" food web. It is the only cave where the limestone walls are being chemically metamorphosed so fast that maps need to change with each expedition. DNA analyses of samples taken during last year's expedition, in fact, indicate that much of the microbial life in the cave exists nowhere else on earth. With such a diverse biological inventory, some scientists believe Villa Luz may be one of the only global habitats to contain all six of life's taxonomic kingdoms. Many microbiologists on this year's expedition joke that it may also be the source of a seventh.

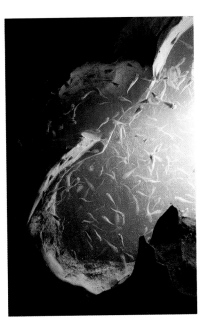

Las sardinas, *Poecilia mexicana,* school in a fingerlike pool carved from the cave's limestone bedrock. Villa Luz is the only cave in the world with such dense concentrations of fish.

"Most of all," Louise explains with visible joy, "it's the only cave where every time you go in, you notice something new." In a world largely "known and explored" by science, that's nothing less than miraculous. Although speleologists have known for years of the existence of historic paleosulfur caves, active sulfur speleogenesis happens about as often as an asteroid strike, and few have ever seen the process actually occur. Yet, in Villa Luz, it's happening right now, in real-time, offering Louise the once-in-a-lifetime chance to study the geological "now" instead of the paleo "then"; to see "genesis" happening in human time instead of earth time. In the process, Louise and her team are learning about much more than just gases, bacteria, and rock. They're learning about the life histories of caves all over the world, and despite the possibly fatal risks, the potential of life itself.

The mouth of Villa Luz erupts from the earth like a ruptured gas pipe, two miles south-southeast of Tapijulapa, a restored colonial village tucked in at the confluence of the Amatan and Oxocotlan rivers in south central Tabasco. Rugged and ruled largely by cattle ranchers, the surrounding region is almost suburban by rural Mexican standards. Unlike most Mexican settlements, main roads are largely pothole-free, and mail often

Selenite crystals encrust a low ceiling in the Yellow Roses room.

arrives unopened. As far as the rest of Mexico is concerned, however, the southern states of Tabasco and Chiapas might as well be annexed to Central America. Chronically neglected, inexcusably poor, and politically impotent, they're the part of Mexico no one seems to want, and as a result, they are custom-tailored for revolutionaries, on-the-run expatriates, and cavers.

"Villa Luz is right in the heart of Mexico's karst kingdom," expedition member Dave Lester explains as we pack equipment for my first day in Villa Luz, "and karst means caves—lots of them."

Karst is a technical geological term referring to landscapes sculpted by chemical dissolution and "breakdown" rather than mechanical erosion from wind and water. Trademark karst features, such as haystack hills, sinkholes, underground rivers, and caves, typically form in soft, soluble bedrock, like dolomite and limestone, in regions with abundant rainfall and active subterranean hydrology. Thankfully for cavers, southern Mexico happens to have all of these in excess.

"Geologically," Dave continues, "you couldn't have better conditions for speleogenesis (cave formation): deep limestone bedrock; rugged, uplifting topography; and aggressive hydrology." Dave is a director of the National Speleological Society, a caver of humbling credentials, and an expert on prime cave country, if ever there was one. He gestures out and upward, pulling pieces of tortilla from his snarled beard, and fades into a deep, almost religious reverie.

"So much karst," he sighs, "and so little time."

The speleological miracles of karst country, however, come at a dangerous price. Malaria and dengue fever, the latter of which is fatal in one out of three cases, are epidemic. Pit vipers lurk head-high in the canopy and can stop a grown person's heart before you can say "antivenom." And killer bees swarm the grasslands like locusts. There is also, Dave reminds me casually, this little problem of a revolution.

Just 50 kilometers south of Villa Luz, over a soaring cornice of mountains marking the border between the southern Mexican states of Tabasco and Chiapas, thrums the heart of the Zapatista rebellion. Unfortunately for Louise's team, the same landscape that gives birth to so many caves also happens to be the ideal venue for an uprising. With its rugged mountains, thick jungle, and deep caves, southern Mexico is the perfect place to duck out and dissolve away. As a result, since the now-famous New Year's 1995 uprising, robberies, stabbings, shootings, and abductions have become a regrettable adjunct to the Chiapas caving package. Testy, unpaid guerrillas prowl the outer perimeters of the jungle, while on the roads themselves, armored personnel carriers and military roadblocks are permanent installations. As far as most tour companies and U.S. diplomats are concerned, Chiapas is about as gringo-friendly as Sudan and Serbia.

"Things are still red hot down here," Louise explains, "and it's open season on anyone for any reason. Innocent situations can escalate quickly. And remember, it's New Year's too. It's the anniversary of the uprising, and if anything's going to happen, it's going to happen now." She pauses, pointing to the military encampment across the river, "And it's going to happen right here."

To the south of us, the looming, emerald flanks of the Chiapas Highlands rear up so high they block out the morning sun. To the north, the landscape flattens out into a broad plain serrated with square, knuckled hills. Silhouetted in the day's early light, they take on the distinct shapes of ankles, elbows, and knees. In many places, the cliffs and vegetation have sloughed away like skin shaved from the bone, and smears of pitted limestone seem to yell out: "CAVES ARE HERE."

Given such ideal geology, Mexico is just about the most logical place to find a cave as unique as Villa Luz. Speleologically speaking, if a karst feature doesn't exist here, it probably doesn't exist anywhere at all, a distinction that has earned Mexico the reputation of being the world's underground Himalaya. In a handful of different locations in southern Mexico, it's possible to travel a dozen horizontal miles underground and still not reach the end of anything. In Purificacion, Huautla, and Cheve, you can drop over a thousand meters down into the earth's crust, to the point where you'd swear it was starting to get hot. Not surprisingly, Mexico has long generated a kind of vortex in speleological circles, drawing cavers by the truckload to drop deep, push far, set records, and flirt with death. Like climbers across Nepal, they fan out and conquer, converging only long enough over rice and beer to up the exploratory ante another notch toward the truly insane.

Given such a voracious appetite for unspoiled caves, the greatest mystery of Villa Luz, ironically, is not so much its biological diversity, but its long-standing geographic anonymity. Cavers, like most explorers, spend a disproportionate amount of time looking for new frontiers. In developing and often war-torn countries, they snoop in places "white people" don't normally go and interrogate locals that tourists don't usually talk to. In short, they do just about anything necessary to find virgin holes. In light of such obsessive efforts, discovering a cave as scientifically significant as Villa Luz, with stairs and boat access, was as delightful as it was embarrassing for many veteran Mexico cavers.

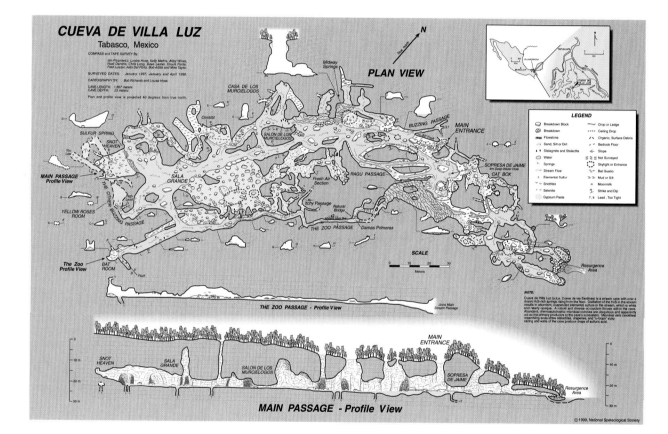

The official plan view of Villa Luz. Careful maps are essential to speleology for both safety and scientific reasons. This map is created by specialized cartographic software using lineplots, compass measurements, and passage descriptions taken within the cave itself. (Courtesy of Bob Richards.)

"The fact is," Louise explains, "no one was looking for a cave like Villa Luz. Cavers come to Mexico for length and depth, not for acid holes in a war zone. If they're going to risk their lives, they want to write themselves into the record books. But that's just not what Villa Luz is about."

Louise credits the rediscovery of Villa Luz to a lifelong caver and a Ph.D. psychologist named Jim Piszarowisc. Since 1972, Jim has braved bandits, rebel roadblocks, bad water, potent tequila, and remote Mexican jails for the sole purpose of finding new holes in the karst kingdom. On one such reconnaissance trip a few years back, Jim was approached by an old woman in a church square in Teapa, just north of Tapijulapa, who spoke to him the only four words of Spanish he knew: *Hay muchas cuevas aqui.* There are many caves here.

Over the next few days, the closer Jim got to Tapijulapa and the Chiapas Highlands, the more he heard locals talking about *azufre*—sulfur. They held their noses, pointed upstream, and mumbled something about white water and an angry God. Not quite sure whether he would find a mass grave or a massive opening in the earth, Jim followed his nose, literally, and within a week, he had found the entrance to Villa Luz. In his mind, he had hit the mother lode. With fellow caver Warren Netherton, he dropped inside, snapped a few photos, and got sick. Jim went home a few days later with a lingering headache and a deep chest cough.

"The problem at that point," he recalls, "was getting people interested in a foul, poisonous hole. We knew nothing about the risks, or even what we were looking at. Most people were just scared."

Finally, however, Jim showed his photos to Louise, and his life hasn't been the same since. Neither, of course, has Louise's. Within weeks, applications were filed and expedition permits received; cartographers, microbiologists, and biochemists were summoned; ropes, lights, vials, and smears were mobilized. With support from the Explorer's Club, Westminster College, and a host of others, the exploration pot was at a rolling boil by the fall of 1997, for a full-fledged Christmas expedition.

"That first trip cracked the Pandora's box for many of us," Louise recalls of the inaugural trip. "As soon as we got into the first room, I knew this was the beginning of something big. I just didn't know how big. If Jim hadn't been so dedicated, Villa Luz might have been one of the greatest missed opportunities in the history of science. . . . There's just nothing else like it on earth."

Physically, caves are as diverse as human beings. Some yawn open into sky-like amphitheaters that would need stadium lights to illuminate them. Others twist, taper, and truncate for hundreds of miles as if on a mission to the very core of the earth.

Over 20 feet deep and still unexplored, *La Sopresa de Jaime* **is the largest of approximately two dozen identified sulfur springs in Villa Luz.**

Some are predominantly dry—*vadose*. Others are fully submerged—*phreatic*. Some exceptionally complex caves are both—*epiphreatic*—fluctuating with seasonal rains or snowmelt, and changing in an instant from silent tunnels to stone-scouring torrents. Caves are found in glaciers near the top of the world, and branching off from the deep trenches of the sea. They form in temporary cliffs and banks of mud and in the oldest bedrock on earth. They are filled with freshwater, salt water, radon, sulfur, and in exceptional circumstances in outer space, possibly nothing at all.

Despite geology's proven artistry, however, no one had ever seen anything like Villa Luz before: a geologic phenomenon with a biological clock. Normally, caves are carved out by carbonic acid, the compound that forms when water reacts with carbon dioxide in the air or soil. Unfortunately for scientists, the process works like climate change—in atomic steps imperceptible to the human eye. Villa Luz, by contrast, seems to change every day. By metabolizing H_2S and O_2 into sulfuric acid (H_2SO_4) instead, the cave's bacteria, mucks, and slimes facilitate a far more aggressive and largely visible biochemical erosion. The process, though rare, is surprisingly simple. H_2SO_4, the acid commonly found in car batteries, reacts with the cave's bare limestone (calcium carbonate) bedrock, quickly converting it to microcrystalline gypsum (calcium sulfate). Highly soluble in water, the gypsum eventually sloughs off into the stream and is swept out of the cave for good. As this process exposes additional bedrock, it too is attacked by H_2SO_4, and the erosional cycle begins anew. As a result of this ongoing process, Villa Luz is literally caving in.

Due to such aggressive speleogenesis, an active sulfur cave like Villa Luz bears more resemblance physically to a clogged small intestine than a subway tunnel. From a bird's-eye view, called a *plan view* in technical cartographic parlance, the cave curves gently from southwest to northeast. Tip-to-tip, the official length is just under a mile and a half; vertical height in most rooms averages 60 feet from streambed to surface. At the cave's upstream end, a spigot from a dam break in the back wall feeds the main current year-round, while from the southwest, two additional streams pour in from passages too small to penetrate. Downstream, outside, the current leaps from an anonymous pile of stones like a blue winter brook, and the sulfur precipitating out from the water clings to the rocks and hanging vegetation in a delicate frost.

Inside, some passages and rooms in Villa Luz are high and wide enough to hangar an airplane. Large boulders sheared from the roof lie haphazardly about, as if a glacier had retreated through the cave only weeks before. Other passages are so small, only stream water can follow them. There are also 27 skylights, 24 springs, and at least 17 additional unpenetrated leads that begin as hallways, taper to crawlways, and ultimately end as wormholes no wider than a toilet bowl.

What makes Villa Luz such a speleological anomaly, though, is not its physical architecture, it's the biological architects themselves. Unlike the rest of planet Earth, Villa Luz doesn't run on solar energy, and the food chain doesn't begin with photosynthesis. The cave's high octane ecology runs exclusively on energy from sulfur oxidation ($H_2S + 2O_2$), and due to the seemingly endless sulfur inputs, life in Villa Luz literally leaps, flies, and drips into your face. It thrives in nameless, faceless colonies in every crack, under every rock, along every wall and ceiling. Technically, the sludges and slimes are called *microbes,* and they're some of the smallest, simplest life forms on earth. Taxonomically, they occupy the very bottom of the evolutionary ladder, kingdoms *Bacteria* and *Protista* to be exact. We know them more commonly as bacteria, algae, and amoebas. Microbes make topsoil fertile, recycle sewage at the bottom of the ocean, help animals digest each other, and kill mercilessly when nature designs them to do so. There are millions of them in your own body, and billions of them in a single room in Villa Luz.

In general, microbes tend to look like they came from a shower drain rather than the artful chisels of natural selection. Yet, not all the biota so far identified in Villa Luz lacks charisma. Down at stream level, swarms of midges graze the rocky breakdown for bacteria, and in the water itself reside rare albino crabs, assassin beetles, and eels. Huddled in small rock pockets, *P. mexicana* vie like feasting trout for the best feeding spots. Their bodies are stout and tapered like comets, their eyes wide, beady, and blue. Lacking pigmented skin, their veins and hearts show through like meticulous anatomical models. Preliminary sampling expeditions over the past two years have also revealed five species of bat, planktonic microbial phlegm, multiple fungi, a turtle, a transient local rodent called a *tepiscuentl,* tarantulas, black widows, and at least seven other species of arachnid.

"Villa Luz is simply the most active, dynamic, and biodiverse cave we know of," Louise confirms. "The first thing we noticed on our initial expedition was the sheer quantity of life. It was the first time we had ever seen such aggressive sulfur speleogenesis, and also so much chemoautotrophic life. Villa Luz is an energy free-for-all, and everything appears to run off of the sulfur."

It is precisely this fact that makes Villa Luz headline news. Typically, caves are the exclusive abiotic territory of geologists, but Villa Luz has turned that logic squarely on its

An albino crab hides behind a travertine dam just upstream from the Cat Box room. Observed infrequently, the crab, like most species in Villa Luz, is a biological mystery.

head. In just two years of blitzkrieg investigation, Louise and her colleagues have found that Villa Luz is in fact a boiling evolutionary pot, stewing with life in many of it's most primitive and endemic forms.

"Villa Luz is literally a planet unto itself," says Louise. "It's a real example of a Gaia environment and what we call 'biogenesis': a situation where organisms actually create and regulate their own world, where everything is totally interdependent—the rocks, the water cycle, the atmosphere, the biota, all of it."

Not surprisingly, the attraction of Villa Luz for some scientists *is* other planets, most notably Mars.

"Mars is a sulfur-based system like Villa Luz," explains Penny Boston, a Ph.D. scientist at Complex Systems Research, Inc., "and so far our best shot at finding extraterrestrial life. But at this point we don't even know what to look for. That's why we're so interested in the microbial life in Villa Luz. It might show us what to expect and where to look." Penny's findings here will ultimately pass directly into the hands of the scientists and planners at Mars mission control. If we can get an idea how sulfur ecosystems operate down here, the logic goes, we just might be able to recognize a similar system up there.

At this point, however, the only characteristic the two environments seem to share with any certainty is the existence of sulfur itself. On virtually every taxonomic level, Villa Luz remains as unstudied as the Red Planet itself, and the potential for original scientific discovery in every field is oceanic. Villa Luz is one of only a handful of places left on earth that doesn't fall into the already established taxonomic paradigms of science—and where first-time discoveries are often a matter of just showing up and pulling something off the wall.

"For all of us, this is shotgun investigation," Louise admits. "We're on the tip of a scientific iceberg and observing these things the first time. To be honest, we're still in what I would call a 'reconnaissance' mode. . . . We don't really even know what to study yet!"

Even after two full-scale expeditions, Villa Luz remains a black hole of mostly anecdotal speculations, which makes it no different from virtually every other cave in

Getting her feet wet. Working in the foul air directly above a sulfur spring, Holly Shugardt compiles a taxonomic inventory of the cave's spiders.

the world. Caves, as a general rule, aren't warm and fuzzy places. There are no slow-burning sunsets, no warbling songbirds. Caves, in fact, are the very essence of many people's most bowel-opening phobias: fear of the dark; fear of cramped, crushing spaces; fear of entrapment; fear of suffocation; fear of drowning; fear of vampire bats, tarantulas, snakes, skinless rodents, and other albino trolls. And, of course, fear of a torturous, anonymous death. Ask anyone, especially cavers, about their worst death scenario and it will often take place in a cave. Without daylight visual references, every room looks alike, and objective risks quickly become impossible to assess. For even the most experienced caver, the regular fear and disorientation are humbling reminders of how visual the human world has become, of how, without the sun, sea, and sky for reference, we are as paralyzed in our own medium as fish deprived of their fins.

Villa Luz's toxic biological stew only makes matters worse. Not only has the cave's ecology turned out to be far more complex than originally thought, but the more scientists learn about the gases, the more they realize they shouldn't be in the cave at all. As an unfortunate consequence, the chronology of original science in Villa Luz has evolved more like a game of Twenty Questions. Vast pastures of observation are only occasionally broken by revelation, and even the most basic accumulations of scientific data have come with geologic sloth. Everything must be noted, described, sampled, and sealed before exhaustive laboratory analysis can commence. No stone, literally, goes unturned, because assassin beetles, crabs, eels, and centipedes gather on the underside. The process, essentially one of detection and description, is very much like what a curious child might do in the woods. Significant features are scrutinized, and sample vials are placed into "like" piles, with one or two specimens reserved for especially obsessive focus.

In the most isolated and scientifically significant areas of Villa Luz, research has amounted to little more than "see-it-and-run" observation. Here, concentrations of H_2S often rev so high that respirators and new filters can clog in less than an hour. In still other areas, like the aptly named Itchy Passage, Tyvek chemical suits are mandatory to protect researchers from what Jim and Louise believe is a fungal-based histamine reaction. Thus far, those who have ventured in without protection emerged with full body welts and feeling like they were wrapped in a hot fiberglass blanket. In the few tight passage leads left to push, squeezes are so small you can't even get in without exhaling. As passage volume shrinks, gas concentrations soar proportionately. It's here that worst-case scenarios begin to rear their heads: What if the O_2 level drops below 10 percent? What if I twist an ankle in a crack? Could I evacuate before my brain shuts down?

Microbiologist Doug Soroka coaxes a toxic snottite into a sampling vial.

In addition to hindering basic mapping and sampling regimes, worst-case scenarios like these have also kept Louise out of Villa Luz's last frontier. Since systematic penetrations began two years ago, only the squirmholes that lie beyond a sedan-sized room called Yellow Roses—named for the rare gold florets on the walls—have remained out of reach. On even the most current map, the area is still marked by a single question mark. Despite repeated attempts, all previous pushes beyond the room's last limestone lip have been thwarted by soaring gas concentrations, bottomless springs, and six-inch airspaces between the water and ceiling. Cavers have registered H_2S levels as high as 156 ppm, O_2 levels as low as 9.5 percent. To top it all, Yellow Roses is so far removed from the Main Passage that should a fatal convergence of gases occur inside, timely evacuation to clean air would be uncertain at best.

Yet, Yellow Roses is the most scientifically unique area of the cave. It is the only place in the world where Louise has observed the yellow roses, technically called *sulfur*

Assistant Holly Shugardt explores a skylight room near the mouth of Villa Luz.

folia, which are stacked, subaqueous formations she suspects were deposited by the stream like geologic bathtub rings as it receded in the distant past. It is the only place she has seen a mammal—a bat—thriving in a fatally hypoxic environment. And it is one of two places in Villa Luz where she has heard the "buzzing," a barely detectable harmonic hum whose source is still totally unknown. For veteran cave junkies like Louise, such a frontier is dangerous—scientific heroin. Despite the known risks, the temptation to go for it is all-consuming.

Given the regular risks and irregular rewards, why speleologize, then? Why would anyone with Ph.D. intelligence endure the fatal risks of the underworld for the dark, indecipherable company of microbes and stone? And why here, in a war zone?

"Caves are the Earth's last frontiers," Louise argues, "and the underground wilderness is the only real wilderness left to study. There's more cave passage yet undiscovered than passage that has been explored. You just can't say that about forests, mountains, or oceans."

Recent discoveries seem to support Louise's view. Specialists in new fields such as geomicrobiology now speculate that more surface area and biomass—more raw "dark life"—exists underground in semisubmerged caverns and deep ocean vents than on terra firma. With respect to sulfur caves in particular, it has even been postulated that the first forms of life on earth were in fact chemoautotrophic, percolating in sulfur-charged cracks deep underground before boiling over into the famous primordial soup. Commercial investigations have also shown that the world's sulfur caves possess a wealth of possibly valuable species and compounds that could cure everything from cancer to oil shortages.

"We're not just finding out about extreme life or paleocaves here," explains Louise. "Villa Luz has a lot of wider applications to economically valuable industries, like lead and zinc mining, petroleum exploration, chemical and genetic engineering, and pharmaceuticals. Any inventory of new and exotic species tends to lead to the discovery of valuable compounds, and in Villa Luz, just about anything is possible."

Caves are also ecological backbones wherever they exist, and any long-term terrestrial habitat management must necessarily take into account their presence. In many karst landscapes, caves are literally the plumbing upon which all other habitats are based. They act as water and nutrient sinks, aerate soils, regulate stream flow and aquifer discharge, and filter out contaminants and sedimentation. Many, although none to the extent of Villa Luz, also harbor species that are critical to surrounding habitats in other, not so obvious ways.

Unfortunately, caves are regarded as nature's dive bars. Like swamps, they have been plugged, poisoned, and paved with little regard for long-term ecological consequences. Some have been pumped so full of sewage, they have literally overflowed like toilets. Others have been so shot-up by Saturday night rednecks that few living things ever returned. Inherently, caves are also low-energy systems. Without the primary active ingredients for decay and regeneration, like water, sunlight, nutrients, and detritivors (microbes that break down organic matter), caves are extremely slow to recover from even the most well-intentioned impact. In some caves, a pile of human feces can sit for a hundred years before even changing shape. In others without hydrological flushing, handprints and footprints can remain on the walls for millennia. When we make the decision to affect a cave in even the most circuitous way, we are necessarily gambling with extinction.

"Caves are also the places no one else wants to study," Louise adds. "As a scientist and explorer, can you imagine a more perfect working environment? I like to get more out of my adventures than just adrenaline. What motivates me is virgin exploration in scientifically fascinating caves and finding things that no one else has seen or described before. That's what we're getting here."

Given Louise's example, it should come as no surprise that world-class speleologists aren't the silk sheet types. Any cave explorer who can't take care of business chest

Penny Boston evacuates from the Buzzing Passage after detecting oxygen concentrations below 10 percent, under half that of normal atmospheric levels.

In an attempt to push new territory, Louise wades under the last lip of the Yellow Roses room using all eight inches of air space available.

deep in a river of guano three days back in a cave is about as productive scientifically as a marine biologist who refuses to get wet. To work effectively, survivalist nonchalance must be automatic. Days of darkness, near-drowning, death threats, and disease must be brushed aside like nuisance insects.

"Cavers are unique among adventurers," insists Louise, who has spent an estimated four years of her life underground, "and speleologists are different from other scientists. We don't just climb, ski, or dive. We're true explorers. We're obsessed with seeing what's around the next corner, and we're prepared to do whatever necessary to push those limits underground. On many expeditions, we're not just squeezing through holes. We're also rappelling in the darkness, lead climbing, swimming, and even scuba diving." Unlike climbers, cavers also aren't into graduating their limits with numerical ratings.

"You either have the balls to do it," Dave Lester likes to say, "or you don't."

Among certain speleological crowds, it's not uncommon to find that everyone has spent at least a week underground. On our expedition, the minimum rite of passage is six days—144 hours without sunshine, fresh air, or flattering afternoon light. On such extended expeditions, feces and urine must be packed out in "Burrito Bags," and food is minimized to such an extent that cavers joke about their wrists shrinking. On the most extreme pushes, mandated prerequisites include effective body recovery skills and the willingness to amputate your own limb in the event it's got you anchored to a certain demise between a rock and a hard place.

The grim reality of extreme caving and speleology, however, is not just that people die; it's how they die. The number-one cause of death is free-falling and splattering on the rocks below, due most often to bad handholds or breaking through a "false" floor. Second is drowning in a flash flood, an experience survivors compare with being trapped under lake ice. The third most frequent, and perhaps most preferable way to go is having your head smashed in by a runaway boulder. It's one of the few ways to die in a cave that doesn't involve prolonged suffering.

Given what she's endured, Louise's own track record of accomplishments is especially humbling. She's been trapped behind a flash flood overnight and lost for hours almost a thousand meters beneath her surface support team. She earned her Master's degree by investigating Mexico's longest cave virtually unassisted, working alone dozens of kilometers in for days at a time. In helping to push Mexico's deepest cave in the early 1990s, she became one of the few people on the planet to squirm, crawl, and climb a full vertical kilometer from the last breath of fresh air. But like most explorers and scientists, Louise is unimpressed with her own accomplishments.

Denied. Jim Pisarowicz is forced out of the Other Buzzing Passage on self-contained air after detecting oxygen concentrations below 9 percent.

"Risk is a reality for any explorer," she explains. "It's an inevitable part of the adventure. Just think about Columbus, Marco Polo, or John Wesley Powell. Without people throughout history who were willing to accept the challenges of original exploration, we'd all still be living on tiny islands of civilization and culture. If you don't want to see what's out there, you might as well stay home, have babies, and get cable."

Louise pauses, as if reconsidering the decision one last time.

"I'm just doing what my Mom told me to do," she finally adds. "I'm getting it all out while I'm young. I guess I'm just having trouble growing up."

With such an awesome track record of high-risk achievements, one would think Louise had no demons left to conquer.

"Not so," she admits. "If you can believe it, my greatest fear is of bats. They're beady-eyed, repulsive, and everywhere. I understand their importance to a cave ecosystem, but I don't have to like them."

Louise's second fear is scuba diving in underwater caves.

"The world's number-one recreational killer," she affirms without even inviting debate, "and a one-way ticket to the grave. In the last 10 years, over 300 people have died cave diving—more than 30 people a year. It's the most seductive thing I've ever done, but it's just too fatal. I already do too many dangerous things. When I'm 83 and have a terminal disease, maybe I'll get into it. Until then, I'd like to stay off the statistical list."

Compared to such extreme penetrations in the past, Villa Luz would seem to be little more than a walk-in closet by comparison. There are no technical free climbs, exposure swims, or 30 rope rappels into the darkness. It's not even particularly deep or long. There's a boat launch to the trail, a trail to the cave mouth, and a set of concrete stairs down to the beginning of the Main Passage. Nevertheless, the nonchalant rating is perilously deceptive. Villa Luz has more potential to kill than most other caves in the world, and unlike Mexico's more technically demanding caves, Villa Luz doesn't kill with avalanches, floods, and thousand-foot free-falls. With a Martian mixture of deadly gases, it steals life like high cholesterol and loneliness—quietly and invisibly.

At this early stage in the research, only one thing about the cave's toxicity seems clear: it's not what researchers know that's terrifying, it's what they don't know. And unfortunately, no one knows enough at this point to make an informed decision about whether anyone should be in the cave at all. In the absence of such certainty, Louise and her colleagues throttle back and stay conservative. They assume death is likely, change filters hourly, and treat gas spikes like puffs of the plague.

Finally outside of the Other Buzzing Passage, under the vaulted dome of Sala Grande, the cave's largest room, Louise and I stand erect and stretch for an unseen sky. The effects of the gases have hit hard and linger ominously. Alone in my own body, I focus on what it's like to overdose on a toxic gas, wondering if what I feel is normal and hoping silently that Louise feels the same way. My head feels too heavy for my neck, my arms and legs as if they're moving through water instead of air. Around my toe, a third-degree flesh burn has spread in a raw, amebic explosion.

Louise soon admits that she too is suffering from a quick onset of symptoms: tunnel vision, nausea, and the distinct feeling she's swallowed a handful of fiberglass.

"I had new filters, too," she adds. "There's something going on in there."

Back in Tapijulapa, cold showers do little to wash away the effects of the hydrogen sulfide. With a total exposure time in Yellow Roses room of over two hours, Louise and I violated every mathematical rule of H_2S saturation to the extreme. Our lung tissue should already be sweet, red puree.

"Today was an intense H_2S experience," Louise acknowledges later over dinner. "I feel like I've been soaked in the stuff."

"One of my cartridges was wet also," I admit, knowing that means I'm even worse off than everyone else.

"Well, you got in and got out alive. That's what counts." She pauses, then smiles slightly. "And we *did* push the cave a little further. At the very least, we know there's more to explore next year. . . ."

Look, but don't touch. Sealed in a Tyvek chemical suit, Lynn Kleina returns from a brief penetration into the Itchy Passage.

AIR
The High Frontier

Since Galileo, the things that we've been seeing [in space] are beyond human comprehension and understanding.

—Neil Armstrong

Little Cayman, British West Indies.

As the new millennium dawns, earth's high frontier is no longer the unattainable universe it once was. In the past century, the human race has summited the planet's tallest mountains, walked on the moon, circled the globe in a hot air balloon, and, most recently, has even stretched the tentacles of exploration to the surface of Mars itself. As a result, the world today is a much less forbidding place. Once vast and impassable chasms between nations have been reduced to brief aeronautical steps, while the dynamics of the cosmos and the secret lives of birds are no longer the abiding mysteries they used to be. With respect to even the loftiest scientific endeavor—whether geographical, chemical, or astronomical—no part of the high frontier now seems out of our reach.

Yet, like the world's underwater wilderness, the high frontier was not always as easily accessible as it is today. For thousands of years, gravity represented one of the most daunting limitations to human knowledge and exploration. Although many of history's boldest thinkers, like Copernicus, Galileo, and Leonardo da Vinci, cast their eyes endlessly skyward and seemed to know intuitively that clouds and forest canopies were as vital to the universe as anything here on earth, the laws of nature confined *Homo sapiens'* flights of discovery to his own imagination. For many early civilizations, such as the ancient Greeks, the sky was also a holy realm where no human rightfully belonged, and those who, like Icarus, dreamed of flying were not heroes but fools. Were humans meant to soar among the gods, the Greeks reasoned, they would have been given the wings to do so.

In 1903, in a small North Carolina town called Kitty Hawk, however, brothers Orville and Wilbur Wright boldly transcended the castes of evolution, becoming the first humans to achieve the dream of powered flight. On a purely technological level, the Wright Brothers gave to stargazers and birdwatchers what Jacques Cousteau gave to early scuba divers and oceanographers: a means of controlled, independent access to a realm where *Homo sapiens* was never designed to go. With the introduction of powered flight, we were no longer mere petals on the wind, but eagles with the power to explore the most remote corners of the universe.

The Wright Brothers' major contribution to the history of science and exploration was also psychological. Their persistent vision and ingenuity demonstrated that no frontier—physical, intellectual, or technological—was beyond the grasp of humanity, that even a pair of bike mechanics from Ohio could overcome the most elemental laws of nature and change our prevailing world view. Ultimately, the Wright Brothers' invention would inspire a generation of pilots, astronauts, and climbers to reach for the sky, unleashing an era of scientific discovery the likes of which the world had never before experienced. Within just 60 years of that first flight in the *Flyer,* on April 12, 1961, humankind would take yet another quantum leap into the high frontier—into space itself.

These days, science on the high frontier encompasses much more than just aeronautical engineering and space exploration. Air at every altitude is the medium in which many of earth's least-studied plants, animals, and other phenomena exist. Thus, it is here, in the "blue wilderness of interminable air," that these subjects must undergo scientific scrutiny if they are to be understood on their own terms.

That being the case, scientists have recently begun to utilize virtually every type of aerial technology—from hot air balloons and experimental hang gliders to elevated platforms and floating rafts suspended in the rain forest canopy—to bring the high frontier closer to home. In the process, they have begun to answer questions *in situ* which only a century ago were considered as unknowable as the stars themselves, such as how fast wind circulates in the high eye-wall of a hurricane, how birds migrate, how weightlessness affects the process of human aging, and even whether or not there is life in outer space.

By gambling their lives on the tenuous assurances of ropes and wings, however, airborne scientists and explorers are also flaunting one of earth's most elemental natural laws—what goes up must inevitably come down—and unfortunately, when technology fails, the results are almost always fatal, as the deaths of Amelia Earhart and the seven *Challenger* astronauts in 1986 so painfully demonstrate. Every year, too, hundreds of nonscientists and explorers are killed as a result of commercial, private, and experimental plane crashes, parachute failures, and ill-fated aerial stunts. Dozens more die falling from cliffs, glaciers, trees, and high mountain summits.

Humanity's bold Icarian explorers are after much more than just data, however. In exchange for their own individual lives, they seek that most universal of human needs—hope. Science on the high frontier has given us room to soar again, and a literal universe of mystery to explore. Most important, it has given us the ability to understand that all life is united by a common thread in the vast and forbidding cosmos—our shared place in space.

Father Swan. Ultralight aircraft are classified by the FAA in their own category. No
license is required to fly them.

Are You My Mother?

The small western–New York town of Alabama is famous for two things these days, the new hot water showers at the T&A truck stop on Interstate 90 and a flock of 20 rare trumpeter swans (*Cygnus buccinator*), North America's largest native species of waterfowl and the largest swan in the world. Given that as recently as 1932, barely 150 members of the species were known to exist at all, Alabama locals are especially pleased with their new neighbors. They pull off the road for a closer look through the fence and offer free bird feed, veterinary care, and open fields of edible roots.

The trumpeters are not in Alabama to stay, though—at least not permanently. If everything goes according to plan this morning, 11 of the 20 *C. buccinator* at the John White Memorial Game Farm will find themselves exactly 40 miles south of here at a remote rural landing strip on the Tuscaroroa Plateau in south-central New York State. There they will become the first of their kind in over 180 years to begin the species' historical north-south migration route from the Great Lakes lowlands to the eastern shore of the Chesapeake Bay along the Atlantic Flyway.

What really interests the locals, however, is not the rarity or the elegance of the birds themselves, nor is it the restorative ecological value of repopulating the Atlantic flyway with the majestic trumpeter after so long an absence. It's the way the birds are going to get from here to there in the first place—by following a "flock" of unorthodox ultralight aircraft.

"Most people have seen *Fly Away Home,* or at least heard of the movie," biologist Gavin Shire explains in his native British tongue, "but when they see us actually flying overhead in formation, it must be quite a shock. . . . They must think they've gone crazy."

Dressed in a yellow flight suit, Eskimo boots, and a thick leather jacket, Gavin performs a last-minute radio upgrade on his aircraft just outside of the game farm barn.

It's just before 5 a.m. on a cold, black December morning. Above an icy, 10-knot wind, we can hear the wind sock snapping ominously at the end of the runway. "Dodgy conditions," Gavin mumbles to himself. Ten knots is the upper limit for safe flight with the swans in his plane. Next to him, the three chase pilots for the migration, Brooke Pennypacker, Joe Duff, and Bill Lishman—whose real-life flights with Canada geese (*Branta canadensis*) inspired the Hollywood hit movie *Fly Away Home*—preflight their own aircraft, double-checking critical attachment points and installing emergency parachutes in anticipation of the remote mountain passes to come.

Combining a light fabric wing, a snowmobile engine, and a fuselage resembling a lawn chair, an ultralight "trike" appears every bit as experimental as it really is. In form, the trike resembles a real-life model of a Leonardo de Vinci flying machine. Forward thrust is provided by a 500cc two-stroke engine, called the power plant, connected to a marginally protected, three-blade, six-foot-diameter prop—a veritable meat grinder from a trumpeter's point of view. The double-surface, Rogallo-style wing design used on virtually all trikes is a cross between a high-performance Mylar racing sail and a full-fledged aeronautical foil. Strung drum-tight along a wishbone boom with 18 offset rigging wires, the wings vary in length between 20 and 40 feet, depending on the balance of speed and maneuverability desired. Functionally, the trikes operate more like motorized hang gliders than actual three-axis fixed-wing aircraft; thus, they permit the fine adjustments in speed and trim required when "flocking" with birds. The French-built Cosmos trike used by Gavin was chosen for its superb safety record and world-renowned sloth. Capable of cruising comfortably at speeds as low as 25 miles per hour, it is one of the only flying machines on the planet that can soar slow enough, precisely enough, to fly with one of the world's heaviest flighted birds.

"When we fly with the swans," Gavin explains about his weight-shift controlled aircraft, "it can be necessary to change your altitude by as little as six inches and hold it there, which is just not possible in a 'stick and rudder' plane. When we started to train the birds, for example, we were flying at barely 25 miles per hour mere feet above the trees. The wing we were using stalls at about 22 miles per hour. This was one of the real risks with the project, and without the Cosmos design, we would have had problems."

Outside, across a windswept field a hundred feet behind the barn, the "ultra-swans" are already wide awake. They line up along the near fence like kids pressing into a baseball game—preening, honking, watching Gavin's every move, oblivious to the history at stake today. Five months old now, the swans are almost fully grown. They have already molted once, and their primary flight feathers are now the color of brushed aluminum. Weighing over 20 pounds and standing over four feet high, they

The test pilots—*Cygnus buccinator*. An eight-week-old trumpeter swan, called a *cygnet*, forages for subaquatic vegetation (SAV) in the pond at Airlie.

measure almost eye-to-eye with assistant biologists Michelle O'Malley, Stephanie Scolari, Kevin Richards, and Donielle Roninger, who ready the birds for their momentous trailer trip to the runaway. Given the pressure for a successful flight, Gavin is preoccupied with his plane, the news crews, the weather, and the state of the swans themselves.

The Trumpeter Swan Restoration Project is a three-year experiment initiated by Environmental Studies at Airlie (a division of the International Academy of Preventive Medicine at Airlie, near Warrenton, Virginia) to demonstrate the viability of reintroducing migratory trumpeters to the east coast by teaching them to fly their traditional north-south routes behind an ultralight plane. Although still largely untested, the theory behind the experiment is as basic as science gets: Given the slightest crack, nature's basic roots will sprout through and reassert themselves. Teach 20 swans to migrate, and they can then teach 20 others, and so forth.

As the project's "flock leader," Gavin himself is something of a modern-day Icarus, boldly endeavoring to transcend the laws of nature in the name of "ecological redemption." In 1997, the project's pilot year, Gavin and three swans made aviation history by proving that trumpeters could, in fact, be taught to follow an ultralight plane. Their two-day, 103-mile journey took them from Airlie to the eastern shore of the Chesapeake at an average altitude of 750 feet. For a bird that typically climbs more than two miles into the troposphere and rides the jet stream for hundreds of miles at a time, the trip to Crapo, Maryland, was barely a workout. For the biologists, however, the message was clear: if you teach the swans correctly, they will follow. This year, after a bit of tinkering to improve the swans' long-distance stamina and ability to "lock on" to the ultralight, the goal is for real: a 10-stage, 330-mile migration that accurately replicates one the swans might have done 200 years ago. If successful, Environmental Studies intends to push the U.S. Fish and Wildlife Service and the Atlantic Flyway Council, the agencies in charge of developing a Flyway Management Plan for the species, to adopt the technique as an official means of reintroduction in the years to come.

"People are always fascinated by the ultralights," says Gavin, putting on his helmet and ski goggles in anticipation of the flight's sub-zero temperatures, "and the romantic idea of flying with the birds and leading a flock 'home,' but what they don't realize is that this is about the return of the trumpeter swan. . . . This is about restoring a beautiful bird to its native migratory ways."

Owing to indiscriminate market hunting for meat, down, quill pens, and fashion accessories during the early years of colonial settlement, *C. buccinator* was almost extinct by the turn of the twentieth century. Those that survived the guns were even-

A flock of trumpeters takes off on the wing of chase pilot Brooke Pennypacker against the backdrop of the Tuscaroroa Plateau in south-central New York State.

tually choked out by agricultural expansion, the modification of wetlands and estuaries, and the fragmentation of previously confluent migration corridors. Despite a pre-European distribution believed to have stretched from the Arctic circle to the border of Mexico, a 1932 coast-to-coast survey turned up only 69 trumpeters in the contiguous United States, all of which were located in a single flock in Montana's Centennial Valley.

These days, due to protection from hunting under the Migratory Bird Treaty Act of 1918, the creation of critical refuges, and the reintroduction of resident flocks to Ontario, Minnesota, Wisconsin, South Dakota, and other midwestern states, the trumpeter swan is no longer endangered nor at risk of extinction. Coupled with the discovery of previously unknown flocks in Alaska and western Canada, the entire North American trumpeter population, in fact, now totals well over 16,000 birds, and more regional restoration projects are on the table. The numbers, however, are misleading barometers of the species' ecological stability. Not only are wintering grounds still threatened by urban sprawl and development, but not one of the current reintroduction programs involves reestablishing the species' historic migration patterns. Trumpeters may be waddling back from the brink, but overall, the species is by no means intact and thriving.

At the heart of the debate for scientists like Gavin is the importance of the migratory process itself, and more specifically, the question of whether any permanent, reintroduced trumpeter population can be considered "wild" or "recovered" in the first place. In the effort to stabilize any endangered species, seasonal migrations are not an optional part of the restoration package. In the trumpeter's case, migratory pathways are passed down from generation to generation like an indigenous oral history. Without the routes, an essential element of the species' wild character is irretrievably lost. From a practical standpoint, without the ability to respond to seasonal variations in prey, weather, and other extrinsic environmental factors, the swans quite literally become sitting ducks, pinned down by the year-round use of a single habitat and constantly running the risk of catastrophic depopulation from disease, large-scale disturbance, overuse of finite resources, and over the long term, lack of genetic diversity and exchange. Ecologically, despite the good intentions of resident restoration projects, raising a migratory species to call a single refuge home isn't reintroduction; it's more like building an outdoor zoo.

Teaching a flock of stubborn, 30-pound waterfowl to migrate isn't quite as simple as sinking some fence posts in the ground and calling it a sanctuary, however. It requires a rare synergy of scientific expertise, physical infrastructure, financial capital, and political will which until a few years ago simply didn't exist. Most of all, it requires

Flying comes naturally to a trumpeter swan. Landing does not.

someone like Gavin, who is not only proficient with the science of captive breeding and the reintroduction of endangered birds but is also willing to risk his life in an ultralight on a day like today. Two-thousand feet in the air on a windy winter morning isn't the place to be doing anything "experimental"—scientifically or technologically. With swans on the wing, the flight becomes potentially suicidal, which is exactly what makes the project twice as exciting as it would be otherwise.

For most people, what makes the Trumpeter Swan Restoration Project sensational is not the thought that they might one day look out the window to see a flock of trumpeters alighting on their local pond; it's the idea that scientists are risking their lives in experimental aircraft to make that happen. In the opinion of most visitors to the John White Game Farm, specifically, Gavin is a hero not because of what he's doing but how he's doing it. The Trumpeter Swan Restoration Project appeals directly to humanity's predilection for martyrdom, and for this reason it is without doubt one of the most visually arresting wildlife reintroduction initiatives on the planet.

"Ultralights are simple machines," Gavin explains, "so there's not really much that can go wrong with them . . . but when something does go wrong, it can be catastrophic. There's no breakdown lane up there. It's not like a car you can just pull over. An engine out at low altitude, [for example], can be very, very dangerous."

Out on the runway, chase pilot Bill Lishman, the original "Father Goose," prepares to take off on a brief test flight to assess the conditions for the entire flock. He pulls the starter cord and the ultralight roars to life with the high-pitched whine of a chainsaw, piercing the still morning air. Bill then hops into the small seat, grabs the control bar, and accelerates down the long hill to the runway. Just beyond the first row of utility wires, northeast of the game farm, he pushes forward on the bar, exposing the wing's undersurface to the airflow, and the plane leaps off the ground as if it's being pulled up, like a puppet. In seconds, Lishman is 200 feet in the air.

With or without the swans, of primary concern to every ultralight pilot is gear failure at altitude. With a single power plant, a single wing, and a Spartan assortment of peripheral controls, ultralights are hailed by advocates as the simplest and safest way to fly. For the very same reasons, they are judged by critics to be the aerial equivalent of high-speed motorcycles.

"In a regular airplane," Brooke tells me as he finishes off his own preflight check, "there are hundreds of bolts and linkages that can kill you. On a trike, there's only one, and if you treat it with appropriate weight and attention, you should be okay."

Brooke reaches up and fingers a single, three-eighths-inch stainless steel pin called the "Jesus bolt," so named because when it shears in half, "Jesus" is likely the

A perfect day for flying. Dawn breaks clear and calm over the John White Memorial Game Farm as assistant biologist Kevin Richards prepares Gavin Shire's ultralight for flight.

last thing out of your mouth before you splatter on the ground. Tucked just above the pilot's head, it represents the only attachment point between the wing and the fuselage of the plane itself, which for most people is precisely the problem. What ultralights boast in simplicity, they sorely lack in redundancy. Should any primary part of the plane malfunction—the Rotax engine, the wing fabric, the steering controls—the results are often fatal. Brooke is quick to add, however, that an ultralight, like all planes, is only as safe as its pilot and how and why it's flown.

The "Jesus" bolt. The three-eighths-inch steel bolt is the only connection between the wing and the fuselage of the ultralight.

"You've got to approach ultralight flying with a healthy degree of paranoia, especially with the birds. You always have to tell yourself that this could be the flight where I die." Like most pilots, Brooke has learned about caution the hard way. In his 15 years of experimental flight, Brooke has had nine friends die in ultralight accidents.

Given the multiple traverses over the Appalachian Mountains on this year's migration, the pilots court even greater risk by violating rule number-one of general aviation: Always have a suitable emergency landing field within gliding distance. Once into the heart of Pennsylvania's coal country, there are no fields or roads where the pilots can put down their planes should the weather deteriorate or a bird decide to break away. For dozens of miles in every direction, the northeast trending faults of Appalachia break in great, geologic tidal waves over nothing but timber.

"We've done this part of the route before and it's all bush," Joe Duff admits. "If a bird or a plane drops out over the mountains, it's over. There's no way you're going to get them back."

Considering today's flying conditions, Gavin and the chase pilots will also be violating rule number-one of ultralight aviation: Only fly when conditions permit safe, controlled flight. By first light, a thick fog bank still hangs low over the runway. High overhead, thin cirrus clouds curl across the sky, a telltale sign of increasing high altitude winds and approaching weather. At the edge of the landing field, the wind sock continues to snap. This is the kind of weather in which accidents happen, Gavin tells me, and it's been like this for months.

As two local journalists hover in anticipation of headline bites, Gavin describes with practiced British understatement some of the countless near-misses he's endured since the team arrived in Alabama. Most dangerous of all has been direct contact with the swans themselves, especially in gusty conditions like today. Without consistent wind, the plane is knocked around by turbulence, making it impossible for the pilots to provide the necessary wing trim to produce "zero bar pressure." Otherwise known as a *slipstream,* it's this envelope of calm, predictable air that underpins the physics of V-flocking in the first place, allowing the swans to draft off the ultralights' wings with optimal efficiency. Without it, the birds lose patience, swerve around looking for good air, and eventually get wrapped up in the plane itself, a scenario which, during practice, has repeatedly threatened to founder the entire flock like cars in a freeway pileup. The problem is further compounded by the lack of hierarchy within the flock itself. Not only do the swans fight among themselves for dominance, but with Gavin himself.

"If I'm dipping and diving all over the place, fighting the turbulence," Gavin says, "the swans can't snug up behind the wing. Instead, they fly up on top, then out in front, and eventually box me in. . . . Having a swan fly in front of the wing makes handling the plane really tough. The birds create vortices, which reduce the lifting properties of the air over the wing, and it can take all your strength just to keep the plane straight and level. Ultimately, I can't go over the top without hitting the ones above me, or slow down to give myself more room without making contact with the ones behind. . . . As a result, it's as dangerous for me as it is for the birds. When a swan gets wrapped in the rigging, it creates some serious problems in your ability to control the plane."

A veteran of five ultralight migrations with three different waterfowl species, Joe Duff adds that the risks aren't just about accidental contact with the birds. He's concerned as well about midair collisions between the planes themselves.

"When you have four planes up there maneuvering, turning, stooping, and climbing, all it takes is one bad radio call or tunnel vision on a single bird and WHAM! . . . It's over. . . . The problem is that the risks come with the territory when you're doing migrations. You can only fly so long before the law of averages kicks in."

Unfortunately, since the birds were first transferred to Alabama from their original home in Virginia, where they were hatched in June, training problems have created the potential for a free-for-all. Morning flight training has been consistently hampered by high winds and bad weather, and insurgent birds within the flock itself have precluded the group cohesion critical to a successful migration. Over the last five weeks in particular, birds have been falling ill, breaking away from formation, competing with Gavin for dominance, and worst of all, tangling themselves in the planes' delicate rigging. Consequently, Gavin, Brooke, and the other pilots have done more chasing and corralling than leading.

"The birds just aren't ready yet," Gavin explains, his frustration clearly evident. "With so little time to practice, they haven't developed the stamina or hierarchy to stay in formation for more than a few minutes. . . . In this weather especially, I'm not sure that they can make it, or that we can either. This is a pretty trashy day to fly."

Gesturing around him to the highways, high wires, antennae towers, and finally to the wind swirling in the top of a nearby oak tree, Gavin wears the look this morning of someone who's been victimized by fate. Time is running out, he tells me. Tomorrow, the forecast is for high winds off Lake Erie, low clouds, and sleet—portents of a long winter only days away. There's no more time for practice. If the birds don't get out this morning, they risk never getting out at all.

Gavin's now-or-never solemnity is not for the cameras; the stakes for today's flight, both physically and scientifically, are as high as they get. The Trumpeter Swan Restoration Project ranks as one of the most ambitious initiatives yet in the embryonic field of *restoration science,* the still unrefined process of reweaving nature's web and cleaning up the messes of human generations past. As part of similar restitutions, rivers are being unplugged, tall grass prairie is being replanted, and apex terrestrial predators like wolves and tigers are being given back small, charitable chunks of the wild. Yet

A remote camera mounted on the nose of Brooke Pennypacker's ultralight
captures a rare in-flight image of migration.

most scientists agree that the Trumpeter Swan Restoration Project is different. Not only are the myth-evoking Icarian means vastly more exciting than planting prairie seeds, but the end goal itself illustrates one of the more ironic twists in the history of conservation biology. The scientists of the Trumpeter Swan Restoration Project are doing more than just releasing swans, they're teaching them how to be wild again.

The problem is that reconnecting nature's ecological circuitry isn't as easy as sticking a plug back in its socket. Brainwashing a bird to follow an ultralight and teaching it to migrate seasonally with the goal of facilitating continental reintroduction are two entirely different things. For the Trumpeter Swan Restoration Project to be truly successful, yes, the swans must follow the ultralights south, but they must initiate the return trip north next spring on their own and identify the difference between wintering and breeding grounds. They must learn to vocalize, socialize, identify themselves as trumpeters, and eventually reproduce with their own kind when they reach sexual maturity as second-year birds. Most of all, they must shed their associations to humanity and learn to live like wild birds in an increasingly civilized landscape in which people, cars, planes, and domesticated animals have all become agents of natural selection.

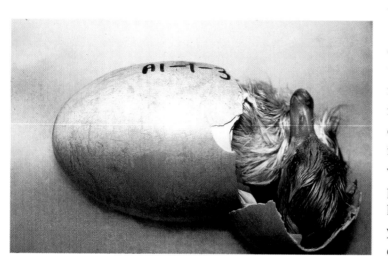

A trumpeter hatches from its egg in the incubator at Airlie. Out of an original clutch of 28 eggs, 23 swans hatched from their eggs healthy and alive. (*Photograph by Gavin S. Shire.*)

Obviously, this is far easier said than done. As experience with myriad species shows, wildlife reintroductions are a lot like human tissue transplants. Although swapping life from one place to another seems simple enough in theory, failures, rejections, and complications are all too often the norm. In the grand tapestry of evolution, life exists where it does for a reason, and it rarely behaves the same way when moved and manipulated for expressly human purposes. The rewilding of any species into any habitat is, as *Baltimore Sun* writer Ted Horton aptly called it in reference to the ultraswan project, a "frontier newer than space."

If the ultraswan experiment proves successful, however, the biologists will have accomplished much more than just the reestablishment of east coast trumpeter migrations. By answering such general methodological questions as how waterfowl maintain flock hierarchy in the air, how much flight training is enough, what a pilot can do to encourage drafting, and most important, how much an ultralight migration must mimic

Flight instruction. One of three training groups follows Gavin Shire and the ultralight down the runway at Airlie.

the real thing in time, space, and technique, Gavin hopes to contribute data to what may one day become the most revolutionary tool in wildfowl conservation since the advent of the National Wildlife Refuge. For other endangered migratory birds, like the lesser white-fronted goose (*Anser erythropus*), the whooping crane (*Grus americana*), and the Siberian crane (*Grus leucogeranus*), standardized ultralight migration procedures may turn out to be the equivalent of planting old-growth forest seeds—an early hand-crank by humans to get the momentum of evolution up and running again.

When Michelle and Stephanie finally arrive with the trailer to take the first team of six swans down to the runway, the birds race to the doors as if being released from prison. Smug and overprotected, the swans carry themselves with the air of trust fund children, oblivious that this is all for them, that dollar-for-dollar, they are some of the most expensive birds on the planet. In the excitement, they unfold their massive eight-foot wings and flap widely with flight intention, sending up a storm of grass, leaves, and white, downy feathers.

In all, only 11 birds will fly today; the remaining nine will be trucked to the Tus-caroroa Plateau with the rest of the support and cargo vehicles and flown locally to build strength and stamina. Because of the weather and the state of the birds them-selves, the flock has been chosen by process of elimination. Overly dominant, inconsistent, and weak birds have been grounded. Five others have been diagnosed with potential avian bronchitis and quarantined. Another named Jack continues to suffer from eye problems. Those that remain are a mixed bag from the project's original three teams— red, blue, and green—and although most have flown together before, the uncertain flock dynamics portend myriad problems.

In spite of the overall risks and today's complexities, the basic theory behind the ultralight technique is perfectly simple. As opposed to songbirds, many of which have their migratory itineraries genetically hardwired to the planet's magnetic field, trumpeters must learn a migratory route from the air. They must be taught by a designated flock leader about different topographic corridors, distinct geologic landmarks, and when to start and where to stop. Thanks to a process called *imprinting*, however, one doesn't need feathers to be the lead bird. Waterfowl, it seems, will follow just about anyone home.

First identified by Austrian biologist Conrad Lorenz, imprinting is utilitarian slang for a uniquely avian characteristic called the *following response*. In his work with Greylag geese (*Anser anser*), Lorenz noticed the tendency among waterfowl to follow the first object they see and hear after hatching, ultimately identifying that "thing," whether animate or inanimate, as their flock leader. Over time, Lorenz and others experimented with various elements of color, sound, and shape and found that the key to manipulating maximum automation from the following response depended less on any one sensory factor and more on repetition and consistency. In other words, given the right technique, waterfowl would follow a motorcycle as obediently as they would a human or their own mother or father. At the time of its discovery, however, the following response generated little fanfare among scientists; no one saw that the phenomenon could be used for an applied scientific purpose.

In 1988, Canadian inventor, sculptor, and ultralight pilot Bill Lishman finally put two-and-two together. Working with a clutch of Canada geese, Lishman applied his own self-styled imprinting techniques to teach the birds to follow him first on foot, then on a bike, and ultimately in his own ultralight plane. By fall, Father Goose and his flock were soaring daily over southern Ontario. For scientists and wildlife managers worldwide, Lishman's experiment held a tantalizing message: the imprinting process works even in the air. For Dr. William Sladen of Environmental Studies at Airlie, news of Lishman's success was the answer to a dream.

Since his early research with Antarctic birds in the 1960s, Dr. Sladen has envisioned the return of North America's large migratory avifauna with childlike surrealism, painting pictures of a restored aerial Serengeti to anyone who would pay attention. As a scientist, however, he has always been acutely aware of the logistical limits which pre-

Assistant biologist Michelle O'Malley gives the first trumpeter team some final words of encouragement before the beginning of a history-making migration day.

Brooke Pennypacker clears the trees with the trumpeters tight on his wing. Within seconds of takeoff, the swans sort themselves into an established flight hierarchy and assume the traditional V flocking pattern.

clude such utopian ecological dreams. Lishman's experiment gave Dr. Sladen what he had been looking for—a methodology. If geese can be taught to fly behind ultralights, he reasoned, why can't larger threatened birds like trumpeter swans and whooping cranes be taught to migrate behind them as well?

With the goal of finding out, Dr. Sladen and Lishman joined forces in 1993 and quickly set about designing imprinting and training protocols for a full-fledged goose migration from Blackstock, Ontario, to Airlie. Up until 1993, Lishman had only flown with his geese for a few miles a few minutes at a time, and rarely out of sight of home. To migrate the 380 miles between Ontario and Virginia, the birds would need greater stamina, more efficient flocking skills, and greater dependency on the plane to ensure cohesion over unknown terrain. In scientific circles, the goose migration was met with widespread skepticism from the very beginning. Citing uncertain potential for rewilding and unnecessary risks to both the pilots and the birds, critics called the ultralight technique a pet trick, and they criticized Lishman's lack of scientific training.

Much to the chagrin of the naysayers, though, the world's first ultralight migration was a roaring success. Out of 18 birds raised on Lishman's farm, every one of them completed the journey to Airlie without incident. The following year, improving on the imprinting and flight training techniques from 1993, Operation Migration blew the doors of wildlife restoration right off their hinges. Of 35 geese flown from Lishman's home in Ontario to the Tom Yawkey Wildlife Center in South Carolina, a distance of more than 800 miles, 33 returned unassisted the following spring to the exact same pond, and many are still migrating along the same route today. Altogether, between 1993 and 1995, 113 Canada geese were led by ultralights along preselected migratory routes between Canada and South Carolina and nearly 65 percent of them returned on their own the following year. With such encouraging results, Dr. Sladen decided it was time to up the ante, and in 1997, the Trumpeter Swan Restoration Project was launched with Gavin at the helm.

"They still think I'm crazy," Dr. Sladen tells me, looming close like a curious bird. "They think this can't work. But they're wrong." He looks affectionately at the first six birds as they depart for the far end of the runway in a dilapidated, wooden trailer and speaks to them quietly, "You'll show them, won't you?"

Partially obscured in the lingering fog, Gavin, Brooke, Bill, and Joe have all taken to the sky and are testing the still-turbulent air over the landing field. As they dive in close over the trailer, the swans respond immediately to the roar of the Rotax engines overhead, honking excitedly, shuffling around the trailer, and bobbing their heads as if wired to an internal musical beat. Silhouetted against the faint light of dawn, the ultralights tear small rips across a brightening sky, diving and spiraling intermittently like wind-blown butterflies. Dr. Sladen turns toward the sunrise, and as the planes come back in for landing, he opens his arms as if accepting something divine.

"In the beginning," he continues, "people thought 'Why would you mix birds with planes? We spend hundreds of thousands of dollars a year just to keep the air spaces separate.' People also criticized the human safety factor. Why not use model or remote planes rather than risk lives in one of these?" Dr. Sladen gestures to Brooke's ultralight as it rolls to a stop with the rest of the planes. In an age of stealth fighters and space shuttles, the aircraft appears appropriately Mesozoic. With its bolts, butt ends, round pegs, and square holes, it scarcely seems airworthy, in fact. "What we've shown them," Dr. Sladen adds with a wry, I-told-you-so smile, "is that there's no better way to do this work. We just needed to learn how."

But it's a fact as well that no one has the ultralight technique hardwired. Like all knee-jerk, animalistic reactions, there are patterns and catalysts to waterfowl behavior but few behavioral guarantees. Large monogamous birds are not machines. They are uniquely expressive, individual animals with peculiar life histories, radiant idiosyncrasies, and distinct emotions, much like humans. A decade of experimentation has also revealed specific differences between waterfowl species themselves, not only in

Dawn breaks over the John White Memorial Game Farm as the swans take to the air between Gavin Shire and Brooke Pennypacker.

how they respond to imprinting but also in how they migrate and how the eggs must be cared for in the first place. Trumpeters, for instance, have turned out to be more "family" than "flocking" birds, which means they are less willing to migrate with ultralights in large groups. As a result, protocols have had to change with each year, each migration, and each new species and scientist brought into the mix. Old tricks have been tossed and fresh ideas tried in their place. As with all raw scientific experimentation, Gavin reminds me, theories are never wrong, just untested.

"Every year," Lishman adds, standing by his plane, ready for final takeoff, "we're building on last year's lessons and trying to correct last year's mistakes, and every year, regardless of the bird species, the process gets more refined." He pauses briefly, taking stock of the four ultralights around him and the collective migratory knowledge of the pilots. "But mostly it gets more complex," he adds. "You start to realize what a difficult, intricate process imprinting and migrations are. . . . There are always a lot of theoreticals." Lishman knows this pain of trial and error better than anyone in the world. In the quest for predictability and the "construction" of a truly wild migratory bird, he has altered his ultralight to look like a goose, dressed up like a whooping crane, and hand-raised his birds so far from civilization that by the time migration occurred, they had yet to see a human being or man-made structure up close, or even to hear a human voice.

Although he hasn't gone to the same extremes as Lishman, Gavin's own techniques with the trumpeters have pushed the envelope equally far, and whether today's migration is a success or not, the value of the knowledge gained over the past six months cannot be understated. Simultaneously drawing from and departing from the precedents set by Lishman over the past few years, the primary goal of the Trumpeter Swan Restoration Project this year was to expose the birds to the plane from day one, and more important, to allow them to follow it only when Gavin was inside. Not only would this ensure greater dependency on the plane itself, it would also remedy one of last year's most glaring mistakes: by the time the swans reached Crapo, they identified themselves more as people than as trumpeters. Instead of mingling with local birds and mastering critical survival skills, such as foraging and predator avoidance, the birds would loiter outside the biologists' doors like stray dogs, begging for corn, companionship, and the comfort of human love, despite the best attempts to haze and "dehumanize" them.

"To prevent the same thing from occurring this year," Gavin explains, sitting back in his seat and waiting for the swans, "our procedure was to start playing the tape of the ultralight [engine] when the embryos broke into the air cell, about two days before they hatched. We would then play the tape to them three times a day after they hatched for the first three to four days. We introduced them to the ultralight without the wing as early as possible, at about day five, but did not turn on the engine. The biggest change for this year was to not let them walk anywhere without the plane. As soon as they were able to swim in the pond, we would only let them go down there by following the plane, minus the wing. The psychology behind this was that the plane, like mother swan, always led them to something they liked, so they would be more willing to follow."

Gavin also experimented with different visual and auditory cues this year to see if certain sensory elements might affect swans in different ways than geese and cranes. From the very start, everyone in the "flock" was required to wear yellow—even the ultralights—and a bicycle horn which mimicked the swans' trumpeting call was used instead of the human voice to rally the birds to attention. Although due to the daily hassle, the team stopped short of wearing costumes, Gavin also minimized the human presence in general, permitting contact only with the plane, the biologists, and their own kind.

Unfortunately, even with the new techniques, the Trumpeter Swan Restoration Project has been hampered by serious problems. Many of the corrective refinements designed to build on last year's mistakes have proven largely ineffective, and the larger flock and more ambitious migratory goals have opened up entirely new loopholes in the imprinting process itself. Worst of all, trumpeters have turned out to be far more difficult to handle and imprint in captivity than anyone originally thought.

"Relative to geese," Gavin explains, "swans are rocket science. Not only are they much larger, but they are much more difficult to incubate, hatch, raise, and keep disease-free until fledging. They also don't seem to imprint as roboticly as geese. . . . Even with the same conditions, total failure has always been a possibility."

To no one's surprise, four swans never made it to Alabama in the first place. Two died from birth defects within five days of hatching, one succumbed to an unknown disease soon afterwards, and the runt of the flock eventually had to be euthanized. Of the 22 swans that made it to New York, two have died on practice flights in the past month. The first snapped its neck on a utility wire, and the second cracked its breast plate on the game farm fence coming in for a landing. Alabama, New York, has also turned out to be one of the windiest places on earth. Out of a total of 69 days at the John White Game Farm, only 21 days have been flyable. The most significant problem, however, has been direct collision between the swans and the ultralights. Since intensive flight training began, there have been six nonfatal entanglements in the rigging.

"On last year's final leg," Gavin recalls, "we had two tangles in the rigging, one right before the runway, but neither was serious. They bumped me, and I dropped them off the back and regained position. The problem is that because it was the last leg, we didn't recognize it as a pattern and consistent problem. We thought it was a fluke. Then when we started having the same problem this fall, we knew it was a significant issue. . . . It's one of the most important lessons we've learned this year: that what we're trying to teach them—namely, to lock on tight for maximum draft—is the very source of the problem."

As far as the project in general is concerned, the consequences of collateral mortality extend far beyond the loss of a swan. Due to its high profile status among both aviation and waterfowl enthusiasts and the scientific community at large, the Trumpeter Swan Restoration Project can't hide its deficiencies; and due to its experimental status, the project can't afford bad press either. Even a single death will give the critics the ammunition they've wanted to shoot the technique dead once and for all. Ironically, at this still-early stage of development, the viability of future ultralight migrations depends less on success and more on preventing egregious failure.

"Killing the birds is just unacceptable," Dr. Sladen explains. "It puts the pilots at risk, the birds at risk, the project in jeopardy, and the whole technique of ultralight migration in a bad light."

Based on last year's track record, there are also more problems to come. Despite attempts to minimize the swans' attachment to humanity, the birds have once again developed a deep affection to the biologists, especially Michelle and Stephanie, with

Timing takeoff. As Gavin Shire pushes forward on the ultralight's control bar, the aircraft leaps immediately into the air.

whom they have spent the most time. It also remains to be seen what impact the swans will have on the habitats and species that have evolved to function without their presence.

"What's most important in a project like this," Gavin asserts, "is that when we biologists go trying to reverse something we messed up years ago, we don't mess that up too. Trumpeter swans breeding in the Chesapeake Bay instead of New York or Canada would be fine for the swans but potentially disastrous for other bird or plant species in the bay."

On a somber note of potential failure, the first flock of swans is finally driven into position just behind the ultralights at the eastern end of the runway. Burying his apprehension, Gavin preflights his plane one last time in a sequence of good luck offerings: he strokes the dew from his wing fabric, checks the knots on the batten sleeves, and wiggles the prop as if worried he might not have screwed it on tight enough. He then turns to the other pilots with a questioning thumbs-up. Yes, they respond, it's time.

"CLEAR PROP!" Gavin yells, pulling down hard on the starter cord. Instantly, the ultralight roars to life, and again the birds go wild. Three-thousand feet overhead, volunteers Bill and Mary Lou Hagan fly top cover for this first leg, directing traffic over the radio and keeping track of wayward birds and plane failures. Soon, all four engines are revving, working the birds into a Pavlovian frenzy.

Then suddenly, with a quick nod from Gavin, the ultralights are off. Seconds later, the gate of the trailer is dropped and the swans rush out like thoroughbreds from the starting block, terrified that their flock leader might leave them behind. With a dozen deep flaps of their wings, they are up and off the runway and tucked in behind Gavin's wing.

In less than a minute, however, things start falling apart. Seeing the pond from the air, one of the swans breaks from formation and begins to spiral downwards. Others soon follow, and the ultralights loop back in an attempt to salvage the flight. In order to keep the swans airborne, Gavin dives in beneath them just feet above the trees, and offers them a good wing. Lishman and Joe ride up from behind and keep the flock moving. Three-hundred feet out in front, Brooke accelerates toward Tuscaroroa, gunning his engine repeatedly as if to say, "Hey swans, this way!" Over the radio, the migration sounds more like a World War II dogfight than a refined wildlife reintroduction. Then suddenly, amid the chaos and confusion, comes a transmission that stops everyone cold.

"Engine out!" Brooke yells. "I've got an engine out!" Out in front of the swans, we can see his plane dropping fast. Responding immediately, Joe peels off from the chase group to lend support and leaves Gavin and Lishman to round up the birds and bring them home. Brooke, however, needs no help. He muscles his ultralight like a

A rare image of a trumpeter on the wing. Brooke Pennypacker says he can see God in the eye of a swan flight. (*Photograph by Gavin S. Shire.*)

hang glider toward a fallow corn field a half-mile from the game farm and eventually disappears behind a stand of trees. Seconds later, his voice comes over the radio.

"I'm down," he says calmly, and then adds, "Do you want me back up there?"

The first flight is over. Back by the game farm barn, the swans have landed by the pens and stand around absently as if nothing had happened. Out on the runway, the ultralights taxi in for landing. Over the radio, Gavin is thoroughly annoyed.

"Bring out the next group," he says. "We'll try this one more time."

The second team of five swans gets airborne immediately, and much to everyone's surprise, locks on tight. As the ultralights disappear over the trees to the south, the birds fan out single file in the sweet spot just aft of Gavin's wing. Against a deep blue winter sky, the flock forms a perfect V.

"Wonderful," Dr. Sladen gushes. "Absolutely wonderful!"

Unfortunately, the project's good luck doesn't last for long. Fifteen miles into the flight, the weather deteriorates. The wind picks up to 17 miles per hour and the air begins to rumble with turbulence, threatening to bring the planes down far short of their 42 mile goal. Then the worst happens. Over the radio, we get news that a swan has hit the rigging above Gavin's plane, fallen into the prop, and dropped to the ground in a remote field just north of a small town named Darien Center. Gavin and

The "V." High above the eastern shore of the Chesapeake, the trumpeters lock on to Gavin's wing in perfect formation, utilizing the slipstream of the bird in front of them. (*Photograph by Gavin S. Shire.*)

the other pilots are okay, but the flight is over. In a shroud of disappointment, the biologists pack up the pens and the rest of the project's equipment and begin the long drive south.

On the ground in Darien Center, about 15 miles from Alabama, the pilots are visibly distraught. Part of the swan's left foot is gone, severed cleanly by the prop. Gavin, thankfully, is alive, as is Brooke, who was hit with two more engine failures en route.

"Steely's a very lucky bird," Gavin says quietly. "Losing just a foot is a miracle. The problem is that it all happens so quick . . . all I feel is the yank against the rigging wires. This time, when I knew a bird was tangled, I pushed forward, pitched up, and tried to lose speed to throw her off, but she must have just dropped straight down into the prop instead. . . . Unfortunately, this problem is not new. It was only a matter of time before a bird got injured."

At a project meeting that night, the collective mood is one of frustration as the day's events are reviewed: three engine outs; eight birds of eleven refused to leave the area; Steely will have to be evacuated to Virginia and undergo surgery; and the mountain legs ahead promise only to be more dangerous. Worst of all, there are no quick-fix solutions to the problem of prop strikes. Once the birds have habituated to a particular way of flying, there's no way to alter their instincts. The process of imprinting, unfortunately, cannot be run in reverse.

By the end of the meeting, everyone is in agreement that only the four best fliers should attempt the next leg. The rest will be trucked. No one will attempt to traverse the mountains.

"Sladen doesn't think it's safe," Gavin tells me later, "and neither do the people at Airlie. When you get off the ground, the first thing you think about is crashing or an engine out. And other than a few small fields, there's nowhere to land on the next few legs." Gavin then pauses dramatically, admitting to himself silently what he may have known all along.

"Well, we do know one thing with certainty: we'll be much better prepared next year."

Following another prop strike on day two, Gavin, Dr. Sladen, Lishman, and the rest of the ES biologists effectively called the point-to-point migration, opting instead to truck the birds to each location and fly them locally in the hope of committing at least part of the route to memory—an on-the-spot, connect-the-dot theory that had never been tried before. But despite superb flying conditions south of the mountains, the swans continued to break out of formation even on these short flights. Thankfully, there were no more midair collisions.

"Steely" recuperates at Darien Center after losing his foot in a midflight collision with Gavin Shire's prop blade.

In the spring of 1999, not one of the 22 ultraswans initiated migration back to Alabama, New York, on its own. In the fall, there was no third-year migration either. Gavin, Dr. Sladen, and everyone else involved in the project spent the year back at the drawing board, incorporating this year's lessons into a superior plan that will be implemented in 2000.

The failures of the Trumpeter Swan Restoration Project are also its successes, however. "It's important to note," Gavin explains, "that out of nothing, we salvaged something from this experiment—that is, important information about the way the swans migrate. Had our join-the-dots theory worked, it would have been a truly fantastic breakthrough, saving tremendous amounts of time, money, and risk [in achieving the same goal of reintroduction]. As it was, it didn't work, but at least we know now that this is not a feasible way and others must be tried and perfected."

What is lost amid talk of the project's deficiencies, of course, is what it feels like when things go right. "Most of the time, this is hard and frustrating work," Gavin adds, "but every now and then, when conditions are just right and the birds are cooperating, you get a really spectacular flight. It is a transcendent experience to be a part of the flock and see every wing beat up close—to look into their eyes and back through the millions of years of evolution that have brought them and us to this point. Brooke is convinced he can see God in the eye of a swan flight. For a nonreligious person, this is quite a concept, and sometimes I'm inclined to agree with him."

Ultimately, the moral of the story is as old as science itself: the progress of science in every field is fueled as much by emotional failures as by publishable successes. With respect to wildlife reintroduction specifically, however, the message is far more ominous: Breaking nature apart is easy; putting the pieces back together again is something even humanity's most creative minds have yet to master.

Sitting on Top of the World

Among many locals, Prairie Creek Redwoods State Park is known as the "garden of the gods." Tucked amid the flat coastal farms, dry lagoons, and second-growth forests of Humboldt County, California, the 14,000 acre Biosphere Reserve is one of only seven significant protected areas on the planet where virgin coast redwoods (*Sequoia sempervirens*)—the world's tallest trees—still survive. Like the rest of the northern California coast during the winter, the weather here is torrential. Fog banks hover over the distant canopies like floating glaciers and a constant drizzle striates the air. For *Homo sapiens*, the conditions are dark and depressing; for *S. sempervirens*, they comprise a meteorological utopia.

"This kind of climate makes Humboldt County home to the forest primeval," canopy ecologist Steve Sillett explains as we make the drive to Prairie Creek from his Arcata, California, home, "and my study area here along Godwood Creek is one of the choicest redwood stands left. Once you get up into Vantage's upper crown, you'll see exactly what I mean."

For those who have never climbed a tree, let alone one of the world's tallest trees, getting acquainted with canopy research in an ancient redwood is the equivalent of jumping into high altitude climbing with a quick Mount Everest ascent: each novice mistake could be fatal. Yet, in spite of logical fears, the coast redwood forest canopy couldn't be more inviting. Hovering up to 150 feet above the forest floor, the first layered reefs of foliage beckon with the magnetism of the open sea. The mystery stirs something deep down; the connection is immediate. Given such natural affinities, it's difficult to imagine that as recently as five years ago, basic information on the coast redwood canopy was virtually nonexistent. Steve's research has changed all that. Steve is the world's first scientist to study the *S. sempervirens* canopy—earth's highest biological frontier. Since he first began his forays into the redwood canopy in 1993, Steve has single-handedly discovered more about these ancient monarchs than the human race has collectively accumulated since the last ice age.

Facing page:
The "garden of the gods." Old-growth redwood trees inspire humanity's deepest inclinations to find spirit in nature.

Researcher Mark Bailey begins the 300-foot climb up one of 10 study trees along Godwood Creek.

Physically, coast redwoods are the blue whales of the plant kingdom. At over 300 feet tall, the average *S. sempervirens* is more than two times the height of the Statue of Liberty, and over a hundred feet taller than the Eiffel Tower. Occasionally measuring over 20 feet in diameter at breast height (dbh), it's as if natural selection decided to create a kind of Super Tree in a rare act of experimental generosity. Temporally, coast redwoods have more in common with mountain ranges than individual life forms. As Steve likes to put it, they are "geologic agents." Individually, many share birthdays with the pyramids of Egypt. The trees he's researching today, in fact, are descended from *Sequoia,* which dominated 60 percent of the earth's land area over 160 million years ago. Not surprisingly, in the larger matrix of the forest community, redwoods rule as ecological tyrants, hoarding light, rain, and fog drip, and stockpiling photosynthetic nutrients in personal grain silos. As naturalist John Muir described them, redwoods are quite simply "kings of their race." From a scientific standpoint, though, the most remarkable aspect of coast redwoods is neither age, size, nor spiritual depth.

"Quite simply," Steve explains, "it's the architecture and biological diversity of the canopy. The size of a redwood is awesome, but what's going on in each redwood crown [the top area of the tree] is far more incredible. This is what keeps us up here despite the risks. There's just so much more to discover."

A full-time professor at Humboldt State University, Steve describes himself as a "redwood canopy ecologist specializing in epiphytes." Loosely translated, that means he hangs at 300 feet in the world's tallest trees researching plant species that are often no larger than a sprig of parsley. Literally, epiphytes are plants that grow on other plants without parasitizing them, and where conditions permit, they thrive as successfully on blades of underwater seagrass as they do on the branches of an ancient Sitka spruce. Ecologically speaking, they're opportunistic hitchhikers. Biologically, they run the gamut from "structural parasites" to largely innocuous loiterers like Spanish moss.

In forests that support them in mass quantities, as do the tropical rain forest belts of equatorial South America and Africa, epiphytes often are much more than just a physical presence in a given tree. They also contribute actively to a canopy's overall structure, function, and composition. They are to the inner ecology of each tree what trees are to the forest itself. From what Steve has discovered since he began his research in Humboldt County, this is especially true in old-growth coast redwood forests.

The fern *Polypodium scouleri* grows in large mats almost exclusively in the redwood canopy.

Contrary to what's expected of temperate conifers, the average crown of a redwood tree overflows with epiphytic plant species: lichens, liverworts, mosses, fungi, ferns, flowering shrubs, and even saplings of other tree species. Not surprisingly, the redwood forest is literally the greatest measured accumulation of biomass on the planet. From a functional perspective, the epiphytes comprising this diversity seem to evolve as vital organs of each individual redwood, like opposing thumbs or the cerebral cortex in personal human ecology.

"The epiphytic diversity we're finding in the redwood canopy is a forest in itself," Steve explains, "very much like what we find in the tropical cloud forests. In one redwood crown alone, I found a flowering huckleberry bush, a salmonberry bush, and a small *Rhamnus* tree . . . and the fern mats are the size of cargo vans. We're blowing conventional wisdom wide open here." In other trees, Steve has also found small, dripping "waterfalls" originating from especially large fern mats; branch-to-branch, branch-to-trunk, and trunk-to-trunk fusions within individual trees; and just recently, adventitious rooting on both Sitka spruce (*Picea sitchensis*) and redwood trees.

As he talks about the coast redwood canopy, Steve enacts a kind of scientific charade, sketching out each of the trees in his five study sites along Godwood Creek. He carves the trunks and branch reiterations out of the air and heaves coils of imaginary

Steve Sillett examines a huckleberry bush growing in the Floating Raft tree over 150 feet off the ground.

rope with mimelike exaggeration. As he describes each move, he fixes on the middle distance intensely, visualizing each detail and feature with what appears to be photographic accuracy.

In the wider field of canopy ecology, Steve's discoveries have obliterated the belief that complex canopies worth the extreme research risks only exist within five degrees of the equator. Although scientists have known for years that redwoods are enormously complex trees, the danger of conducting scientific research in the canopy has prevented anyone from working in them long enough, regularly enough, to make any defensible assertions about what's really going on in them.

What inspires Steve to work from single support ropes at 300 feet is not isolated epiphytes, however. It's the mysteries of how, where, and why these specialized plants exist together. Instead of simply asking what's what, Steve is looking into processes, dynamics, and the macro-relationships at work in the redwood canopy, not simply the liverworts and lichens that comprise it.

"Literally," he explains, "my specialty is lichens and bryophytes, but that's only a small part of what I'm looking at here and what makes redwoods so awesome. Rather than simply cataloging what lives in them, I'm interested in the larger systemic questions of how these trees operate and what they're capable of."

"My main focus right now," he continues, "is canopy architecture, and one of the main things I'm personally doing is mapping individual trees to create three-dimensional diagrams of canopy structure. Each tree is different in its architecture, composition, and diversity, and I want to find out how and why. My students' masters theses will provide preliminary data sets on biomass and species diversity, and my canopy mapping will give a structural context to these emerging data." In total, Steve has five students who make up his team, and with their collective work, he is stitching together the first and only inquiry into the loftiest canopy on the planet. Despite the early flood of discoveries, however, Steve's findings are still frighteningly embryonic. In the truest, Platonic sense, they prove most of all that the only thing we really know about the coast redwood canopy is how much we don't yet understand.

"Basically," Steve admits, "we still know next to nothing. We're cracking a Pandora's box here, but at this point the only thing we're sure about is that the canopy is complex enough to warrant us being up there in the first place. As a canopy researcher, there are enough scientific questions to keep me in the redwoods for a lifetime."

We arrive at Prairie Creek beneath a lid of low-level stratus clouds. Hanging in the uppermost branches, they make the trees appear even taller, as if, like titans, they are

holding up the sky itself. With us are four of Steve's students: Mark Bailey, Billy Ellyson, Brett Lovelace, and Anthony Ambrose. Our goal today is Vantage, a 280-foot specimen located at Study Site V. For the three-mile hike in along the meandering course of Godwood Creek, the load is divided among us into six packs, each containing 50 pounds of ropes and climbing and sampling equipment.

Once we've reached Site V, Steve uses a thin black pilot line to set a climbing rope in Vantage's crown. Billy and Brett rig a separate rope in Site V's "control" tree just 50 feet away, a 296-foot Sitka spruce named Sunny Delight. This allows two climbers to ascend into the canopy simultaneously, saving precious minutes in deteriorating weather. Just below Sunny Delight's summit, Billy and Brett will traverse between the two trees over a 40-foot gap and join the rest of the team in Vantage's crown. Despite the protection of thick leather gardening gloves, Steve and Billy wince under the weight of the 60-pound ropes as they haul them into the crowns. Akin to raising sail on a tall ship, rigging both trees takes over 10 minutes. As the ropes snake up out of sight into the burls and branches, Steve sheds light on one of the most obvious questions about his work: How do you make the first ascent into a 300-foot tree in the first place?

"What you have to understand," he begins, "is that rigging trees and climbing trees are two entirely different things. Getting the first rope up there and doing the

The Atlas Giant.
Photographs, laser
measurements, and
Steve Sillett's canopy
data were used to
create this immaculately
detailed and
"anatomically correct"
illustration. (*Courtesy of
Robert Van Pelt.*)

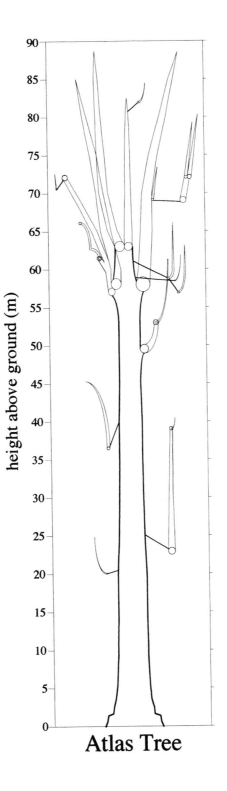

Atlas Tree

The Atlas Giant laid bare. Canopy maps like this one created by Steve Sillett are vital to understanding redwood trees. They mark the precise location of branch reiterations and significant canopy features and they provide a physical context for all subsequent research projects. (*Courtesy of Steve Sillett.*)

original ascent work is where the real risk and challenge are. What makes it so dangerous are the endless unknowns." After shooting the first monofilament pilot line into the crown with a powerful hunting bow, nothing can be taken for granted. With no idea what kind of branch the rope has run over, what it's rubbing against, or what kind of debris is about to be dislodged onto your head, you're gambling your life on myriad unknowns. Thankfully for all of us, Steve rigged both Vantage and Sunny Delight over a year ago.

With the bitter ends of both ropes finally on the ground and secured to small spruces nearby, Steve, Mark, and the rest of the team step into their harnesses and begin assembling the equipment they'll need for today's work. At minimum, each climber has a harness; two ascenders, commonly called "jumars," for scaling the main rope; a 60-foot split-tail lanyard, which allows the climber to move freely around the canopy on his own; extra steel climbing clips called carabiners; and a rappel device to get back down. For even the most experienced big tree climbers, it's precisely the paucity of this gear that makes climbing redwoods so nerve-racking. If any one of these five objects is improperly used or installed, you stand to die.

While Mark attaches his ascenders to the main rope and begins to climb, a process called "jugging," Steve uses his technique to explain the safety mechanisms and how ignoring them could cost an inexperienced climber his life. Even Steve's graduate students, with dozens of climbs under their belts, listen intently as he talks, gravely committing each step to memory. They know their lives depend on how well they remember what goes where and when.

Steve knows only one person who has fallen from a giant tree and lived to tell about it. According to firsthand account, the climber, a professional arborist, had his rope lanyard tied into a branch at 90 feet, and it simply snapped under his weight. He fell too far too fast to grab another branch, hit nothing else but foliage, and proceeded straight to terminal velocity.

"It's so easy not to fall," Steve adds. "Just don't do it."

So far neither Steve nor any one of the students working under him has had a serious accident while working in the coast redwood canopy. The near-misses have been because of rope slips, knots that begin to untie themselves, and moves that require them to unclip for a step up. Steve's injuries have come primarily from broken branches and steel climbing clips rather than from unintentional experiments with gravity. The only blood ever drawn came from accidentally impaling himself on a sharp, broken branch. Ironically, Steve's most painful accident happened near the bottom of a tree. Tired and mentally absent after a day of hard climbing, he rappelled off the end of his rope 10 feet short of the ground.

The main reason Steve has never fallen is simple. When it comes to tree climbing, he's as qualified to do what he does as an Everest-level mountaineer. In fact, when it comes to rigging and working in giant trees, many of Steve's colleagues consider him to be the most experienced in the world. Since his first major climb in 1987 while at Reed College, Steve has scaled approximately 25 miles of trunk. That doesn't include a substantial amount of inner crown climbing once he's off the main rope. Combined, the total would be enough to carry him well into the ionosphere.

As Steve and I talk, we watch Mark ratchet up the main rope at a plodding, almost imperceptible pace—10 jugs, rest; 10 jugs, rest. Ever so steadily, his silhouette shrinks into Vantage's lower branches at 200 feet as if sinking out of sight into an abysmal, green sea. Twenty feet to the south in Sunny Delight and just as high off the forest floor, Billy keeps pace with him, stopping periodically to take in the expanding view.

"Off rope!" Mark finally yells. He's off the main rope, anchored on his own lanyard, and it's Steve's turn to climb next. Within minutes of leaving the forest floor, he, too, disappears into the crown. Finally, it's my turn to ascend. I go over my equipment one last time: harness; ascenders; rappel device; lanyards; carabiner clips—check. For my last earthbound gestures, I experiment with a few small good luck offerings, cleaning a smudge of pitch from the ascender cam, readjusting the leg straps on my harness, then finally turning to the tree itself and clipping my ascenders to the rope. The furrows of Vantage's fibrous bark are moist, coagulated, and slippery to the touch. I slide my top ascender up the rope and jug my first few feet. So far, so good.

With each successive ratchet of the ascenders and each three feet gained, the world below ceases to exist. At a hundred feet, the forest floor is barely recognizable and all signs of our temporary encampment at the base of the tree have vanished. At 150 feet, I'm hyperaware of having reached the "you-fall-you-die" point. It's the height at which any tree climber faces the ultimate fear.

"Orgasmic, isn't it?" Mark is smiling down through Vantage's dense lattice work of burls and branches from a large fern mat. "The forest, the trees, the fog . . . everything. It's orgasmic." Not waiting for a reply, he turns back to his work with Steve. His conversational nonchalance so high in the air unnerves me even more.

At 220 feet, just beyond Vantage's lower branches, the climbing experience changes completely. As the crown begins to close in and restrict the vertiginous views

of the surrounding trees, the redwood forest's embrace becomes intimate and reassuring. The branches and foliage offer the illusion of a safety net, like they might be capable of breaking a fall.

Scientifically, this is where the core of Steve's work begins. Each branch literally drips with epiphytic life. Even within the deep vertical gutters of the trunk itself, a living film is thriving—a colonial lichen, Steve explains. As the crown continues upward, the branches gather in an increasingly complex thicket, a quality Steve describes affectionately, though unscientifically, as "gnarl." Gnarl illustrates well the claim that structurally redwoods "are capable of just about anything."

In contrast with most other temperate evergreen trees, redwoods seem to possess a conscious desire to break free from evolution's selected formats and be physically unique. In even small sections of redwood crown, there are "bombers" (irregularly large branches), "stobs" (broken off branch stumps), "downslopers" (geotropic branches that grow toward the ground), and "reiterations" (secondary trunks that bulge from the main trunk like the bicep of a bodybuilder). Why such complexity and creativity? No one yet knows.

Structurally, Vantage is no prodigy. Steve has climbed many other trees here in Prairie Creek which make Vantage seem like a backyard maple by comparison. Yet Vantage does have one distinguishing feature that ranks it among the finest redwoods on earth: fern mat FR637, nestled in the enormous elbow of a reiterating branch at 240 feet. Currently, Mark is bellied up next to the mat as if it were a large sushi bar. He dictates precise, sequential numbers to Steve, who leans off the main trunk 10 feet away with nothing behind or below him except open air. In size, the fern mat dwarfs both of them. Four feet wide and almost 10 feet long, it's thick and luxuriant, underlain by a foot of dark, rich soil. Over five feet in diameter where it grows out horizontally from the trunk, the branch on which the mat sits seems even more imposing compared to the small, human bodies next to it.

When I finally join them just above the mat, Steve starts right in with the science. To get in better position for his on-site lecture, he kicks himself off the trunk, swings on his lanyard into the gap above Mark, and lunges for a reiterating branch on the outer edge of the mat. Looped over a branch some 20 feet above us, the rope slides out and down toward the branch's tapered end. Steve takes hold on his new perch at the last minute, digging his nails into the fibrous bark like a rock climber holding a thin granite rail.

"This mat illustrates perfectly one of the most exciting things we're finding out about the redwood canopy," Steve begins, "how truly terrestrial in nature each redwood crown really is. Just look at the soil buildup—there's over 12 inches of humus here, an

Facing page:
Steve Sillett ascends Sunny Delight, one of four spruce trees growing sequentially out of a decaying *S. sempervirens* that fell hundreds of years before.

Steve Sillett releases a rare salamander species, *Anneides ferreus*, back into the canopy.

indication that this mat is hundreds of years old. And look at the fern growth. You rarely find this in any other tree, even in the tropics." Spread out between us is a dense garden of *Polypodium scouleri*, a fern species found almost exclusively in the redwood canopy. With different age classes, a multilayered canopy, spiders, millipedes, and a species of salamander (*Aneides ferreus*), the mat is like an old-growth forest itself.

"Take a look at this one here," Steve continues, separating out one of the largest ferns near the middle of the mat. "Each pair of symmetrical fronds indicates one year of growth, which means this one is in its eighteenth year. Some of the other ones here look to be over 20. This high up, we don't even know how long individual ferns can grow, let alone how long a collective mat this size can survive. Just think about how many generations of ferns have lived and died here, how an entire family tree of salamanders has rooted itself here—without any need for going to the ground."

Obvious from their well-distributed presence is the fact that such *P. scouleri* mats play an instrumental role in the coast redwood canopy ecosystem. Spread throughout Vantage's crown are no fewer that a dozen similar gardens, ranging in size from living-room sofas to oven mitts. Each clings to its host branch with the nonchalance of car keys tossed on the front hall table and overflows with ferns, rainwater, and sweet,

Facing page:
Research assistant Anthony Ambrose pauses to take in the expansive view from Ying and Yang. Even at 200 feet, trees of this size are still up to 10 feet in diameter.

organic debris. At the core of Steve's research program is the question of how each of its physical characteristics contributes to the life cycle of each individual tree and the canopy ecosystem as a whole. How many mats do coast redwoods sustain, for instance? How much biomass and photosynthetic energy does each mat add to the crown? How long do they retain and store water? Do they fertilize the tree?

Billy Ellyson inches his way along a traverse between Vantage and Sunny Delight.

For his part, Mark is addressing the first of these questions in his master's thesis. Today, as part of Stage I sampling, he's doing a stem count, a rather unpleasant research method combining the physical tedium of weeding with the intellectual minutia of statistics. By counting how many actual *P. scouleri* stems there are on each fern mat he samples, Mark can make some assumptions later about the amount of fern biomass in each mat, and by extension, in each tree. From a logistical standpoint, however, Mark's research is not simply academic, it's life-threatening. To maneuver himself into a position so that he can reach the fronds on mat FR637, Mark has to regularly release his hand- and footholds, putting his entire weight on the ropes he's set for himself.

As Mark and Steve complete the stem count, Billy and Brett, now at Sunny Delight's summit, set a 40-foot traverse into Vantage's crown 30 feet above us. Like a tightrope, the traverse runs between the two main trunks through a wide, wind-blown gap. Eyeing the straight drop to the forest floor, both Brett and Billy look nervous. Unlike all other moves in the canopy, traverses are leaps of faith. Once away from the trunk, there are no supports other than the rope itself. There are no second chances or backups, no branches to grab, no foliage to pad the fall.

A more experienced climber, Billy attempts the traverse first. He eases out slowly to test the rope, sliding the slip knot toward us just eight inches at a time. Without warning, the knot gives and Billy drops 10 feet before he can even scream. All we hear is the snap of branches and the windlike rush of falling matter. By the time we figure out what's happened, Billy has already reset his own knot and is cursing quietly. He is cut, but alive. After dusting himself off, he and Brett continue the traverse—this time without problems.

Aside from extreme moves like traverses, Steve, Mark, and every team member has his own style when exploring the coast redwood canopy. Steve moves around with the smooth, deft explosions of a big cat, slinging his lanyard around successively higher branches like a rodeo cowboy and standing unsupported on the ends of wind-blown branches with the arboreal equivalent of sea legs. Bolstered by complete confidence in his ability, yet always cautious, no move is out of reach. In comparison, Mark's moves around fern mat FR637 are more methodical. As he ascends and descends, his labored lunges betray the effort it takes to move around such a massive crown.

"The key to studying such an enormous tree," says Steve, "is horizontal mobility. When I started climbing in Costa Rica, we'd jug up these tiny trees and sample whatever was close enough to reach from the main line. Such limited techniques might work in the tropics, but in a crown like this, you miss everything that's important. The key to our system here is the split-tail lanyard, originally developed by arborists in Europe. We've been refining it for years. The result . . . ," Steve unhooks a steel clip from its ring on his right hip, coils the line, and prepares to toss it over a limb about 15 feet over his head, "is the ability to get as far out on any branch as we want."

Perfectly emphasizing his point, the clip glides over the intended branch without touching it and drops back down to within four feet of Steve's other hand. He throws two rolls of slack through the rope, lowers the clip into his palm, and fastens it to his belt. Now secure and self-belayed, Steve begins immediately to ascend to another layer of the crown. He needs to take some final diameter measurements for Vantage's still incomplete crown map, and daylight is waning.

On the way up, Steve points out some of the other epiphytes which call the redwood canopy home. The first specimen we find is an amebic clump of moss the size and weight of a loaf of wet bread. Cast like a shin pad where it clings to its host branch, it is textured like chartreuse steel wool on one side and shredded wheat on the other.

Out on a limb. Billy Ellyson marks his samples at the top of an
ancient Sitka spruce.

Relative to the evolution of zebras and three-toed sloths, the moss is unremarkable—the epitome of a species we find difficult to protect because it lacks charm and charisma. Next, we find a lichen, a fungus enslaving an alga or cyanobacterium, which resembles wilted iceberg lettuce. According to Steve, it is one of the most important nitrogen fixers in the crotches and armpits of a redwood crown.

"Ecologically," Steve remarks, gesturing to another toaster-sized specimen, "these epiphytes are as amazing as anything I've seen, in part because of how subtle they are. This one mat here is probably hundreds of years old and has endured repeated storms that have destroyed entire trees. . . . What's more is that we've found these mats are literally part of the redwood itself. They've been developing as long as individual trees, and in second-growth forests you just don't find them."

In one of his recent experiments, Steve transplanted fern mats established in ancient trees to younger trees without them and found to his surprise that they did just fine. What this tells him is that redwoods need to reach a certain level of gnarl before they can even begin to develop complex epiphytic communities. Once they do, they can support an interior epiphytic forest unto themselves. It also reveals that epiphytes are part of what it means to be an old-growth redwood. They provide what forest ecologists call "ecosystem services," such as micro habitat, nitrogen fixation, and water retention.

Near the end of the day, at the tree's summit, a twisted grid of horizontal branches with barely enough space for two people, it becomes immediately apparent why Vantage is so named. To the west, the azure Pacific rolls hypnotically on toward Hawaii. To the north, south, and east spreads nothing but old-growth coast redwood canopy, as far as the eye can see. Even at 280 feet, the branches we're standing on are still almost a foot in diameter. "This is one of the only spots in the world where you can still get this," Steve laments, "where you can still surround yourself with a sea of coast redwood crowns."

The view is as stunning as it is rare. Broken, desiccated treetops spear above the canopy like church steeples, and each crown jockeys aggressively for space and light. For the nonscientist, the view is a text of biological hieroglyphics, which is precisely why Steve's work is so critical to understanding, appreciating, and protecting the last remnants of redwood forest. Where most people would see an unknowable pattern of creation, Steve sees gaps, angles, architecture, and predictable three-dimensionality; in negative structure, he sees a positive one. The redwood canopy is like a language that needs to be translated, and thankfully, Steve's research is finally breaking the code.

The following day, we move on to Study Site IV. Usually, the hike to the Floating Raft Tree is a pleasant two-mile walk up Godwood Creek. Today, however, it might as well be at the other end of the Lewis and Clark Trail. Last week, a four-day El Niño drive-by ripped through northern California and the damage is near catastrophic. More than a dozen trees, including the world's tallest western hemlock (*Tsuga heterophylla*), are down along the trail, and Floating Raft, the Site's key study tree, stands right in the middle of it.

After only 10 minutes of hiking, the carnage from the storm begins to rear its ugly head. As is often the case after such a tempest, massive limbs sheared from their trunks have speared into the earth and stand like lampposts. Epiphytes ripped from their lofty perches litter the forest floor in a triage of dismembered body parts. In many places, domino lines of trunks have fallen and now lie stacked on top of one another, resembling the wreckage of a derailed train. In the gaps left by the fallen trees, light pours through for the first time in a thousand years, and the small understory plants respond instantly to this fortuitous chance to reach for the sky. All in all, the falls probably took less than a few minutes; it will take nature's recycling team over a thousand years to clean up the mess.

Another mile further, the damage begins to thin out, allowing the massive redwood trunks still standing to take center stage. All around us are the signature features of an ancient coast redwood forest: standing snags (leafless, dead trees), nurse logs (decomposing dead logs on the ground), and a dense, multilayered canopy. On the forest floor, the gaps between the trunks are wide enough to land a jet.

Steve, Mark, and I finally arrive at Site IV to find that three massive trees around Floating Raft have been felled by the storm. Floating Raft itself, though, is still standing and intact. Steve let's go a sigh of relief.

"Floating Raft would have been a tragic loss," he says. "Now let's get climbing while we can."

The goal today is to remove all 120 pounds of fern mat FR521. That means cutting it from its host branch, stuffing it into garbage bags, rappelling it to the ground, and hauling it back to Steve's lab—all without losing so much as a fern frond. On paper, the task is a dry, required part of Mark's Stage II sampling for his master's thesis. At 240 feet in the crown of Floating Raft, it'll be like getting an injured climber down from a storm-besieged mountain summit.

Unlike most other redwoods, Floating Raft begins to bristle with the quintessential redwood gnarl at just 60 feet. The branches weave themselves into impenetrable thickets, making a clean path of ascent virtually impossible. And with almost a

Facing page:
Steve Sillett's research team earns its just reward for a day of hard climbing and research: sunset at the top of Flat Top tree.

Storm damage from a catastrophic wind event is capable of toppling multiple old-growth redwoods. Steve Sillett is standing on top of the root wad to the right for size reference.

month of steady rain, Floating Raft's trunk is running today like waterfall. In such conditions, hand- and footholds cannot be trusted, each branch becomes a potentially life-threatening obstacle. It takes an hour and a half to get the team up into the crown.

Climbing conditions notwithstanding, Steve and Mark already have their strategy for removing the mat from its host branch. Steve has set one 70-foot rope over a limb high above the mat and a 60-foot lanyard to the reiterating trunk on which the mat sits. This will allow him to maneuver into an open gap where he can work unencumbered by branches and foliage. Mark is strung on the other side of the mat from a similar belay. Together, their rigging tangles up the work area like the cables of a suspension bridge. The wind is blowing lightly, and Steve and Mark swing back and forth like human wind chimes. Two hundred and twenty feet below us, the silver wire of Godwood Creek snakes along the forest floor, a nagging reminder of just how high and exposed we really are.

Once into position, Steve pulls out a pocket knife and begins to cut away square sections of the fern mat. The soil is at least 10 inches deep, and Steve buries his arm up to the elbow to get at the roots that bind the mat to the limb. Despite his best efforts, the mat refuses to come free. He ascends two feet higher, braces his boots against the limb itself, and tears part of the mat away like green muscle from a behemoth bone. As the section rips free, Steve snaps back into the open air as if propelled by a bowshot. He does this five times, each time handing a section to Mark, who hangs over the gap with garbage bags in his lap. Under the mounting weight, Mark's support branches 15 feet above begin to bend and creak. He surveys them warily each time he adds another slice of soil. Twice, the lanyard slipknots give way under the pressure and he drops a foot before they reset.

By the time Steve has cut away the last section of the fern mat, three 40-gallon garbage bags have been filled, weighing close to 300 pounds in all. It's 5 p.m., and barely an hour of daylight remains. The mat removal has taken the better part of the afternoon, and although Steve and Mark are clearly exhausted from the effort, neither the work nor the risks are over. Getting the bags to the other side of Floating Raft's 12-foot trunk and down to the ground represents a whole different challenge altogether. The path back to the main rope is a vast, open vacuum in the crown. There are no limbs to climb or branches to help support the excess weight of the bags. The solution: Steve and Mark have to shimmy along a traverse, six inches per push, with constant readjustments to the balance of the bags in their laps. Luckily, there are no rope slips.

Steve Sillett and Mark Bailey remove a fern mat from the Ying and Yang tree as part of Stage II sampling for Mark's master's thesis.

Getting down a giant coast redwood is far easier than going up. Reattached to the main line and loaded with two bags each, Steve and Mark use the added weight to their advantage as they rappel down Floating Raft's trunk one at a time. Kicking off the trunk, they hit the "sweet spot" and drop to the forest floor as smoothly and silently as a stone sinks in a lake. The excess loads cause their rappel devices to burn with the stench of scorched hair. Small curls of smoke rise from the rope where it twists through the device and linger on a vertical trail along the descent line to the ground.

By the time all the bags have been rappelled down, the light blue shadows of the understory have darkened to deep shades of twilight gray. The team will have to hike out along the carnage trail in almost total darkness.

Once underway, we walk at a measured pace, meditating to the soft percussion of our own footsteps, deep in our own canopies of thought. Despite the minefields of broken branches and debris along the trail, Steve still can't resist occasionally looking up into the canopy, and smiling broadly.

"Tree boating" in the canopy of the Atlas Giant. Says Steve, the redwood forest
"gives me everything I need in life."

"I'm so fortunate," he says finally. "I have something that gives me almost everything I want in life . . . something that nourishes me in almost every way. . . . Sometimes, I even climb in the canopy just to sleep."

By the time we reach the car, I, too, am feeling so fortunate.

"Can you feel it?" Steve asks in the parking lot. "The sweet pain of a climbing day, the magic of having been up there?"

I can say I now know why the locals call Prairie Creek the garden of the gods.

Santa Rosa Island, in Channel Islands National Park, California, provides ideal peregrine habitat: steep cliffs, big skies, and lots of prey.

Bridge over Troubled Waters

From the girders beneath the Vincent Thomas suspension bridge in south Los Angeles, the view is post-apocalyptic. To the south and west, the 250-foot container cranes of Long Beach harbor loom over the docks of the world's largest commercial shipping port like *Brontosaurus* at a waterhole. At their feet, thousand foot factory tankers lie berthed together in a train of self-contained cities. Beyond the miles of warehouses and highways for as far as the eye can see, the only green is the color of the bridge itself.

Shell fragments taken from the Golden Gate Bridge eyrie. The Santa Cruz Predatory Bird Group maintains one of the most extensive databases in the world on peregrine falcon eggshell thinning.

For a variety of reasons, however, the girders of the Vincent Thomas Bridge are also prime nesting habitat for one of America's most celebrated endangered species: *Falco peregrinus anatum,* better known as the American peregrine falcon.

"When the workers sandblasted the bridge for painting," raptor biologist Brian Latta yells above the din of traffic, "the debris settled down into the I-beams and created ideal nesting substrate. . . . Caltrans [California Department of Transportation] was providing habitat for peregrines here and they didn't even know it." Balancing an incubated plywood "chick carrier" in one hand and a dynamic climbing rope in the other, Brian charges down the catwalk just beneath the roadbed. Every so often, a convoy of tractor trailers rolls over above us, shaking the entire bridge with seismic tremors.

According to Brian's nesting data, Caltrans and other state transportation authorities have unknowingly attracted peregrines to the Desmond Bridge, the San Francisco–

119

Falco peregrinus anatum—the "cloud runner." (*Courtesy of Hans Peters.*)

Oakland Bay Bridge, the Antioch Bridge, the Petaluma Bridge, and San Francisco's Golden Gate Bridge as well. In fact, just about everywhere in urban and industrial California these days, there seems to be a pair of nesting peregrine falcons. After 50 years at the brink of extinction, *F. peregrinus anatum* now seems to be not only surviving humanity but thriving in spite of it, readily accepting artificial, pseudogeologic structures for surrogate habitat and living royally on a smorgasbord of nonnative urban prey. Driving the phenomenon is the fact that peregrines don't see the world the way humans do—in terms of habitat wars between industry and wildness. *F. peregrinus anatum* lives in the air. In the apocalyptic sprawl of Long Beach harbor, they see open sky, big wind, lots of prey, and plenty of high urban monoliths for hunting and stooping.

"Unfortunately," Brian adds, "they also now recognize the bridges and other vertical structures as suitable nesting sites, and they're laying eggs here on a regular basis."

The presence of peregrine falcons in centers of humanity is in itself no surprise. For as long as people have cared enough to notice, peregrines have been nesting on human structures, from the castles of Spain to the Brooklyn Bridge. With dozens of natural nest sites along California's wild coast currently unoccupied, however, the current raptor renaissance in California's cities is a mixed blessing. Given the species' recent brush with oblivion, any peregrine is no doubt a good peregrine, but the

To go or not to go? Brian Latta and Golden Gate Bridge Authority officials consider the dangers of a wet and windy nest entry.

species' urban success raises a complex array of questions for biologists about the mechanisms of pollution, the biology of the bird itself, and the underlying principles of endangered species and raptor protection in general.

That a recovering endangered species should choose to reestablish itself amid the industry of Los Angeles in preference to its natural southern California habitat is not simply thought-provoking, however, it's dangerous. Like radio towers, suspension bridges and high-rise buildings are considered "high mortality" nest sites. Subject to crosswinds and downdrafts instead of the predictable updrafts of sea cliffs, they provide little margin for error when fledging chicks make their first attempts at flight some five to six weeks after hatching. In some places, such as building ventilation shafts, cramped nesting conditions also prevent the chicks from sufficiently strengthening their wings before takeoff. As a result, instead of leaping into a warm El Niño wind and landing on a ledge five feet away, chicks often fledge from bridge eyries to their deaths, drowning in the water below or getting blown up onto the asphalt above and splattered. As part of the Santa Cruz Predatory Bird Research Group's (SCPBRG, or the Bird Group) ongoing effort to mitigate such scenarios, one of Brian's primary mandates as a field biologist is to translocate chicks from these high-mortality nests to natural sites elsewhere in the state.

Brian Latta descends the superstructure of the San Francisco–Oakland Bay Bridge
on his way to the nest.

At the midway point between the bridge's suspension towers, Brian stops, drops his gear, and scans the girders anxiously, as if something were about to break. On either side of the catwalk, the superstructure of the bridge protrudes out over the water in a steel skeleton of interconnecting balance beams. For 200 feet below us, there is nothing but air. A warm 20-knot wind blows in from the ocean, mixing the smell of salt with the sweet stench of grease from the roadbed.

Suddenly, Brian grabs my shirt and yanks me onto the gridiron floor.

"Duck!" he yells.

Drowned out by the roar of traffic, an adult peregrine swoops through the I-beams like a heat-seeking missile and glances off the duffel bag two feet from my head, leaving a small, efficient laceration. Looking up, I see her bank sharply, arc back just overhead, and flap to a stop on an outlying girder just 20 feet away. Her eyes are big and black and set sharply against a throat of ivory white. On her breast, her contour feathers flare up with nervous rage; on her wings and back, the feathers are the color of polished steel. As peregrines always do, she stands flat-footed, letting her talons fold out from beneath her legs like steak knives. She eyes us anxiously and vocalizes her agitation in short, machine gun bursts—*kak, kak, kak, kak, kak, kak*. Without rising, Brian points to the beam just to her left, where, set down inside the I-beam itself, a single, 21-day-old chick rocks back and forth.

"This female is fearless," Brian says with a wry, adversarial smile. "She knows why I'm here, and she's drawn blood before to defend her chicks." He stands hesitantly, opens his duffel bag, and begins to pull out an assortment of harnesses, slings, and aluminum D-shaped *carabiners*. This is the fourth time in as many years Brian has climbed the Vincent Thomas Bridge to translocate the chicks. On the same mission, he's also rappelled off the top of Long Beach City Hall and traversed the ledges of the Union Bank building and another major skyscraper in downtown Los Angeles.

In addition to standard research projects in peregrine reproduction, population status, and toxicology, such rescue-style heroics—technically called "salvage"—have long been a trademark of the Bird Group. Through the 1980s and early 1990s, when the peregrine was still considered a lost cause, the primary missions were nest manipulation, cross-fostering, hacking, and captive breeding, under the direction of Bird Group coordinator Brian Walton and climber-biologist Lee Aulman. By removing eggs that were chronically breaking in natural eyries, hatching them safely in captivity, and then releasing the chicks back into the wild, the Bird Group ensured an accelerated level of repopulation and geographic recovery throughout California during the most precarious years of intensive care. Since its founding in 1975 by Dr. James C. Roush, III

Brian Latta pulls a chick from the ventilation shaft of a building in downtown Los Angeles.

and Dr. Kenneth S. Norris, the group's biologists and volunteers have released over 800 peregrines, from the border of Mexico to Washington State. These days, however, now that more pairs are reproducing naturally in the wild and the overall population continues to increase, the Bird Group no longer augments nests, and Brian no longer salvages eggs. Now, he salvages the chicks.

"If we didn't do this," Brian explains of the translocations, "30 to 50 percent of the peregrines fledging from urban nests in California would die. As it is now, they'll be fledging from wild sites just two weeks from now and most likely surviving those first few flights." So far, the Bird Group's success rate with urban transplants is superb. Thanks to dedicated nest attendants and release crews, over 70 percent of the chicks make it to independence, and an estimated 50 percent go on to breed and fledge chicks of their own.

Despite the charitable intent, a decade of working with peregrines has not come without a price. Although a traditional rock climber at heart, Brian's not climbing traditional routes for chicks and eggs. Instead of clean lines and clear cracks, peregrines prefer scree slopes, hanging boulders, and greasy suspension girders. They look for depressions in the cliffs where they can't be seen and forbidding overhangs with air-only access. When other climbers ask Brian to put a number on the difficulty level of the routes he's putting up to get at the nests, he jokes that there are only three gradients: "ugly," "really ugly," and "I'm not that stupid." In almost 300 climbs on natural cliffs and 65 bridge and building ascents, Brian has been showered by rock slides, almost knocked clear off an I-beam, and hammered by a protective female more than 14 times during a single nest entry.

"In the beginning," Brian remembers, "the climbing was much more urgent because the population was in critical danger. . . . We'd be jumaring back up [ascending on a fixed rope] this horrible face, knowing that we were carrying some of the only peregrine eggs in the state. These days, it's not so life-or-death."

Despite the obvious risks of these climbs, Brian and a dedicated group of climber-biologists before him have developed techniques that effectively reduce the inherent danger. "We are extremely careful and efficient," Brian explains. "We put a lot of thought into each climb before it is started. We know how to get to otherwise daunting locations to transport fragile chicks and eggs safely, and we know when to back off. We may seem extreme but we're not stupid. No Bird Group climber has been seriously injured and no peregrine hurt or viable egg damaged in our 20-plus years of field work."

Today, as always, Brian's route is sketchy at best. The nest lies almost midway between two perpendicular support intersections along the outermost bottom girder of the bridge superstructure, 30 feet directly out from the catwalk and 10 feet from the last possible anchor point. If Brian gets knocked off by the female, that's how far he'll swing into empty space before his protection theoretically arrests the fall. Complicating the route is an oily, carbon-based paste from last night's rain, which covers the beams

The tender side of science. Brian Latta with one of three chicks salvaged from the San Francisco–Oakland Bay Bridge.

like car wax. Given the conditions, Brian checks his primary anchor and harness twice, then reconfirms the lead of the rope with his belayer and local peregrine expert, Jeff Sipple. As he visualizes his steps one last time, he repeats out loud some of the first advice he ever got about climbing with peregrines. Keep your sunglasses on. Always look behind you. Always keep "one hand for the cliff." And watch out for "testicular pinch" when putting your full weight onto the rope.

"And just remember," he adds, "all of this is to save one bird."

For those who know their birds of prey, that someone like Brian would be willing to put his life on the line for a single peregrine chick is no surprise, nor is it shocking that the peregrine falcon continues to ride first-class on the endangered species arc. Peregrines for centuries have been conferred royal status by falconers, and especially in the last 40 years, the species has become one of most indelible symbols of American wildlife conservation.

Of all the world's birds of prey, *Falco peregrinus* is widely considered to be the ultimate avian predator. Roughly the size of a crow, the peregrine combines the speed of sound, the shape of a bullet, and the carving skills of an internal surgeon. Diving in thousand-foot vertical "stoops" at over 200 miles per hour, the species can change direction on a dime, hit like a meteor, and eviscerate its prey like a down pillow, all

Easy does it. Brian Latta takes his first tentative steps out onto the superstructure of the Vincent Thomas Bridge in Long Beach harbor.

without missing a wing beat. Using a specially evolved notch in its beak, it can unlock the neck vertebrae of most birds with a simple twist of its head, minimizing the aerial struggle and the possibility that prey might escape. Utilizing the same cutlery for feeding, even a hatch-year peregrine can shred a seagull into string cheese.

The greatest mark of the peregrine's evolutionary success, though, is not any one superlative physical trait but rather the species' near-ubiquitous geographic distribution throughout the world—from Greenland and Siberia to Tierra del Fuego and Africa's Cape of Good Hope. Peregrines are among the most adaptable avian predators evolution has created, living from sea level up to 9000 feet, feeding on prey as large as ducks and as small as hummingbirds, and requiring only a remote gravel slab to breed. Derived from the Latin word *peregrinus,* meaning "traveler" or "wanderer," they are the cloud runners, and true to the

A male *Falco peregrinus anatum*, otherwise known as a *tiercel*.

nickname, they conduct their activities from the sky, largely oblivious to the terrestrial world below them. In a migratory phenomenon called "leap-frogging," some northern species travel as far as 10,000 miles twice each year.

North America itself is home to three distinct peregrine subspecies: the American peregrine (*Falco peregrinus anatum*), Arctic peregrine (*Falco peregrinus tundrius*), and Peale's peregrine (*Falco peregrinus pealei*). As little as a 150 years ago, the American subspecies in particular was a fixture throughout much of the continent, carving its distinctive aerial script wherever there were songbirds and sky. In the latter half of the 1800s, however, the peregrine, like most North American birds of prey, began a steep and relentless decline. At first, the root cause was hunting, under the euphemistic crusades of predator eradication and game augmentation. Similar to the cases of wolves and bears, farmers were advised to shoot every raptor they saw in order to protect their livestock. For sportsmen, the justification was less admirable and the result equally damaging to the species as a whole. But it wasn't until after World War II and the introduction of the chlorinated hydrocarbon pesticide DDT (dichloro-diphenyl-trichloroethane) that *peregrine* and *extinction* were ever used in the same sentence.

First touted as the ultimate all-purpose weapon against agricultural pests, DDT was a killer from the very start, endangering not only peregrines but osprey, brown pelicans, bald eagles, and a host of other species as well. Through a process called *bioaccumulation,* DDT takes over an ecosystem much like cancer does—once absorbed into the soil, the fat-soluble pesticide is passed from plant to insect to rodent to bird and finally to the apex predators, infiltrating the food chain from top to bottom. The farther up the chain DDT gets, moreover, the more concentrated it becomes. In the beginning, some peregrines died directly from consuming contaminated prey. Over time, however, it became apparent that the scope and consequences of DDT pollution ran much deeper than anyone thought. As DDT applications became more widespread, falconers and ornithologists began to notice that perennially active peregrine eyries were turning up vacant and that the skies over much of North America were falling increasingly silent.

Convened to address the worldwide decline of peregrine species, the 1965 Madison Conference concluded that chlorinated hydrocarbon pesticides had "led to persisting widespread reproductive failures [and] combined with other environmental stresses, may also involve increased adult mortality rates in some populations." Conclusions further asserted that "the initial effect of the reproductive failures was to wipe out the extraordinary nonbreeding reserve that had previously characterized the peregrine populations of the past. This phenomenon was impossible for ornithologists to measure. What they saw was the second stage, the steady numerical decline in the 1950s of the breeding adults in many regions."

Through examinations of eggshell fragments—a methodology the Bird Group continues today—English scientist Derek Ratcliffe had largely isolated DDT and its metabolite DDE (dichloro-diphenyl-ethylene) as the primary cause of the species' reproductive failures. By interfering with the process of calcium deposition, the pesticide was causing peregrines to lay eggs up to 20 percent thinner than normal, leading to fluid loss, embryo failure, and physical breakage during the 33-day incubation period. As a result, adult breeders were unable to reproduce and repopulate the species as a whole. By the 1960s, more peregrines were dying of natural causes than were being born, dooming the species to extinction.

The smoking gun. Collected from the Diablo Canyon eyrie in 1988, this eggshell measured 19.8 percent thin. (Photograph courtesy of Kit Crump.)

As both a primary manufacturer and user of the pesticide, California was hit especially hard. Not only was DDT sprayed throughout the state, but an even greater quantity was introduced into the marine ecosystem, both directly from waste-dumping and indirectly from surface runoff. From an environmental standpoint, the pesticide was everywhere, in soils, rivers, ocean sediments, plants, phytoplankton,

Brian Latta displays eggshell fragments collected from the Vandenburg Air Force Base eyrie.

insects, rodents, songbirds, and even the largest marine mammals. In Palos Verdes, near where DDT was originally manufactured, solid chunks of DDT littered the ground like softballs. Elsewhere in California, tissue samples from various animals revealed an even more noxious witch's brew—PCBs, dieldrin, endrin, aldrin, toxaphene, and kelthane, an organochlorine miticide that also breaks down into DDE.

As a result of such widespread contamination, California peregrines by the 1960s were vanishing at an almost exponential rate, even as sensitive habitat throughout the state was being set aside for the distinct purpose of wildlife protection. By 1970, *F. peregrinus anatum* was almost gone entirely. In a survey that sent climbers into some of the highest and wildest falcon habitat in the hemisphere, the official head count stood at only two nesting pairs—at Morro Rock at the southern end of Big Sur and a cliff called Fat Chance in the state's northern interior. This represented a decline from an estimated 300 pairs just two decades earlier.

In the same year, diagnoses for *anatum* populations elsewhere in North America offered no better news. Across the continent, more than 95 percent of an estimated 7000 territories that had existed prior to European colonization were silent. East of the Mississippi, all 133 known eyries were deserted, and not a single bird was known to have fledged since 1957. By the end of the year, the peregrine, along with the bald eagle and brown pelican, finally received protection under the original Endangered Species Act. Two years later, in 1972, amid vast public outcry, DDT was banned in the United States almost entirely.

Given the peregrine's mythic status, the species' worldwide free-fall was a soul-shaking cataclysm. For falconers, especially those with peregrines of their own, the questions revolved primarily around stewardship. How, they wondered, could we have allowed such a magnificent predator to vanish? Why did we not notice sooner? For scientists, the searching ran much deeper. Not only did the raw toxicity of DDT take everyone by surprise, but many, most notably Rachel Carson, who voiced her fears in the now-classic book *Silent Spring,* suspected that the general raptor die-off indicated a much more worrisome trend. Given their place at the top of the food chain, peregrine falcons are ecological barometers in the same way as the proverbial canary in the coal mine. In times of purity and plenty, populations flourish in direct proportion to the health of those species and resources upon which they depend. In times of scarcity and crisis, however, they crash and burn with everything else. In North America, the peregrine's precipitous decline was the first sign for many that what ailed the land ran much further than skin-deep, and that the links between flora, fauna, and the impacts of humanity were far more complex than anyone had initially thought. Most ominous of all, scientists and falconers like Brian Walton began to argue that the peregrine's fate would eventually become our own, that in a world of ubiquitous, industrial contamination, no one is immune.

Against these seemingly impossible odds, *F. peregrinus anatum* has fought back and recovered—just not quite in the way most experts expected. Drawing on a vast store of falconry techniques and scientific expertise, the SCPBRG, The Peregrine Fund, the Raptor Center, the Canadian Wildlife Service, and a network of falconers and volunteers around the country collectively released more than 4000 peregrines over a span of 20 years—literally hand-placing the species back into the wild, one egg, one chick, one bird at a time. At the last official head count, the U.S. Fish and Wildlife Service, citing data from multiple sources, reported 1388 peregrine pairs throughout Canada, Alaska, and the western United States, with a minimum of 205 east of the Mississippi. In California the peregrines have expanded not only numerically but territorially as well. The state is now home to over 150 geographically diverse pairs, and the number of active nest sites expands every year to include bridges, buildings, and other human structures.

Given impetus by the political push for a conservation success story, and despite ongoing and often bitter debate, the U.S. Fish and Wildlife Service officially delisted *F. peregrinus anatum* from the Endangered Species List in the summer of 1999. At the heart of the controversy is the tortured spirit of the Endangered Species Act itself,

All in the family. A remote camera portrait of the Muir Beach hack birds just prior to fledging.

which gives rise to the fundamental question of when enough is enough. At what point do we consider a species self-sustaining and sufficiently prepared to face the lions of natural selection again? And with what scientific criteria (i.e., raw numbers, breeding pairs, rate of population increase, etc.) do we judge a species to be "recovered?" In California, that the peregrine is back is not in question; whether it can continue to thrive without "management" and habitat protection amid a rash of new chemical threats is still hotly debated. As far as Brian is concerned, listings and technicalities obscure the real issue. Despite healthy numbers in some places, peregrine eyries are still failing in others, and if the Bird Group biologists were not out here doing something about it, nobody would be.

Proving the point, Brian is already 20 feet out from the catwalk of the Vincent Thomas Bridge, toed up on a two-inch steel lip and hanging by rivet heads. He stops short of the superstructure's outermost beam and wraps a nylon sling and carabiner around a support strut to establish his last protection point. With 10 feet of open exposure still to come, he checks it repeatedly. As he steps around the corner and comes into full view of the nest, the chick immediately begins to wail above the roar of traffic. Brian freezes instantly, as if he's set off an alarm system, but it's already too late. The female has reappeared. Perched in the shadows opposite the nest, she cries three times, giving Brian one last chance to reconsider his trespass, then bows her head like a rhino and dives.

Backed against the support beam, Brian squats low into his knees and raises his arms to deflect the blow. At the last second, the peregrine flares her talons and lands a direct hit on Brian's helmet, briefly knocking them both off balance. Five feet before an intersection of I-beams, the peregrine brakes, drops through a gap in the sky, and recovers in a series of graceful, acrobatic turns. The chick continues to wail.

"Keep an eye on her," Brian yells. "Tell me where she's coming from!" Anticipating another pass, he sits down, braces the girder between his legs, and begins to shimmy quickly out to the nest. Still a stranger in its own body, the chick can do nothing to defend itself. Brian pulls his chick carrier around in front of him, places the bird gently inside, then pulls up instantly.

"Where is she?!" he demands. "Where is she?!"

The female, however, is nowhere in sight, which is the worst of all possible scenarios. It means she's "up there" somewhere, gaining altitude, looking for speed. Brian glances quickly over both shoulders, stuffs shell fragments from all four eggs and prey remains into separate plastic bags, and begins to inch back toward the safety of the support beams. The wind blows hard in 20-knot gusts and the air is eerily quiet. Then

The Vincent Thomas female defends her nest by taking a shot
at Brian Latta's head.

suddenly, the peregrine banks hard out of a terminal stoop, transferring a thousand feet of vertical momentum into a single centrifugal blow. At the last instant, Brian ducks and braces against the beam, sending the female glancing off his back and down into the aerial abyss beneath the bridge. He is shaken but manages his way quickly back to the support intersection. From a girder just 40 feet away, the female has landed and wails. Glaring at Brian intensely, she emanates a deep maternal rage.

Back in the safety of the catwalk, Brian opens the chick carrier and plastic bags. Among the prey remains are the feathers of a cockateel, a green parrot, starlings, and the leg bands from four racing homer pigeons—toxically speaking, the equivalent of organic hand-raised veal. According to Brian, at first glance the shell fragments are thick and robust. Just three weeks old, the male chick is healthy and powdered with fresh, snowy down. Calm and quiet now, he looks up at us curiously as if to ask, "Are you my mother?"

"I've taken some birds off the bridges that look like they've been dropped down a chimney," Brian notes, pointing to the chick's ivory white down. "They're covered with road dust, exhaust, and sooty coke debris. . . . That's another reason in itself we need to get these birds off of here." Brian nods to the female, still wailing some 40 feet away.

"Now if we could only convince her to nest somewhere else."

Back in the bridge superintendent's office, Brian gets on his cell phone with Bird Group coordinators to relay nest data and to double-check his itinerary for the rest of the southern California coast. Next stop: Big Sur. Next week: the Oakland Bridge, the Golden Gate Bridge, and a major skyscraper in downtown Los Angeles.

Brian looks at me and shrugs, "We just release them into the area," he says. "We don't tell them where to lay their eggs."

As we're leaving, we pass a sign outside the employee's lounge that says:

"No job is so important and no service so urgent that we cannot take the time to perform our work safely." Given what's just taken place, we all smile at the irony.

Unlike the industrial sprawl of Long Beach harbor, the coast of Big Sur, California, is arguably the most wild and scenic stretch of land on earth. Backed by the hulking 5000-foot spine of the Santa Lucia Coast range, and shearing into the Pacific in an endless procession of 400-foot headlands, it has the raw, geologic feel that the end of a continent should have. For over 70 miles, there are just 6000 people, five towns, and except for California Route 1, no major roads. There are also no landing strips, railroads, or anchorages for sailboats or fishing fleets. Thanks to a 1972 coastal conservation initiative which put the coast from Carmel to Morro Bay under protection virtually in perpetuity, the entire landscape has been literally left to the birds.

Big Sur is also perfect peregrine falcon habitat, providing high cliffs, lots of overhangs, consistent updrafts, diverse prey choice, and miles and miles of wild blue yonder. With so much open territory, one would think an aggressively rebounding avian predator like the *F. peregrinus* would simply move in and take over. The purity of Big Sur is misleading, however, and the area's peregrines are as endangered now as they ever were.

"Don't let the scenery fool you," Brian says, pulling his pickup off the road onto a gravel cliff top, "the birds on the Vincent Thomas Bridge are in better shape than they are here. . . . Failure is the norm for most of these nests."

In near-perfect opposition to Long Beach harbor, the view from the top of the cliff at Cape San Martin is one of the wildest in the hemisphere. It's just past eight in the morning, and the sun has yet to clear the coast. Blocked out by the shadow of North America, the cliff below us crumbles away in a series of smudged charcoal etchings. At the bottom, steep blue rollers break over small beaches of wave-crushed stone where seals and sea lions lounge in the sun with Roman pomp and nonchalance. Offshore, the distant geysers of California gray whales moving north are the only signs of life on an otherwise empty horizon.

For local peregrines, however, Big Sur and the rest of the central coast is far from

Facing page:
Negotiating an obstacle course of large boulders called "widow makers," Brian reaches an eyrie at Vandenburg Air Force Base south of the Big Sur to band the chicks and collect eggshell fragments and prey remains.

idyllic. In contrast to the reproductive successes in Los Angeles and San Francisco, eggs here continue to break during incubation, nests fail, and despite fledging from some eyries, the reproductive success rate for the area is abnormally low. Currently, within 40 miles of Cape San Martin, there are just nine active peregrine eyries, only four more than one can find within two miles of the Vincent Thomas Bridge in Long Beach harbor. The reason for the continued nest failures, according to Brian, is, once again, eggshell thinning. According to the Bird Group's toxicology data, California's average thinning ratio continues to hover at 17 percent, the point at which reproductive failures begin to skyrocket. In the wilder territories like Big Sur, however, the values remain much higher.

"All of the central coast, from Monterey to Point Conception, including the Channel Islands," explains Brian, "has higher levels [of thinning] than just about anywhere else in the world that we know of. The arithmetic mean of all midcoast clutches collected from 1976 to 1998 is 19 percent thin. During those years, 86 out of 196 clutch sample means were over 20 percent thin. Morro Rock tops this list with a clutch mean of 29.9 percent thin in 1980. Eighteen of the 28 clutch samples from Morro Rock were over 20 percent thin. In 1998, the midcoast averaged 17 percent thin. Five of the 19 samples were over 20 percent thin, and Anacapa topped the list at 26 percent."

"The key point here," Brian adds, "is that 17 percent is a state average. Most urban pairs in Los Angeles and San Francisco have a percentage of 10 percent, so relatively speaking, they're doing great. The birds in Big Sur, however . . . are clearly still in danger of failing on a regular basis." So far this year, two out of the five nests have already come up empty.

Citing extensive data, Brian explains that the root cause of the thinning and failures is no different now than it was 40 years ago: chemical pollution. Beneath the central coast's wild veneer, Big Sur is an underwater wasteland. Thanks to more than 30 years of pesticide manufacture and dumping between 1947 and 1982, the entire Palos Verdes Shelf (PVS) off of southern California is now saturated with over 100 metric tons of DDT, and is an EPA-designated Superfund site. A recent University of California Sea Grant study has also confirmed that the chemical is coming unbound from deep-water sediments and working its way directly into the water column, dramatically increasing its lethal range far beyond where the original dumping occurred. The Bird Group's recent analyses of eggshell fragments and prey remains from nearly 200 central coast peregrine clutches have also turned up elevated concentrations of PCBs (polychlorinated biphenyls), HCBs (hydrochlorinated biphenyls), and dioxins, a byproduct of paper and Agent Orange production and one of the most carcinogenic substances on earth. Given that neither DDT nor kelthane has been sprayed or introduced into the environment for decades, it's plausible that some synergistic cocktail of all these chemicals in the marine web is causing the continued nest failures throughout the area.

Ironically, the data also suggest that the success difference between urban and wild peregrines in California may have less to do with habitat, as was originally thought, and more to do with prey. Due to the high stability of DDE in aqueous solutions, Brian speculates the coastal peregrine's diet of seabirds, ducks, and migratory waterfowl ultimately is a lethal pill. Urban peregrines, by contrast, dine on the relatively less toxic flesh of pigeons, starlings, and exotic pets, accumulating smaller concentrations of chemicals into their systems. From a conservation standpoint, the result is a complete reversal of logic: the wildest birds have the worst chance of survival.

Regardless of the specific mechanisms, the uncertain status of *F. peregrinus anatum* along coastal California sends another clear message about wildlife, wilderness, and the accumulated consequences of industrial pollution: If peregrines are indeed the ecological barometers scientists say they are, something is still dangerously wrong with the system. Unfortunately, now that the species itself is no longer endangered, no one really seems to care. The public passion has faded, the big-name supporters are gone, and money for monitoring and continuing toxicology studies is virtually nonexistent. Even more distressing to biologists is the fact that the peregrine is no longer afforded the amenities of first-class travel under the Endangered Species Act. Were another catastrophic free-fall to occur, the process of getting the peregrine back onto the list to increase protection and clean up contaminant hot spots would take years.

Not surprisingly, the peregrine's recent discharge from intensive care has only increased Brian's personal commitment to monitoring the species' recovery, especially here in Big Sur and in the Channel Islands. Now that there's no more free ride—no more "fostering," "augmentation," or "management"—up-to-date data on the reproductive success and population status of coastal birds are more critical now than ever before. The problem for Brian is that the price of getting them remains just as high.

According to nest attendants, the Cape San Martin eyrie lies somewhere 150 feet below us amid a gnarled obstacle course of loose boulders and sharp granite overhangs. Although the exact location and reproductive status of the nest itself is still unconfirmed, the attendants have observed the telltale signs of successful reproductive behavior since the first weeks of nesting season, now almost two months ago. In the last 13 days, specifically, the young male falcon, called a *tiercel,* has been returning with prey up to six times a day, a good sign of multiple chicks. Brian takes in all the information, leans out over the edge, and contemplates the route. Beyond a steep scree slope 20 feet in front of us, the cliff slices away precipitously into deep, blue space.

"Well," Brian says finally, unraveling his rope and feeding it over the edge, "there's only one way to find out what's down there."

With their love of wild terrain and vertical faces, technical rock climbers and peregrine falcons have been cohabitating the high frontier since the first days of American alpinism. In the early years, especially on the big walls of Yosemite Valley in California, their relationship served as proof for many that wildness and humanity could coexist on the simplest of terms. Big Sur, however, is no Yosemite, and what Brian does, specifically speaking, isn't rock climbing. It's so much worse, in fact, that most any climber with real experience would take one look at a coastal peregrine cliff and head home. As opposed to the hard faces and straight cracks of America's climbing meccas, the cliffs of central coast California are minefields of hanging tombstones, eroding slopes, and landslides waiting to happen. There are few solid hand- or footholds, and every few feet a sharp overhang threatens to rip through the climbing rope like jagged steel.

"No matter how many climbs I've done," Brian sighs, pulling the same arsenal of slings and carabiners from his backpack as he used on the bridge, "or how hard or easy they've been, I still get this tightknit ball of nausea in my stomach beforehand. Lee [Aulman] said he felt the same thing for years, then told me if you're not scared, you're just stupid." With the help of the nest attendants, Brian sets up a primary anchor of three metal re-bar stakes, driving them deep into the top of the cliff. Tethered by all three points, we will rappel down along the same route on the same rope to minimize disturbance to the eyrie itself.

By the time the ropes are ready, our presence here is no longer a secret. The female peregrine swoops from the cliff and shoots out over the water on an updraft, gaining a hundred feet in short order with a dozen quick pumps of her wings. At the top of her arc, she banks left and glides parallel to the cliff for a panoramic view. Above the waves crashing below, we can hear her agitated cries—*kak, kak, kak.* Brian briefly watches her circle, trying to gain some hint about the location of the eyrie, and double-checks his harness one last time. Finally, he gives the thumbs-up and backs over the edge. Releasing the rope slowly through his hands, he takes five steps down the slope, picks two large boulders from the route, then disappears over the edge. For the next few minutes, all we can see is the sawing of the rope.

Then from below, Brian's voice rolls up over the lip of the cliff. "All clear!" he shouts.

The end of the continent at Big Sur. Brian Latta clears the last overhang and
rappels into the eyrie proper at Cape San Martin.

I clip the rope through my own rappel device, grab a backpack with climbing and banding equipment, and follow his route over the edge of the cliff, keeping a safe distance from the largest boulders, aptly called "widow makers." A quarter of the way down, the cliff turns totally vertical and yawns open into clear views both north and south. Just below my feet, Brian releads the rope around a series of three knife-edge overhangs and leans back into open space to reconfirm the path to the eyrie. The female is nowhere to be seen.

As soon as we begin the next pitch, however, the female reappears, banking in from the south and climbing hard. At 500 feet off the water, she "kaks" three times, tucks her wings, and dives. Her body tapers into an iron bullet and accelerates instantly, as if somehow operating outside the laws of gravity. At the bottom of her stoop, she banks directly into Brian's head, nicking his helmet, and then veers off downwind. Brian brushes her off like a nuisance insect.

"When climbing like this," he explains casually, "you have to be so focused on safety for yourself and the birds, getting to the nest, doing your job, and getting back up with a minimum of disturbance, that you don't have room for worrying about the adults. They rarely hit us anyway."

Brian then points beneath him and nods as if to say "we're here." He kicks off a small ledge, drops past one more overhang with a hiss of the rope, and swings just right of the eyrie proper into view of the chicks themselves. When the rope slacks, I quickly follow behind him. Not yet able to defend themselves, the chicks screech, shiver, and roll into a single downy ball in an attempt to hide. Brian maneuvers quickly onto the outer lip of the eyrie and secures himself against the southern wall, blocking off the entrance to protect the chicks and shielding his own back from attacks. The two chicks are almost 20 days old. Their skins fit like baggy snowsuits, and their down is pure and new. Already, their beaks and claws are full-grown, honed into hard, anodized tools. Relishing the finer details of a beautiful bird in its own home, Brian smiles with a pleasure only he and a few others on the planet have ever known. He smiles especially wide today because the species as a whole is two birds bigger.

"These are the real Veloca raptors," Brian says, picking up one of the chicks. "Forget that Lost World, Jurassic Park nonsense. This is the real thing." He then kicks his feet into two footholds in the cliff, readjusts his rappel device, and settles into the eyrie face-on. From his backpack he pulls a Tupperware container holding two types of leg bands, Ziplocs, and data sheets. As Brian collects eggshell fragments and prey remains from the tasseled substrate, the chicks shuffle around the back of the eyrie like windup toys, gurgling to themselves lightly and eyeing us with nervous curiosity. Amid the peb-

The real Veloca raptor.

bles and guano lie the remains of a least tern, a swift, and various seabirds, as well as the addled remains of two eggs which never hatched. Brian takes samples of everything and seals them in Ziploc bags. He also sifts through to the bottom of the eyrie looking for feather lice, insects, and other detritivors. Brian then picks up one of the chicks and extends its wing.

"In just the first few weeks after fledging," he explains, "these chicks will have a significant mastery of their acrobatic potential. I've seen them stooping dragonflies, flowers, falling leaves, and even each other for practice. They're like kittens with jet engines. . . . The amount of G's they probably pull in their everyday lives is incredible."

As the female stalks the perimeter of the eyrie, she demonstrates Brian's point aptly. Mixed in among the circling gulls, her speed seems surreal, as if she were moving in an entirely different time-space continuum. Unable to stoop in close for a direct hit, however, the Cape San Martin female is helpless today. As she screeches a hundred feet above us, Brian bands both chicks on both legs, then photographs the eyrie for the Bird Group's long-term records.

"I only wish she knew it was all for her own good," he says. "I don't really like to do this either."

Front-row real estate on Big Sur. Brian Latta settles into the eyrie at Cape San Martin to band the chicks and collect eggshell fragments.

As we ascend back up the cliff, we are forced to dodge small rock slides jarred free by the rope above us. To the left and right of our ascent line lie boulders (poised to fall) not removed on the descent. Nevertheless, we make it past the three overhangs safely and intact. At the top of the scree slope, Brian pauses to take in the clouds, the cliffs, and the wide, open sky one last time. Just over the lip, the female turns in tight circles around the eyrie, then swoops in to regain her nest. Above the waves, we can hear her chicks welcome her home.

"We've done our job," he says, "now it's up to them."

FIRE
The Infernal Planet

Man is the animal that has made friends with the fire.
—*Henry Van Dyke*

Lava fountain at Stromboli. (© Roger Ressmeyer/CORBIS.)

Humanity has always had a love-hate relationship with fire. As sunlight, magma, and physical flame, earth's "yellow wolf" is as vital to the planetary ecosystem as air and water, ultimately providing the energy that sustains all life. Fire is the solar heat which warms the atmosphere and the fuel that builds atoms into rocks and continents. Via photosynthesis, fire nourishes plants at the base of the food chain, and by extension, the diversity of all living things. As an ecological mechanism, fire creates rich, fertile soil, replenishes forests and grasslands from the Arctic to the Amazon, and occasionally, as in the case of California's giant sequoias (*Sequoia giganteum*), catalyzes the process of seed release and species regeneration in the first place. Without the cyclical dependency on fire, with which almost every plant and animal species on earth has evolved, the planet as we know it would cease to exist in its current form.

Humanity's relationship with fire is not simply one of innate physical dependence, however. It is also fiercely spiritual, stimulated by some of our deepest inclinations to worship nature's ultimate powers and run for our lives. At the most elemental level, everything about fire is magical—its transcendent dance; its invisible, yet inexhaustible appetite; the way it looks and feels like something we can touch, but can never actually hold it. Psychologically, it's this essential magic that lures us to the flicker of an open hearth and that underlies the pain when lives go up in flames. On a more practical level, our religious covenant with fire is also sound evolutionary logic. For thousands of years, the "fire stick" has been humanity's greatest ally in our struggle to survive on earth, bestowing upon us the gifts of light, warmth, food, and industry that have brought us here today. Yet fire has also been our most merciless foe, burying entire towns under volcanic lava, incinerating cities like Rome and San Francisco, and most recently, threatening the entire human species with thermonuclear annihilation.

Given such power, fire, in all its physical forms, has played a central role in the belief systems of societies worldwide. So fierce was the ancient Aztec belief that all of life emanated from the sun itself, for example, that they were willing to sacrifice the blood of their own citizens to ensure its continued munificence. For other early societies located in volcanic regions, such as Central America and the Pacific Rim, the gifts of divine fire flowed forth from the volcanoes themselves. For still others, like some early Christian denominations and satanic cults, fire symbolized an entirely different kind of power—evil. Instead of being revered for its power to give life, fire was worshipped for its ability to take it away. Ironically, what modern fire science and applied research has proven is that everyone is correct: fire is indeed the planetary dynamo from which all things are born and eventually return—humans included. As renowned fire historian Stephen Pyne has accurately described it, "We are uniquely fire creatures on a uniquely fire planet."

Despite our complex relationship to earth's infernal essence, scientifically speaking, fire couldn't be more simple. In the presence of oxygen and heat, the molecular bonds of organic fuel matter are broken down, releasing carbon dioxide and the visible energy we know as flame, lava, or smoldering coals. In this way, fire is inherently different from its elemental counterparts, earth, air, and water. As an object of scientific study, fire is not a physical, geographic frontier but an analytical one. As a result, there are as many branches of fire science as there are manifestations of fire itself, encompassing disciplines as diverse as chemistry, physics, biology, geology, mathematics, and engineering.

The most obvious and well-traveled realms of fire science are the studies of volcanism and forest fires. At first, the primary goal of both disciplines was to tame the wrath of the yellow wolf and reduce the loss of human life. By better understanding how fire came about and behaved, we could more effectively suppress it and stay out of its way. Over the past 50 years, however, the study of volcanoes and wildfires has shifted from its early humanitarian roots to the goal of understanding fire as a vital planetary process. Erupting volcanoes and burning forests give scientists a physical medium to document fire's essential role in the life, death, and rebirth of earth's living systems. Scientists these days are also studying fire at the less conspicuous level, analyzing things such as fuel chemistry and flame behavior, heat transfer, combustion and ignition processes, and fluid mechanics. Ironically, what all the data have shown is that fire is not a god to be feared and a monster to be contained; it is an ecological miracle to be celebrated and deployed.

At the same time, however, modern science has done little to reduce fire's violent appetite. The yellow wolf is a reckless, savage beast. It can turn on a dime, leap across rivers and firebreaks, erupt spontaneously, rip whole trees from the ground in swirling convection currents, and with respect to real-life phenomena like "back drafts," even possess a devilish life of its own. In all its manifestations—wildland, residential, and volcanic, to name just a few—fire has killed more people in the history of the United States than all other natural disasters combined. Even today, thousands die each year, hundreds of thousands are injured, and billions of dollars of property are destroyed by runaway conflagrations.

For those who choose to work with fire hands-on—whether as scientists or firefighters—the infernal element is no less deadly. In what is perhaps the best-known incident, French volcanologists Maurice and Kattia Krafft were engulfed in flaming debris and burned alive on Japan's Mount Unzen in 1991 as they attempted to film an escalating eruption. More recently, in 1994, 14 wildland firefighters battling a blaze on Storm King Mountain near Grand Junction, Colorado, were trapped high on a ridge and swallowed whole by the rapidly advancing flames. The moral of the story for anyone working with fire is brutally clear: Regardless of what is at stake—original scientific data or a single human life—fire shows no mercy. It is the elemental force with the power to reduce everything on earth, from forests to human flesh, to nothing more than chemical fuel. Our willingness to risk our lives to understand the yellow wolf is kindled by much more than scientific curiosity or professional heroism, however. Understanding the mechanics of fire is ultimately a matter of life, death, and human destiny.

Too Hot to Handle

At 19,000 feet above the top of Mexico, the air is thin, odorless, and ether-clear. The only sound is the thrumming of our helicopter as it bites hard into the shallow waves of turbulence. Fifty feet below our fragile metal bird, a gnarled fin of rock and ice marks the crater lip and summit proper of Citlaltépetl, better known as Pico de Orizaba, North America's third highest mountain and one of the tallest volcanoes in the world. A step to the north, the mountain slides away for 2000 feet in a sheet of sheer glacial ice. Today, it disappears in a boil of gunmetal storm clouds. A step to the south, the first of a hundred vertical headwalls drops off into Pico's cavernous crater. Out of sight, a quarter-mile deep in the crater, a small emerald lake has begun to gather—an ominous sign.

Perched on the crater rim itself and partially obscured in downdrafts of snow, Mexican volcanologist Hugo Delgado Granados motions with theatrical bows of his upper body for the helicopter to drop. The pilot acknowledges him with barely a nod and begins to set the chopper down an inch at a time. Around the windows, the snow builds to a blinding whiteout and visibility drops to zero. Every few seconds the entire helicopter is rocked by a gust of wind from off the crater's rim. "Heavy turbulence," the pilot yells. It would have been much safer to try this an hour ago.

Without even a bump, however, the helicopter touches down astraddle the crater rim, one landing bar on the glacier and the other in the crater itself. Not willing to rest the full weight of the bird on either of the fragile slopes, the pilot keeps the rotor humming, the power up, and waits for the air to clear. For an instant, we are in perfect balance at the top of the highest volcano in the hemisphere, 18,410 feet (5611 meters).

"GET OUT!" the pilot finally yells, his tone communicating clearly that there's no time for reflection. I grab my crampons, ice ax, two hard-shell cases of global positioning system (GPS) equipment, and leap into the lingering blizzard. As soon as I'm clear of the prop wash, the pilot powers up and lifts off. Within seconds, the chopper is

Facing page:
Dawn light bathes the low saddle of Paso de Cortez between the volcanoes of Popocatépetl and Iztaccíhuatl.

151

The expedition helicopter ascends to 19,000 feet over the crater of Pico de Orizaba, the third highest summit in North America.

hundreds of feet below us, riding the air cushion off the surface of the volcano itself back down to a more comfortable atmospheric viscosity of 14,000 feet. Hugo and his assistant, Lorenzo Ortiz Armas, quickly emerge from the swirling snow like ghosts.

"Don't move," Hugo yells, grabbing the cases, "or you'll pass out. Four thousand feet in four minutes will put anyone flat on their back." Because of Pico's high altitude, two of Hugo's expedition members have already left the mountain with blood in their lungs. Three others remain incapacitated at base camp almost a vertical mile below us with migraines, nausea, and tunnel vision. Heeding Hugo's advice, I kneel on the crater rim, face the sun, and take deep gulps of the thin air. At 18,410 feet, ambient oxygen in the atmosphere is barely half what it is at sea level, threatening even seasoned climbers with everything from hallucinations to comas. Not surprisingly, mountaineers call the region above 15,000 feet the "death zone."

Hugo himself seems unaffected. He scampers up the snow slope to the summit, squats on the crater's highest, flattest point, and begins pulling cords and antenna parts from the GPS cases. The helicopter is now long gone, and the world above the clouds is completely silent. Only occasionally can we hear the tremors of rock falls rising up from deep inside the crater itself. Owing to natural erosion, Pico is gradually caving into itself these days. According to Hugo, Pico may also be awakening from a

500-year repose. Recent aerial surveys and net mass balance models indicate that the volcano's once-vast glacial ice fields are melting, while temperature data show that the high flanks are heating up, in some places reaching 162 degrees Fahrenheit. This recent escalation in activity has some people in the nearby town of Hidalgo on edge these days. Barely 10 miles from the crater proper, Hidalgo and myriad other Mexican pueblos are built on the thick, fertile mudflows from Pico's last cataclysmic eruption. Were the volcano to erupt today, it would rearrange the landscape for dozens of miles around.

"It is easy to see why volcanoes will always scare people away," Hugo explains, "but how will we ever know how important something is until we understand it? . . . And how will we protect ourselves?"

As he begins to assemble a rock cradle for the GPS antenna, Hugo hands Lorenzo a small portable thermometer and points to locations downslope where temperature measurements need to be taken. By monitoring annual increases in Pico's overall temperature and taking water samples from the small crater lake, Hugo is determining to what extent the volcano is heating up each year and generating critical baseline data in the effort to forecast just when Pico might eventually blow. On a more global level, Hugo is attempting to correlate temperature and other environmental data to estimate how much Pico's loss of glacial ice is attributable to internal heating, local low-level ozone pollution, and the global greenhouse effect in general.

"This is why I want to do things that aren't normally done," Hugo says, gesturing to the crater over his shoulder and the long dark plains of central Mexico far beyond, "to get data that can't be gotten any other way. When we try new things like this, we never know what will happen, what we'll find, or what the conditions will be like. The risks are always higher, but so are the rewards." As he talks, Hugo's obsession with volcanoes—*los vulcanes*—radiates from him like heat from the sun.

With the goal of always breaking new ground in the field of volcanology, Hugo has spent the better part of 20 years rappelling into hot, smoking craters and closely monitoring Mexico's three high mountain volcanoes—Pico,

The highest crater landing in history. The expedition helicopter touches down on the summit of Pico de Orizaba straddling the crater rim. (*Photograph by Hugo Delgado Granados.*)

Iztaccíhuatl, and Popocatépetl—as if they were intensive care patients. He has executed one of the world's highest helicopter landings on an active volcanic crater rim, mounted a half-dozen penetrations into the smoldering craters themselves, and spent far more time in Mexico's glacier-riddled death zone than any human should. With respect to Popocatépetl specifically, Hugo has been treading the fine line between life and death every year for more than five years now. Popocatépetl, better known as Popo or Don Gregorio, is the tallest *eruptive* volcano in the world.

Since Popo's first explosion on December 21, 1994, the 17,930 foot (5230 meters) "Smoking Giant" has remained a ticking time bomb. Of the dozen violent explosions since, four have been large enough to warrant preliminary evacuations of over 100,000 people from nearby villages. The longest eruption buried seven miles along a major river channel under 30 feet of mud and debris, and another blasted magma more than a mile into the air. Lately, seismic tremors have been increasing, ash plumes (called *fumaroles*) tower up to nine miles overhead, and the skirting summit glacier is retreating at a record pace. In the villages of Xantlicinta and San Nicholas de los Ranchos, huddled close against the volcano's fertile flanks, people say they can feel the ground rumbling, and their annual ceremonies to honor the Smoking Giant have become solemn requests for mercy. As far as active volcanoes go, Popo is as ready as they get.

With over 36 million people living within 70 miles of the volcano's blast zone, Popo threatens apocalyptic ruin should a full-scale eruption occur. Just 50 miles east of Popo's blast zone is Mexico City, the world's most populated metropolis. According to current models and hazard maps that Hugo has helped to generate, over 400,000 people fall in Popo's red "run-or-die" zone, in which mudflows and searing avalanches of gas and debris would sweep down established river valleys and flood plains within minutes. Another 30 million people, including the residents of Mexico City, fall within the volcano's extended yellow zone, where, if historical data serves us, ash and particulate debris could pile as high as two feet, contaminating the air and water, crushing buildings, roads, and other urban infrastructure, and destroying local crops, livestock, and wildlife. Worst-case extrapolations derived from the geologic record indicate Popo would not only scorch every living thing for tens of miles around but would also release an estimated 2 million gallons of meltwater from the near-instant vaporization of the volcano's two large glaciers. The result, Hugo's topographic mudflow models tell us, would be a flood of biblical proportions which could bury dozens of towns in up to 25 feet of fast-moving volcanic cement (called *lahars*).

Such situation-specific data on Popocatépetl have come at significant risk to Hugo himself. With the notable exception of not actually being on the volcano during

The active crater of Popocatépetl. Since the volcano's first eruption in December 1994, the mountain has spewed forth towering plumes of gas, ash, and incandescent debris over a dozen times. (*Photograph by Hugo Delgado Granados.*)

an explosion, Hugo has recently met face-to-face some of volcanism's nastiest facets. In the most perilous experience yet, Hugo rappelled down the volcano's 400-foot headwall into the center crater itself, penetrating a Martianlike netherworld of gas and fire that few people on earth have ever seen.

"It looked like the surface of the moon," he recalls, reliving the experience with the armchair understatement of a seasoned explorer, "very hot and steamy. When we walked on the sulfur near a fumarole, we would sink in and ideas would come into our minds like 'How far will I go down? Will I be cooked like a chicken?' I forgot all about the danger of the rappel itself." Based on Hugo's reports of pooling magma, sulfur deposits glowing in the middle of the day, and lake water temperatures of 149 degrees, up from 84 degrees just weeks before, Popo was officially closed to everyone except scientists in early February 1995. In April, Hugo rappelled into the crevasses of Popo's summit glacier to test for changes in volcanic trace gases like sulfur, chlorine, fluorine, and phosphates. As expected, concentrations were highest toward the surface, indicating that Popo's rebirth had been a long time coming.

"This was extreme science at it's best," Hugo muses. "The adventure was much more than just moving the muscles. We ice-climbed, moved the muscles, and got the samples. I believe in the cutting edge of the mind, and using adventure for something

The pilgrimage. Villagers from towns located on Popocatépetl's flanks ascend
the volcano en route to the annual ceremony to honor the "Smoking Giant,"
affectionately called Don Gregorio.

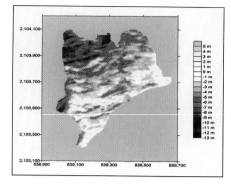 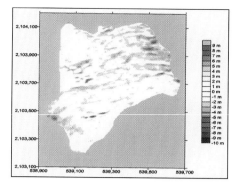

Mexico melting. Created from high-altitude GPS measurements, annual net mass balance models, like these of Popocatépetl in 1997 (left) and 1999 (right), are critical in determining to what extent glacial ice is retreating each year, and more important, how much water will be released if the volcano erupts and where it will go. (*Models by Hugo Delgado Granados*.)

more. Getting these cores was an intellectual adventure. The sense of discovery was just as strong here," he points to his head, and then hits his chest, "as it was here. In this way, even when the body decays, there is no end to the adventure."

Soon afterwards, Hugo flew repeatedly through Popo's towering 30,000-foot gas plume in a small unpressurized plane carrying a COSPEC (correlation spectrometer) and found that sulfur dioxide (SO_2) emissions had more than doubled to 4000 tons per day. Mount St. Helen's, by comparison, discharged only 600 tons of sulfur per day even while erupting. Confirming beyond a doubt what many already assumed, a system of infrared lasers, reflectors, and fixed poles that Hugo installed on Popo's glaciers over the summer revealed that the mountain itself was actually bulging from expansion of the magma chamber.

Popocatépetl's interior hell. Juan Jose Venegas unpacks monitoring equipment deep inside the volcano's crater in order to take samples from the crater lake. (*Photograph by Hugo Delgado Granados*.)

"Bulging is the most obvious sign of clogging," Hugo remarks, pointing down Pico's slopes for effect. "That rapidly building pore pressure must eventually be released. . . . You see now why we have installed [GPS] stations and [infrared monitoring] poles both here and on Popo. We check them twice a year to see what the mountains are really up to."

These days, thanks largely to Hugo's persistent research, 12 seismic stations now ring Popo's lower flanks and feed real-time readouts to computer screens across Mexico. A permanent video camera set up on 17,160-foot (5230 meters) Iztaccíhuatl, just

11 miles south of Popo, monitors the size and shape of the volcano's fumarole 24 hours a day, and when activity starts jumping, a fixed infrared gas spectrometer measures CO_2 and SO_2 gas emissions twice daily.

More remarkable than the current state of alert itself, however, is the fact that Hugo has stayed alive in the process of pulling the alarm. Unlike getting wedged in a tapering cave passage, where dislocating one's own shoulder might buy another shot at life, no amount of shrewd wit or Herculean strength can contend with a volcano's wrath. If there's one thing in nature that shouldn't be messed with, it's anything connected to the center of the earth.

Enveloped by a paper-thin crust of continents and ocean, the earth's interior is a four-layered nuclear hell consisting of a moon-sized, nickel-iron inner core; a viscous outer core; a broad lower mantle; and a liquid upper mantle that boils in some places just 20

The path of Popo's destruction. Mudflow models are vital to evacuation and disaster planning by CENAPRED, Mexico's national disaster prevention agency. Generated from a combination of glaciological and topographical data, they inform residents around Mexico's active volcanoes how far and how fast they need to travel to avoid getting killed. (*Model by Hugo Delgado Granados.*)

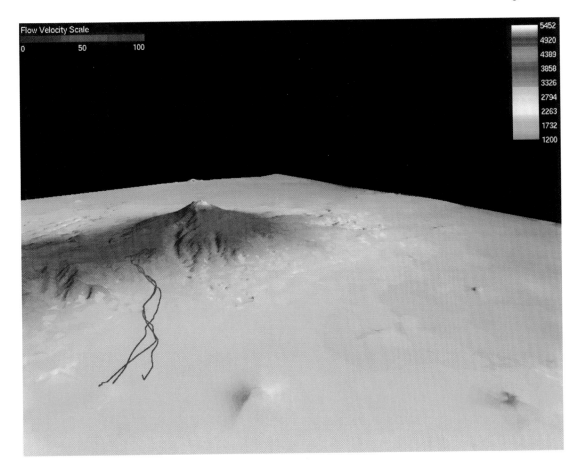

Flow Velocity Scale

| 0 | 50 | 100 |

5452
4920
4389
3858
3326
2794
2263
1732
1200

miles beneath our feet. Volcanoes occur where this pressurized magma overflows to the green surface world above. Often, the magmatic release happens where the planet's 15 or so tectonic plates shift, collide, or break apart, like water breaching the cracks of a great planetary dam. In some rare instances, however, the explosive release of interior pressure can literally shake the earth for thousands of miles around.

"No Pase." Since February 1995, Popocatépetl has been off limits to everyone but scientists and authorized government officials.

Technically, volcanoes fall into three categories, each varying significantly in its physical characteristics and the associated risks to people and scientists. Hot spot volcanoes, like those of the Hawaiian Islands-Emperor Seamounts chain, form when a localized magmatic plume in the upper mantle burns through a soft spot in the planet's crust like a penetrating laser. The resulting eruptions are often more spectacular and predictable than they are dangerous, giving birth to glowing, magmatic fountains; oozing lava flows; and upon solidification of the molten material, towering knife-edged mountains. From a human safety point of view, the only way one could die in a hot spot eruption would be to walk up and fall right into it.

Rift volcanoes, most often found underwater, and now recognized to be a primary source of oceanic crust formation, occur where the earth's tectonic surface plates are pulling apart, such as the Mid-Atlantic Ridge or the African Rift Valley. Generally speaking, rift volcanoes don't erupt in the explosive sense. Instead, they exude and ooze like thickened blood through a jagged geologic laceration. As the magma hits air or salt water, it cools and metamorphoses into igneous, volcanic rocks like granite and basalt, eventually forming entirely new accumulations of earth. Like hot spot volcanoes, rift volcanoes are rarely responsible for any swift and catastrophic loss of human life.

The third and most violent type of volcano—the towering, parabolic kind we imagine when we say the word, the kind that actually erupts—occurs at coastal subduction boundaries where a dense oceanic plate is forced beneath a "floating" continental plate. As the ocean floor melts in the molten upper mantle, a rising volcanic stew is trapped beneath the continent itself, eventually pressurizing under a delicate seal of rock and vegetation. Over thousands, sometimes millions of years, the resulting *magma chamber* swells like a geologic boil and deforms the earth itself. The solitary peaks we know more commonly as Mount Rainier, Mount St. Helen's, Mount Fuji, and

Mount Kilimanjaro were built in this way. Eventually, of course, this pressure must somehow be released, and in the case of a true subduction volcano, it happens explosively. Depending on both the rate and the duration of pressurization, as well as on the persistence of the surface bedrock itself, the effects can range from small local earthquakes and sulfur gas flatulence to mass global extinctions and long volcanic "winters" during which the sun disappears for months.

"Once you learn the damage volcanoes can do," Hugo explains, "you understand why living with them is so risky, and why working with them closely is even worse." He stomps his boot on the glacier as if in reverent acknowledgment to Mexico's volcanic king. "In April 1996, for instance, five people trying to get television video of Popo's crater illegally were caught in a large explosion [1500 feet] down from the rim. They were right in the path of the lava bombs and ballistic debris and died instantly." The effect on the climbers, Hugo goes on in more detail, was akin to being shot at point-blank range by a geologic shotgun. Rescue crews discovered the bodies three days later embedded with countless shards of volcanic glass.

Unfortunately, due to the same need for proximity to their subject, scientists often have no better odds against volcanoes than film crews. Depending on how you perform it, field volcanology can be as safe as watching it happen on television, or it can be downright suicidal. Understandably, most practicing volcanologists choose to work ex situ in the relative safety of offices and computer labs. To unlock the deepest secrets of "Planet Fire" and get the real, pulsing data, however, volcanologists must, quite literally, get into the hot seat. They must have at their disposal diverse physical and intellectual skills, unlimited audacity, and most of all, to quote Lorenzo, *cojones*—balls, courage. Why? Because having *cojones* saves lives. Thanks to a flood of in-your-face data over the past few decades, many of the previously unfathomable mechanisms of volcanoes are now largely understood. Occasionally, however, things spin out of control and people don't come back.

The most renowned American eruption veteran is University of Arizona volcanologist Stanley Williams, who, while monitoring Colombia's Galeras volcano back in 1987, got caught in an avalanche of hot ash and mud and ended up in the intensive care unit with severe burns over a large part of his body. Experienced French field volcanologists Maurice and Kattia Krafft weren't so lucky. Attempting to film a pyroclastic flow on the flanks of Japan's Mount Unzen at the height of the volcano's eruption in 1991, the Kraffts were caught in the path of an explosion, and neither bodies nor film were ever found. The Kraffts, not surprisingly, are revered these days in the scientific community,

Popocatépetl is a classic subduction volcano—high, conical, and violently eruptive. Popocatépetl is also the kind of volcano volcanologists pray for—massive, active, and easily accessible.

and their names are often invoked in a kind of knowledge-at-all-costs rallying cry. In spirit, however, the Kraffts were no different from other deeply driven scientists; they were impelled by one of science's most irresistible forces—the need to see. In field volcanology, closer is almost always better. It's where the real action happens and the most important data are documented. Hugo prefers to see a more obvious moral in the Kraffts' story: Fly too close to the flame and you will eventually get burned.

"Unfortunately," he explains matter-of-factly, "this is exactly the dilemma of field volcanology and the issue we face here with Popo: more data means more risk." He spreads his arms wide, encompassing the vast view of Pico's crater, the storm clouds pacing in and out around the lower Jamapa glacier, and the thin rock wire on which we stand. "This will be the most accurate measurement of Pico's height in over 50 years," Hugo declares, fumbling against the inebriating effects of high altitude to finish the antenna setup, "and we've risked our lives just to do it."

In reality, just about any task on any of Mexico's high volcanoes is a potentially life-threatening endeavor. Ranking as the three highest subduction volcanoes in North America, Pico, Popo, and Ixta are known in Mexico as the Big Three, and as the early victims from this year's expedition amply demonstrate, an 18,000-foot volcano doesn't have to erupt to put people at risk.

"I have had many friends die in the mountains over the years," Hugo laments. "They are dangerous places in subtle ways. Just when you think you are fine, you die." To emphasize the point, he motions to a crude metal cross erected just down slope from us, built as much to honor those who have died here as Pico itself. "Like many others, I have learned the hard way what not to do high in the mountains, and I bring these experiences with me on my scientific expeditions so that, hopefully, we all come back safe and complete."

On the Big Three in particular, what concerns Hugo more than freak volcanic accidents are the inevitable hazards of just being up so high in the first place, things like ice falls and avalanches, glacial crevasses, rogue storms, chaffed ropes, sulfur inhalation, helicopter wrecks, and, most of all, altitude sickness. At over 18,000 feet, with even the slightest exertion, a climber's lungs quickly undergo a kind of respiratory famine, technically called *hypoxia*. In its more moderate forms, hypoxia can cripple even seasoned death-zone veterans with chronic fatigue, nausea, hallucinations, and unconsciousness. In its worst expressions it can kill. To exacerbate the risks, there is also high altitude pulmonary edema, or HAPE, a fast-developing condition in which the lungs fill with bodily fluids, precipitating rather obvious symptoms like bloody sputum and gurgling breath. In most fatal cases, which have been known to occur in as lit-

tle as 40 hours, victims literally drown in their own blood. High altitude cerebral edema, or HACE, in which fluid begins to fill the cranial cavity, is even uglier. Early symptoms include staggering and hallucinations, and can rapidly proceed to coma and death.

High mountains can also kill from the outside, most often by swallowing climbers in freak avalanches, rock slides, or open glacial crevasses. Influenced by a multitude of physical factors, crevasses can be as vast and obvious as the skyscraper chasms of a Manhattan city block, or when newly opened and covered by fresh snowfall, as deceptively inconspicuous as quicksand. On the Big Three, Hugo worries most about the smallest ones.

"The danger with these is not that you'll fall in and disappear," he cautions. "You'll fall in, break both your legs, and get wedged in at the bottom. It's worse, because you have to live through it." For this reason, Hugo and his assistant climbers stay roped up at almost all times when conducting research on any of the Big Three.

Notwithstanding the dangers, to focus simply on the risks of high altitude field volcanology is to overlook the value of Hugo's data. As the only tropical volcanoes in the world that support glaciers of significant size, Pico, Popo, and Ixta comprise a rare physical juxtaposition of fire and ice, a phenomenon almost totally unstudied in the field. As Hugo's data have increased in both quantity and scope, the glacial ice has proven not only to be a critical barometer of local volcanic activity but also a frozen time capsule of equatorial climate change and global warming. Popo, Pico, and Ixta also comprise the ultimate volcanic trinity, forming, respectively, a before, during, and after chronology of volcanic escalation and remission. Scientifically, the Big Three offer Hugo a rare opportunity to study comparatively just what happens to seismicity, glaciers, gases, and people when the planet's innards begin their inexorable course outwards. From the standpoint of human safety, this research might help Mexico avoid a cataclysmic tragedy.

In a worst-case scenario, a subduction volcano can discharge with a force greater than all the Cold War nuclear arsenals combined. When Mount St. Helen's erupted in 1980, the explosion flattened every living thing within a dozen miles of the crater itself, including 57 people, and buried towns as far away as Idaho under a foot of ash. Seismic tremors were registered as far away as northern Canada and southern California. Scientists later estimated the energy from the blast to have been greater than that of 180 atomic bombs. When the Philippines' Mount Pinatubo erupted in June of 1991, its fallout reached even farther, spewing clouds of ash and gas so high into the stratosphere that they literally encircled the earth. Three years later, the drifting volcanic haze was still suppressing temperatures worldwide. The largest eruptions, like one documented in central Siberia that engulfed more than 600,000 square miles of land in lava flows over two miles

Facing page:
Dawn breaks over Iztaccíhuatl's high glacial summit and the valley of Mexico below.

The expedition helicopter makes a cargo drop at base camp, despite low oxygen and high winds.

deep, are considered at least partially responsible for the mass extinctions during the Permian and Cretaceous periods, the latter of which included the killing of the dinosaurs.

Since *Homo sapiens* entered the scene, the collateral damage from large volcanic eruptions has grown even larger, as two of modern history's most lethal human disasters demonstrate. In the first, what began as an imperceptible earthquake off the coast

Treading lightly. Expedition assistants carefully pick their route across the glaciers of Iztaccíhuatl.

of Pompeii in central Italy, shortly before midnight on August 24, 79 A.D., ended as a holocaust. In minutes, over 16,000 people were melted in searing clouds of volcanic gas, which surged down the flanks of Mount Vesuvius at over 150 kilometers per hour. When Pompeii was rediscovered in 1706, the victims' skeletons were found entombed beneath 66 feet of solid ash and mud just as they had died—huddled under their beds and running for their lives.

Almost 2000 years later, on November 13, 1985, 17,800 foot Nevado del Ruiz struck the town of Armero, Colombia, with equal fury. After months of menacing explosions, the mountain finally stopped the dancing and erupted with full force, melting its vast ice cap instantly and unleashing a tidal wave of super-heated laharic mud before scientists could even turn on their instruments. The flood covered the 30 downstream miles to Armero in minutes, cresting to 130 feet just southwest of town and drowning its 21,000 residents in volcanic cement as they lay asleep in their beds. In the three days of mayhem that followed, three helicopters crashed while flying rescue missions; many more people died from disease, exposure, and lack of food and potable water; and many bodies were never recovered. Given the undeniable moral of the story, the town itself was never rebuilt.

Tragically, mass burials like those at Pompeii and Armero, while somewhat rare, are nothing new. Since humans first planted seeds in a volcanic mudflow and watched them grow faster than anywhere else, unforeseen eruptions have claimed hundreds of thousands of lives. And despite constant advances in volcano science and monitoring technology, they will undoubtedly happen again. As in any landscape where human communities coexist with possibly catastrophic natural phenomena—flood plains, fault zones, hurricane belts—disasters are an inevitable consequence of ecological plenty. Despite what volcanologists like Hugo can now do to monitor and predict explosions, no one can stop them. We can only help to get potential victims out of the way.

"God helps those who help themselves," explains Hugo, finishing up with his rock cradle, "but someone has to get up here and figure out what's going on in the first place."

The ultimate goal of Hugo's research, then, is as much humanitarian as it is purely analytical. He intends to avoid an Armero here in Mexico. By providing information on exactly when people should pack their bags and get out, Hugo's data may eventually save lives.

"Mexico doesn't need any more tragedies," Hugo asserts. "Mexico needs to change and get better, but I am not a politician." He pauses and looks proudly at the assembled GPS setup. "I believe this change can happen through science, through better information, and through knowledge."

Hugo, Lorenzo, and I have been on Pico's summit for almost two hours now, and the sun has climbed steadily overhead, filling the volcano's perfect crater in brilliant blue light. Almost a kilometer across the crater itself, thick cumulus clouds have begun to pile up from behind the 800-foot headwall, a result of the mountain's increasingly unstable air. Snow swirls up off the rim, giving shape to the rising wind. In the rush to acquire the GPS position before a change in the weather, we pick up the pace of the work, and Hugo immediately pulls out the large, yellow GPS receiver and locks in on the appropriate satellites. Within minutes, the radio waves are streaming from space to us.

The city of Cholula, located in Popocatépetl's "yellow zone." Were a catastrophic eruption of the volcano to occur, towns like Cholula would be threatened by falling ash, mudslides, loss of livestock, and contamination of crops and drinking water.

Big risk, big reward. On this year's expedition, Hugo Delgado obtained the most accurate GPS "fix" of Pico de Orizaba's peak ever.

First developed for military use and now integral to virtually every scientific expedition in the field, the global positioning system employs an array of satellites to provide users with accurate readouts of where exactly on the earth's surface they are at any given time. Appropriately called a "fix," the position is given in altitude and minutes and degrees of latitude and longitude, and depending on the sophistication of the receiver, the margin of error can range from 300 feet down to as little as an inch. Specifically, Hugo is using a differential GPS, and he will ultimately be able to pin down Pico's summit proper to a single small stone. Using this point and two others farther down the mountain as digitized references, he can later extrapolate the approximate three-dimensional location of any other single point on the volcano, resulting in what's called a *digital elevation model* (DEM). Compared over time, annual DEMs graphically depict the extent to which glacial ice is accreting or retreating, and whether the volcano is swelling with unreleased interior pressure.

"Under different circumstances," Hugo explains, "we'd be getting a similarly accurate fix on Popo as well." According to the most up-to-date information, however, the rate of small seismic "events" emanating from deep within Popo in the past 10 days has increased to almost 90 per day, and larger volcano-tectonic quakes associated with stresses at work inside the volcanic edifice have been detected for the first time in months. Six days ago, sulfur emissions also increased fivefold. Most recently, Popo's activity shut down almost entirely.

"Popo has been too quiet recently," Hugo warns. "Seismic activity is down, and so is the level of off-gassing. When both are low, we know an explosion is very close. With volcanoes in general, calms are never good. It means the conduits are clogged, magma and gases cannot escape, and that pressure is building . . . it means the volcano is being a good economist, trying to save energy for the Big Show." He pauses briefly from his work and gazes down into Pico's crater to where the small crater lake boils away. "The hard data on Popo is the data we just can't get now," he adds finally. "It's just too risky—things like gas emissions inside the crater, water samples from the crater lake. They are . . . How do you say in English? . . . a flip of the coin, and I don't like those odds with my own life. If a strong explosion hit when we were [three miles] from the crater, the shock waves would knock us to the ground. You would feel the vibrations in the ground and through your feet. If it hit when we were on the glaciers, you'd be blown apart. Now, you see why we are so nervous about going up right now? Now you see why we are here instead."

"When was the last explosion?" I ask, expecting a man of such sound mind to put at least a few months between volcanic events and his own scientific expeditions.

"Oh, two weeks ago." Hugo is breathing heavily as he talks now. Three hours of work at 18,410 feet is beginning to take it's toll.

As the GPS completes its fix, Lorenzo finishes up his temperature profile of Pico's summit, taking one last measurement 50 feet down the crater's sandy slope. Around his boots, small sulfur fumaroles rise up like so many boiling tea kettles and permeate the air with the stench of rotten eggs. On the far headwall across the crater, a massive rock fall crumbles from high atop the rim, tearing ever-larger blocks of stone on its slide into the crater. Looking up from the GPS, Hugo smiles reassuringly.

"It was definitely a good day to cancel the crater entry here."

When Hugo, Lorenzo, and I finally pack the GPS cases and prepare to descend to base camp, I groan at the thought of another two hours on my feet. Ever the optimist, Hugo is quick to remind me that the greatest hazard of the day was probably just getting up here in the first place—in the helicopter. As a general rule, helicopters and mountains mix about as well as ships and icebergs. Unpredictable weather swings, whiteouts, gusty winds, and an almost total lack of emergency landing sites conspire to make even a brief ride a treacherous undertaking.

"I'm afraid most of a stall in the thin air," Hugo admits, beginning the posthole down Pico's cone through the wet and heavy snow. "If this happens while we're trying

Hugo Delgado's assistant, Lorenzo Ortiz Armas, measures the soil temperature of Pico de Orizaba's crater. The data show that the mountain is warming.

to land on the crater rim, we die. If it happens higher up, we'll probably die too, but at least we'd have a chance to recover. We have the only pilot in Mexico that will do this kind of work. . . . Think about it: for us, there is only one trip, one chance for something to go wrong. For him, transporting people and equipment on and off the mountain, there are 10 chances to die every day."

Hugo gestures up into the open sky and then back toward the crater rim itself, as if trying to reassure us both that our odds of survival on foot couldn't be better. Reliving the morning's flight, he shakes his head with retrospective awe. "I don't think I'll ever do that again," he says. Hugo then stabs at the snow mound ahead of him. It shatters into a deep and narrow crevasse, chiming like broken glass from a skyscraper window all the way to the bottom. Our wave of security is appropriately short-lived.

Later the next day, the helicopter transports our equipment down from base camp, and on our way back to Mexico City, we stop at Popo's base camp to check the condition of the volcano one last time. Hugo still wants to get inside. The twilight landscape for miles around, however, is cool and quiet, and overall activity is still ominously low. Around the lower flanks of the mountain, pine trees huddle together against the wind, high hummocks of mustard grass gather in large herds, and haphazard ejecta from recent explosions litter the highest slopes like glacial erratics. Some are as small as

The expedition helicopter departs from base camp down to the safer altitude of Pico de Orizaba's lower flanks.

172   Fire

batteries, others as large as a minivan. With the exception of a few tenacious lichens holding on around their bases, life here is virtually nonexistent. It is obvious that Popo is quickly reclaiming its ancestral lands, in some way a deeply satisfying thought.

So when will Popo blow?

Hugo just shakes his head, "All the data tell us for sure is that Popo has much more to say."

WATER

Planet Water

Water is H$_2$O, hydrogen two parts, oxygen one, but there is also a third thing
that makes it water and nobody knows what that is.
—D.H. Lawrence

Gansbaai, South Africa.

Since humans first ventured out to sea, mariners have joked that whoever named the planet "earth" must have lived in Kansas, a lifetime's journey from the nearest ocean. Without the thunder of waves and breaching whales, how could that person ever have known that his world is, in fact, an island, that this so called planet "earth" is fully three-fourths water and would be more correctly called planet "water"?

Yet even today, we persist in a predominantly geocentric view of the world. For some, the aversion to water stems from rather obvious phobias, like drowning or getting lost at sea. For others, the nightmares are more primal, animated by mythic boat-flipping, flesh-ripping beasts. For still others, it is simply geography. In almost every country I visit, I meet someone who has never been to the beach.

Whatever our personal reasons for preferring terra firma, a simple rock-solid truth about water remains: We are all aquatic in origin. Whether blessed with fins, feathers, or four legs, all life shares the evolutionary womb of the planet's oceans, humans included. Biologically, it is this very bond that synchronizes female fertility with the rhythms of the lunar tides, and that regulates the human body:water ratio in almost identical proportion to the land:water ratio of earth itself. On a more psychological level, it's why many of us have our ashes buried at sea, vacation at the beach, and find deep solace in the cadence of the waves. Oddly enough, though, no one seems to care. In spite of the ancestral connections, we currently know little more about the world's marine and freshwater ecosystems today than we did about wolves and redwood forests 200 years ago.

Until as recently as World War II, the primary obstacle to underwater science and exploration was technology. Constrained by surface-supplied air and an anemic understanding of submersible technology, most scientists focused their inquiries on the 25 percent of the planet one could walk on. In the summer of 1943, however, in a small cove on the French Riviera, Frenchmen Jacques-Yves Cousteau and Emile Gagnan changed all that. Gambling on a garage-shop invention aptly called the Aqualung, a crude predecessor to modern scuba, Cousteau became the first human to experience extended, self-sufficient access to the planet's underwater wilderness.

For science and exploration, Cousteau's dive was the aquatic equivalent of the discovery of the microscope or seeing the earth from space. In giving "earthbound man the key to the silent world," Cousteau changed the way we look at the planet and our place in it. From the standpoint of experimentation and technology, Cousteau's first "flight" was one of the most extreme endeavors in the history of science. In his youth, Cousteau dreamed about flying underwater—literally—and ultimately, he was willing to risk his life trying to make that dream a reality. But Cousteau's pioneering role in underwater exploration didn't end there. Until his death in 1997, his expeditions would prove again and again that human discovery isn't constrained externally by planetary geography. Its most daunting limit is internal, human ingenuity.

More than 50 years have passed since that first aquatic flight, and most scientists would agree that we now know enough about the underwater world to be certain only of our own ignorance. Popular opinion about the importance of understanding Planet Water is still mired in fear and misinformation, and research initiatives are consistently hampered by economic and political agendas and incoherent scientific collaborations. On a more practical level, access still remains a significant problem. Even with today's cutting-edge technology, like diver penetration vehicles and deep-sea submersibles, scientists can still only survive underwater long enough to "get in, get out, and get what you can," as one explorer expresses it. Normally, too, circumstances are far from ideal: equipment fails, budgets break, subjects dive and disappear. In exceptional circumstances, the power of the water cycle can also get out of control, swallowing boats and scuba divers whole. These are the instances that remind us that any subaquatic venture is, by its very nature, extreme.

As a result, even as we master the hardware to use and abuse aquatic resources for every conceivable human enterprise, from a scientific standpoint, the majority of Planet Water remains as enigmatic as deep space. Mountain ranges, volcanoes, and rift zones on the bottom of the ocean still haven't been surveyed. Great white sharks and blue whales still can't be followed. Giant squid can't even be found. Despite a global armada of research vessels, submarines, remote sensing and sonar equipment, and institutes full of Ph.D. experts, only a small percentage of the world's oceans, remote lakes, and glaciers has even been observed and sampled firsthand.

The upshot for those scientists willing to carry the Cousteau spirit of exploration forward is a virtually inexhaustible world of biological, chemical, geological, and archeological discovery. In 1998, for example, University of Arizona icthyologist John Lundberg trawled over 2000 miles of the Amazon River with sampling nets and pulled up 35 species of fish previously unknown to science. That same year, an exploratory expedition off the southern coast of Cuba turned up a similar bounty of deep reef fish and invertebrates. Elsewhere in the world over the past few decades, scientists looking for precedent discoveries have found rare prehistoric sharks, deep-sea sulfur vents, the shipwreck of Revolutionary War traitor Benedict Arnold, and evidence that the Biblical account of a great flood is indeed true.

Unfortunately, most people don't grow up intending to swim with great white sharks or scuba dive into glaciers and caves. On the contrary, elite underwater scientists and explorers seem somehow predestined for their roles in the history of human discovery. Like Cousteau himself, they share not only an elemental love for water but also that defining moment when they peered into the "silent world" and realized that earth is but an island, and that instead of Planet Earth, it should have been called Planet Water.

Inner space. A WKPP support diver descends into the mouth of the cave at Wakulla Springs, south of Tallahassee, Florida.

One Small Step
for Inner Space

Taped inside the back door of George Irvine's cargo van, between the decompression tables and a photo of his family, is a small weathered Post-it note which says simply, "No BS. No Excuses." Like George himself, the message is curt, pitiless, and in-your-face with a chilling paramilitary indifference. For the 158 cave divers of Florida's Woodville Karst Plain Project (WKPP) working under him, however, it's an unequivocal reminder of what it takes to stay on top, and more important, to stay alive.

"We don't like to talk about doing things," George says bluntly, spinning a scuba regulator onto a stage bottle for decompression. "We do them first, then tell everyone else how fake they are." He pauses theatrically and winces in the bright summer sunlight. "While the rest of the cave divers are out there getting killed, we're getting data."

Known as the silverback gorilla of underwater cave exploration, George is a man of harsh words, little patience, and infrequent compassion, and in the cave-diving community, he's got the enemies to prove it. But, as he explains frankly, he doesn't really care. Like most WKPP divers, George doesn't tolerate "windbags" who don't deliver, and he'll tell them so right to their faces. WKPP's cave divers *do* deliver, which is exactly what makes the swaggering sting even worse.

"George is the worst kind of winner," admits WKPP geologist and lead diver Jarrod Jablonski, "because he's right to brag about what we do." Along with George and a local Tallahassee diver named Brent Scarabin, Jarrod is the third member of WKPP's current "push" team, and other than George, he's the team's most recognizable member.

Since its founding in 1986 by Florida cave divers Parker Turner, Bill Main, Bill Gavin, and Lamar English, WKPP exploration divers have quietly become the world's best at two things: (1) obtaining firsthand data about north Florida's underwater caves, and (2) "going downtown," which means finding deep, virgin passage where there was none before. As a consequence of the group's 13-year effort to model the subsurface hydrologic profile of the 288,000-acre Woodville Karst Plain (WKP) south of Tallahassee,

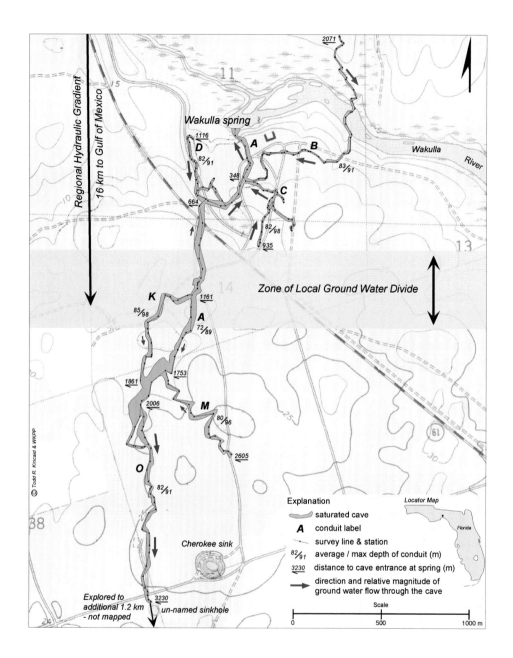

Inner space underfoot. This map shows the terrestrial features south of Tallahassee superimposed over the primary tunnels of the Leon Sinks Cave System, illustrating clearly the direct links between the region's surface and subterranean environments. *(Courtesy of Dr. Todd Kincaid.)*

WKPP dive teams have written the record book on underwater cave exploration. Relying on up to 50 support divers, who come from as far away as Texas, they have pushed over three miles into the world's largest freshwater spring, farther from the last gulp of air than any humans in history. They have surveyed a total of more than 300,000 feet of cave passage. And they have helped to physically connect over 17 miles of contiguous *phreatic* (beneath the water table) conduit—now officially recognized as the Leon Sinks Cave System, the longest and deepest underwater cave in the United States and the third longest in the world, after Mexico's Dos Ojos and Nahoch Na Chich.

Today, WKPP push divers hope to set another record: to confirm a contiguous underwater connection between Big Dismal and Cheryl Sinks, two of the more famous geologic windows into Florida's crystalline aquifer. Although permanent guidelines extend 6000 feet in from the entrances to both caves, explorers have yet to link them because of an estimated thousand feet of obstacles and rubble that pile up from the bottom. If successful, the dive will not only add over two miles of new passage to the total of the Leon Sinks Cave System, but it will also rank as the world's longest underwater traverse between two entry windows.

Despite the personal rivalries now broiling in the cave exploration community, no one's going downtown for bragging rights—because they're not worth dying for. Simply put, WKPP divers are scientific mercenaries. They provide firsthand data about the Woodville Karst Plain where only speculation existed before. In collaboration with dozens of government agencies, the team's lead divers have installed flow meters, collected rare troglobytic (cave-dependent) and troglophylic (cave-adapted) species, and generated water chemistry data sets from places few other humans could go. On a larger level, WKPP scientists, like team hydrogeologist Dr. Todd Kincaid, are helping to determine how, in the first place, such macro-level geologic controls as lithology, stratiography, and local groundwater flow have affected the overall process of phreatic karst development in the Woodville Karst Plain.

First recognized as a distinct geologic unit in 1966, the Woodville Karst Plain proper is a heavily settled agricultural area of some 450 square miles located south of Tallahassee, Florida. Geologically speaking, the region is only one small part of the greater Floridan aquifer system (FAS), one of the world's largest reservoirs of subsurface freshwater which underlies southern Alabama and Georgia, eastern South Carolina, and most of Florida. A plateau composed of porous limestone—in some places more than 10,000 feet thick—the FAS functions like a great continental sponge, storing an ocean's worth of freshwater within its honeycomb of cracks and caves in much the same way the human body holds blood through its intricate system of capillaries, veins, and arter-

The endemic Woodville Crayfish—*Procambarus orcinus*. (*Photograph by Steve Auer.*)

ies. On the surface, the result is a total of 320 identified springs that pour forth an estimated 12 billion gallons of pure freshwater every day.

Biologically, the FAS conduit system also nourishes freshwater habitats that exist nowhere else on earth, providing unique niches for species as diverse as the American alligator (*Alligator mississippiensis*), an albino crayfish (*Procambarus erythrops*), and the least killfish (*Heterandria formosa*), the smallest vertebrate animal in North America. Farther back into the caves dwell rare and endemic troglobytes such as the Hobb's cave isopod (*Caecidotea hobbsi*), the Hobb's cave amphipod (*Crangonyx hobbsi*), and the Woodville cave crayfish (*Procambarus orcinus*). On land, the aquifer's abundant overflow nourishes dense forests of old-growth cypress and live oak and dilutes the turbid flow of surface rivers soiled by agricultural and storm-water runoff. Nearer to the coast, the springs provide regular freshwater input to wetlands and low-lying marsh habitat, countering the brackish ebb and flow of the Gulf of Mexico.

Much as it was when naturalist William Bartram recorded his first observations here 200 years ago, the landscape of the Woodville Karst Plain today remains relatively rich and primeval, lush with longleaf pines, lounging crocodilians, and swelling emerald springs. Lost rivers rise unexpectedly in one place, slither briefly southward, then snake back underground in another. Sinkholes and spring-fed lakes hardwired directly

Facing page:
Dawn breaks over the prehistoric landscape of Wakulla Springs, by volume, the largest freshwater springs in the world.

to the aquifer fill one week and then, just as curiously, go dry the next. Scientifically, however, what makes the region so rare is not necessarily what you see. It's what you don't; as Bartram put it, "the gloomy vaults," "secret subterranean conduits," and in words borrowed from the poet Coleridge, "caverns measureless to man."

Warm, wet, and underlain by almost 500 feet of soluble Suwannee limestone, the Woodville Karst Plain is blessed with near-perfect conditions for phreatic karst development. As surface water percolates down through the region's sandy soil on its north-south run to the Gulf of Mexico, it reacts with molecules in the atmosphere and decaying organic debris to form a mild carbonic acid ($CaCO_4$). In a chemical process called *dissolution,* the acid slowly eats away at the rock, carving ever-larger cavities until, after countless millennia, there exists a Swiss cheese matrix of underground rivers, sumps, sinks, and fully submerged passages that range in size from soda straws to concert halls. From data accumulated both on the surface and within the caves themselves, scientists estimate that the conduits of the Woodville Karst Plain system date back more than 100,000 years, and most of them, despite the accomplishments of WKPP and two long-term expeditions by the U.S. Deep Cave Diving Team (USDCDT) in 1987 and 1999, remain unexplored.

The ultimate goal of WKPP's extreme cave explorations, of course, is to change all that by creating maps—an erudite and often fatal realm of underwater science called *subaquatic speleocartography.* Using distance reels, compass readings, and survey tapes, the team's lead divers are building a road atlas of Florida's aquifer. To no one's surprise, their data, in conjunction with maps and information from the USDCDT, are showing what many scientists have long suspected anecdotally: that what happens above ground happens below it as well, a dynamic hydrological state called *reciprocity.* Unfortunately, the confirmation of reciprocity reveals another, more disturbing connection: the ubiquitous tentacles of urban sprawl in north Florida are contaminating the underground wilderness. Metropolitan Tallahassee is now the fastest-growing region in the state of Florida, and as construction, habitat loss, and groundwater pollution have steadily increased, so have the stresses on the springs and other groundwater resources. Using water quality analyses from WKPP's deep cave samples, for instance, government scientists have discovered high-level traces of nitrates, radioisotopes, and fecal coliform bacteria in various springs throughout the Woodville Karst Plain exactly where one would expect them to be—beneath farms, feed lots, gas stations, trailer parks, and suburban developments. In some of the most popular commercial springs, average visibility has dropped to less than 50 feet, and sometimes blacks out for months, threatening to affect the region's booming

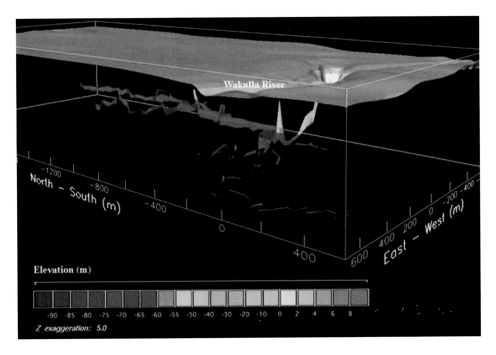

Wakulla Springs in three dimensions. Cutting-edge mapping software and systematic survey measurements are used to create maps that depict Wakulla's primary underwater tunnels in accurate detail. (*Courtesy of Dr. Todd Kincaid.*)

tourist industry. For two and half years, in the mid-1990s, much of the Leon Sinks Cave System was simply undivable.

By decrypting the overall course of water movement, WKPP hydrologists and land-use planners have been able to determine how contaminants originating in one spring system end up in the subsurface flow of another. More important, they have also been able to do something about it. Using sophisticated three-dimensional mapping technology, team cartographers have created dynamic conduit models of over five miles of passage, and these models have recently been used in topographic/land-use overlays to buttress arguments for official protection.

"[WKPP's] maps are vital in determining subterranean connections between sinks receiving surface runoff and pristine groundwater sources," explains Frank Rupert, a geologist with the Florida Geologic survey. "[They] have already been used by local officials to establish a 'blue-

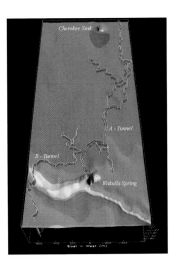

Topographic overlays. These maps help land-use planners to understand the connections between the underwater caves and surface topography. (*Courtesy of Dr. Todd Kincaid.*)

A WKPP push diver penetrates the lunar darkness of Wakulla Springs. Says WKPP project director, George Irvine, "Data gathered here might as well be from the surface of the moon." (*Photograph by Steve Auer.*)

belt' area along the conduit trend within which potentially polluting activities on the surface, such as gas stations, are restricted."

Characteristically unsure of anyone's intentions except his own, George Irvine isn't convinced the maps and blue-belt restrictions will be enough.

"The fact that so much water is moving through here is bad in terms of pollution because things are carried a long way in a very short time," he argues, pulling out a pile of dive slates. "We've hit walls of dirty 'black' water coming in from side passages that are still totally unexplored, and we don't know where the water is coming from. . . . We're running a race to get as much information about this system as we can before it's destroyed."

On the front and back of each of the slates are survey notes, passage and restriction diagrams, compass headings, and coordinates from the "O" tunnel at Wakulla Springs, which, as of June 24, 1998, became the longest penetrated underwater cave passage in the world, exactly 18,000 feet. George flips through each slate as if he were reminiscing through the pages of an old photo album, mumbling casually about cathedral ceilings, a strong in-your-face current, and how "pulling on the rocks at 295 [feet] while 14,000 feet out is not too cool." For everyone who couldn't be there with him—which is everyone in the world except Jarrod and Brent—the slates are scientific postcards from one of the planet's final frontiers. For reasons unfathomable to that same percentage of humanity, they are also worth dying for.

Like all extreme data, knowledge about the hydrology of the Woodville Karst Plain, and north Florida in general, has come at the ultimate price. Compared with other underwater cave systems around the world, like those in Turkey, Mexico, and the Bahamas, the WKP's dendritic systems aren't just long or cold or deep. They are all three. Averaging 69 degrees Fahrenheit and running out to record lengths from air at depths of up to 315 feet, north Florida's caves offer as little margin for operator or equipment error as a space walk. Restrictions around sinkholes, rubble zones, and collapses can be so small that divers have to take their gear off and push it through in front of them to squeeze through. In other places, rooms are so vast, even the strongest underwater lights can't provide sufficient illumination to guide the way. Currents can turn during the course of a deep penetration, pinning divers to the walls, and tight passages can "black out" with silt or tannic water in seconds. In WKPP's 13-year history, three divers—cofounder Parker Turner, Bill McFaden, and Scherwood Shile—never returned. Many others have been temporarily trapped, lost, or otherwise stricken with one of many dive-related traumas.

The inner architecture of Woodville Karst Plain ranges from rooms as high and wide as amphitheaters to passages like this one, which is no wider than a human body. (*Photograph by Steve Auer.*)

Due to the depth and duration of the penetrations, the greatest risk for all WKPP push divers is decompression sickness (DCS), otherwise known as the "bends." Logging bottom times of four to six hours at pressures 10 times what they are at the surface, the divers' tissues absorb nitrogen into solution to the point of total saturation. Were the divers to rise immediately to the surface without stopping at regular intervals to let the nitrogen respire naturally back out of solution—a technique known as *staged decompression*—the excess gas would bubble from their blood like boiling water and literally fry the skin from their faces. DCS comes in many other shapes and sizes, with symptoms ranging from tingling and numbness to crackling joints, paralysis, and death. Unfortunately, although serious "hits" are rare, most WKPP divers are forced to tolerate mild DCS symptoms as a regular consequence of such experimental decompression.

"When we started our initial work in Wakulla," Jarrod remembers, "no one had done that kind of time at depth before. In terms of deco [decompression], there were no precedents to work from."

A WKPP support diver "off-gases" at a designated decompression stop just inside the mouth of the Wakulla Springs cave. (*Photograph by Steve Auer.*)

With the help of the world's top hyperbaric specialists, however, George and Jarrod began writing their own profiles. They tinkered with mathematical equations, honed their bodies to maximize cardiovascular efficiency, experimented with multiple mixed gases, and at great risk to themselves, became their own hyperbaric guinea pigs. Now, four years later, they're successfully pulling off dives of 22 hours at depths of 300 feet that would twist a recreational diver into an egg noodle. For hyperbaric physiologists, the accumulated decompression data from each dive profile have proven to be as scientifically valuable as the 3-D passage maps the divers are bringing back.

"The hardest thing to get in decompression research," WKPP hyperbaric expert Eric Baker explains, "is hard data about bubble formation and the individual physiological factors that affect the patterns, but that's what these guys are giving us." To no one's surprise, George is doing things that no one on earth has yet attempted—skipping deco stops altogether, shaving hours off total decompression time where others are counting seconds, and driving the eight hours back to Fort Lauderdale before the rest of the lead team is even out of the water.

"If a normal person did one of George's profiles," adds Eric, "you'd better have the ambulance running."

To focus simply on WKPP's ability to manage the risks of deep cave diving, however, would miss the true magnitude of the group's contributions to underwater speleology and human discovery. Physiologically, technologically, and scientifically, their work probes the extreme frontier of hydrological exploration, and as a result of their unwavering determination, they've shown that there are always new frontiers if you look in the right places. The best way to grasp how far WKPP has pushed the envelope underwater, however, is to understand where the limits stood just 40 years ago.

Cave diving, like most exploratory endeavors, began in somebody's garage. In the United States, it was in the early 1950s, and in north Florida, as was the case almost everywhere, no one had a clue about what was happening underground. With only ex situ data, state hydrologists and land-use planners were managing regional groundwater flow under the dominant environmental paradigm of post-World War II America: out-of-sight, out-of-mind. That the state's Panhandle and north-central counties were blessed with an abundant and abstruse hydrology had been common knowledge since Ponce de Leon first arrived in 1513. To determine to what extent surface patterns were possibly driven by underground conduction, however, was far beyond the scope of reasonable inquiry at the time. Scientists, among them E. H. Sellards, the first to head the Florida Geologic Survey, had reasoned for almost a century that the entire Woodville Karst Plain was somehow interconnected, but until the advent of scuba, no one could say how with any certainty. Confined to surface-supplied air and wary of the unknown processes behind deep decompression, even the most courageous divers of the era were shackled by overwhelming technological limits.

As usual, however, there were an enterprising few who couldn't accept ignorance as an answer. At just about the same time the early astronauts started exploring outer space, these pioneers borrowed Jacques Cousteau's basic Aqua-lung design and applied it in their own frontier right here at home. They called it "inner space."

At Wakulla Springs, then the best known of all Florida's watering holes, the aquanauts were named Wally Jenkins and Garry Salsman, and in a string of 200 dives, the pair helped to change the face of underwater exploration forever. Using little more than flashlights and sweatshirts, they penetrated over a thousand feet into Wakulla's main passage at an average depth of 285 feet. They returned not only alive but also full of accounts of underwater architecture and phenomena no scientist had ever before imagined. They found rooms as high and wide as amphitheaters and water as clear as deep space. They discovered albino crayfish and eels living hundreds of feet into a darkness 10,000 years old. Most remarkable of all, they found that at the end of the line, the caves kept on going. When Jenkins and Salsman finally hung up their regulators, the frontier was still wide open for the generation to follow.

Times change. Early divers at Wakulla Springs, circa 1930. (*Courtesy of the Florida Geological Survey photo archive.*)

WKPP project director, George Irvine, checks his gear and prepares mentally for another world record dive.

A WKPP support diver returns from an extended penetration dive—relaxed, fluid, nourished.

As a result of their pioneering dives, Jenkins and Salsman also helped to change the way scientists thought about water. In conjunction with similar cave penetrations throughout Florida, those first dives showed that Wakulla's record flows were in fact due to multiple conduits, not just one gaping subway-sized tunnel; that the Woodville Karst Plain functioned more like a circulatory system than a sponge; and that the hydrology of the entire region was fed by a complex matrix of subsurface piping. Ultimately, no one had any idea how far the caves went, how rare and complex the underlying conduit system would turn out to be, or how susceptible the hydrology of Woodville Karst Plain really was to the impact of development, industry, and urbanization.

"There's nothing on earth like the caves here," Jarrod exclaims, stomping his foot on the ground. "We just needed to get inside to find out."

For people like Salsman, Jenkins, and thousands more to follow, the payoff of this new "inner space" was what cave explorers today call the "rapture"—the unyielding urge to go around just one more corner, and from a scientific standpoint, to answer just one more question. Lifelong aquanauts speak of being pulled by invisible blue force fields, losing their sense of mortality, and ultimately of developing a fear of open spaces. In other words, underwater caves can become an addiction, an inescapable obsession that eventually consumes a person.

"The first time I dove in the springs here," Jarrod remembers, "I swam around three or four times, then saw this big black hole at the bottom. . . ." He pauses and opens his arms wide, embracing the empty space. Then he smiles, "I had to peek in."

On the tail of his van, Jarrod stands a stage bottle up—one of five decompression gases for today's traverse—and labels it: *19% helium/46% oxygen/35% nitrogen*. On the side of the tank is the number 120, stenciled in large black letters. That's the exact depth where setup divers will stage the gas at Cheryl Sink for Jarrod's calculated decompression ascent back to the surface. Mistakenly breathing the wrong gas at the wrong depth, he tells me, has killed far more divers in Florida's underwater caves than unexpected acts of God. He then pulls out two reels. Spooled with 1500 and 1800 feet of thin nylon line, respectively, the reels are to WKPP lead divers what the ball of string was to Greek hero Theseus in the Minoan Labyrinth. They mark the only way out in the event the cave goes black. Knotted at 10-foot intervals for measuring the length of passages, the reels are also a critical tool in the creation of "stick" maps and three-dimensional conduit models.

Twenty feet away, shirtless and barefoot in the sandy soil, George sets up his own equipment behind his cargo van. He attaches a dive light to the front of his Diver

The quintessential sinkhole of Big Dismal. Perfectly round, prehistoric in appearance, and opening up directly into the pure water of Florida's aquifer, "Big D" is everything a sinkhole should be.

Propulsion Vehicle (DPV), otherwise known as a scooter, and greases the O-ring seal on a watertight food canister that he'll carry with him on the dive. Inside both vehicles is enough equipment to invade a small island nation: two semi-closed circuit rebreathers originally designed for stealth military infiltrations; four thermal dry suits; six high-powered electric scooters capable of pulling divers through the cave at up to 200 feet per minute—three times faster than they could swim; 10 high-intensity argon lights; dozens of scuba regulators; 20 scuba cylinders; and enough tools and parts to overhaul it all. Jarrod smiles with obvious pride. In order to overcome the limits that first stymied Jenkins and Salsman, WKPP divers have invented virtually everything they use.

Behind the vans, through a screen of stunted longleaf pines, the 75-foot sheer vertical walls of Big Dismal Sink drop away out of sight. Two hundred feet wide and 70 feet deep, "Big D" is the quintessential sinkhole; it provides immediate, unobstructed access to Florida's aquifer. On the walls themselves, ferns, liverworts, and a variety of other flora hang heavy with the morning dew, while around the upper rim, palmetto palms and cypress trees lean in curiously as if trying to see what all the fuss was about. In the gauzy fog, the entire ecosystem seems deeply prehistoric.

Despite the abundance of sophisticated equipment, WKPP's ultimate goal is no different now than it was for Jenkins and Salsman 40 years ago. Adhering to the group's founding mantra, WKPP divers are looking to stay ahead of everyone else—technologically, scientifically, and, of course, measurably—because that's where the original science and exploration are. Skiers call it "fresh tracks." Climbers know it as the "vertical horizon." To the rest of us, it's good old-fashioned "terra incognita." Unfortunately, there's not much of it left. Where these frontiers still exist, however, they are often worth dying for.

"Information and data gathered at 14,000 feet in an underwater cave might as well be from the surface of Pluto," George explains, "and must be treated accordingly. If we don't come back with it, no one else will. This is why we are here. Our job is to produce the data."

The problem is that many people *don't* come back. Worldwide, subaquatic speleology has claimed more lives in its brief history than a small war. In the four decades since those first Wakulla dives, Florida's freshwater caves alone have swallowed some 350 divers, an average of almost one every six weeks. Some victims, like Parker Turner, were seasoned pioneers, always pushing the frontier, until the walls came crashing down—literally. Turner drowned in 1991 at Indian Springs after getting trapped behind a freak underwater avalanche. Other victims, untrained and ill-equipped, were open-water divers who simply misjudged their limits. They could as easily have died playing chicken with a bus instead of an underwater cave. Cave diving fatalities aren't just frequent; they're also ugly. Most, like Dr. Harry Kendall, a physicist who died in 1999 working in shallow water as part of the U.S. Deep Cave Diving Team's Wakulla2 expedition, die from "escalation," in which a small error cascades quickly and irretrievably to death. In the most tragic scenarios, trapped divers have written their last will and testament on a dive slate before running out of air.

For most elite underwater cave explorers, the fatality statistics bear witness to a simple truth, one that says less about submerged caves and more about humanity: *recreational cave diving* of any kind is an oxymoron of superlative proportions. Reinforced by their naive faith in technology, novice divers often enter enclosed underwater passages without knowing the stakes and end up leaving in a body bag. As Dr. Kendall's death demonstrated, even small mistakes near the surface can be fatal for the most experienced divers.

Not surprisingly, George and Jarrod don't talk about death much. After being on the edge so many times, the philosophical questions have become superfluous. Deep down, pushing inner space is an act of faith more than anything else, and the spiritual commitment for each diver is extremely personal. When I ask Jarrod, just before he gets in the water, about acts of God, he just smiles nonchalantly.

"You are pretty much on your own, especially on the long dives," he says. "There's really nothing anyone could do for you if something went wrong. Your only hope is to make haste and get to safety. Then, living through the decompression is another issue. If you don't come back at all, the support divers just say a prayer, and then eventually call the authorities. Dead people are beyond help, and time is not critical. A recovery effort would likely not be mounted until the next day."

He then nods to his girlfriend, Rebecca, who shuffles nervously in the dirt around the back of the van. "Besides," he says, "she does all the worrying for me."

For his part, George shrugs off the danger as if it were nothing more than a Florida horsefly. With so many things that need to go right to get in and out of these caves alive, there's no time for fear.

Although vastly more complex, a successful push into a cave like Wakulla or Big D unfolds like a game of leapfrog. Given the limits of gas supply when breathing at extreme depths and the need for emergency air reserves, divers can only get about 2000 feet into the caves on the tanks they are able to carry physically. (Tanks worn on the divers' backs are strictly for safety. "Drive" bottles for actual bottom time are clipped under the divers' arms). To triple or quadruple that distance, then, additional bottles must be staged by setup teams at 2000-foot intervals farther in so that the final push divers can get to the end of the line, exchange tanks, and push farther into the caves with full air supplies. In addi-

A WKPP setup diver heads into the darkness of Big Dismal to remove stage bottles left by the lead divers. (*Photograph by Steve Straatsma.*)

tion to the stage bottles, support divers also cache extra scooters, food, water, and safety bottles at set depots every 4000 feet so that lead divers know exactly how long they have to survive in the event of an emergency before finding backup. For decompression, up to 50 additional tanks are stashed at 240, 190, 120, and 70 feet so that divers can follow precise, 10-foot decompression profiles back toward the surface, letting the nitrogen bleed slowly from their systems. At 28 feet, divers finally enter the "habitat," a large, air-filled, upside-down trough that permits them to get out of the water, take off their equipment, sit down, and read magazines for the final six hours of pure oxygen decompression.

Not surprisingly, major penetrations like these don't come cheap. Jarrod estimates that each record dive into a cave like Wakulla requires 17,000 cubic feet of specialized nitrox (O_2/N_2) and tri-mix gas solutions ($O_2/N_2/H_2$), at a cost of over $5000 per dive. George figures the worth of his van, fully outfitted for such a dive, at over $100,000. As of 1998, WKPP push divers also began using Halcyon semi-closed circuit rebreathers instead of conventional scuba to push the tunnels even further. These specialized life-support systems "scrub" carbon dioxide from a diver's exhaust and recycle it back into breathable oxygen, thus precluding the need for tanked air. Halcyon rebreathers also run about $10,000 apiece; between them, WKPP divers have 15.

George shrugs at the expense. He feels you can't put a price on the value of the WKPP's data or the sensation of original exploration. He also notes that the group's investments pale in comparison to those of other teams that have attempted the same deep penetrations into the Woodville Karst Plain and Wakulla systems and come back with more bills than they have data.

The moral of the story, he insists, is that WKPP's successes have less to do with technology and equipment than with tools that are far more human, like teamwork, selflessness, fitness, and faith. Reflecting the thinking and approach of the group's original core members, those foundational elements have evolved into an integrated philosophical system WKPP calls "Doing It Right" (DIR), which means that all things being equal, the simplest solution tends to be the best one. At the heart of the group's logic lives the controversial issue of overgearing in any extreme endeavor, and, more specifically, whether anyone who needs significant technological assistance should be diving the Woodville Karst Plain in the first place.

"People have become overdependent on gadgets and technological solutions," Jarrod argues, "when in reality, the only thing they lack is discipline."

In an underwater cave environment, as on any possibly fatal frontier, the greatest tool a diver has isn't manufactured on an assembly line. It's the human body—compliments of nature. Elite levels of fitness enable a diver to swim long distances effortlessly, acquire and respire oxygen, nitrogen, and other gases with maximum efficiency, and recover rapidly from gas- and pressure-related trauma. For his part, Jarrod spends a minimum of two hours twice a day on an Olympic-level training program—swimming, running, biking, or lifting weights—and as part of his experiments with the physical corollaries to efficient decompression, he has sworn off meat, dairy, and all nonorganic foods entirely.

"I can dive for 20 hours," he says, "and bounce right back the next day."

George, predictably, keeps up an equally masochistic regimen.

"I run five miles every morning and swim at least 5000 meters in the ocean every night," he says. "That gives me a resting heart rate of 40 beats per minute." George also hasn't had a drink in 12 years. "All of my divers have to be in top physical condition," he adds, exhaling like a frontal system. "Fat, out-of-shape people are just plain dangerous."

Not surprisingly, fat, out-of-shape divers looking to go downtown with WKPP are told bluntly by George to hit the gym or die elsewhere. Drinkers and divers with high cholesterol diets are told they can carry tanks. And smokers? "You might as well just go down to the bottom and spit out your regulator," says Jarrod. "It's suicide." The bottom line: under George's autocratic watch, not a single diver has died or suffered a serious dive-related illness.

Breathing easy. WKPP science director, Bill Mee, takes his first breath of *real* air after 3 hours of breathing on the Halcyon rebreather.

When it comes to equipment, Doing It Right is no less militaristic in it's adherence to efficiency and austerity. Unlike many other underwater explorers, WKPP divers don't regard their gear as high-tech toys, but rather as an integral life support system designed to accomplish a distinct scientific task. Called the Hogarthian rig, the system is based on certain inviolable precepts about keeping it simple. Don't trust your life to underwater electronics, for instance; let form follow function; minimize all links in all chains; and so forth. Quite appropriately, the DIR approach to personal choice isn't very complicated either—there is no choice. Simply put, if you don't do it WKPP's way, it's the highway.

"The uniformity is one reason we operate so well as a team," Jarrod explains, stepping into his dry suit. "Everyone knows the setup and the system. We can interchange parts, communicate clearly, and help each other out in emergencies without thinking. . . . Any diver can swim into a cave alone with almost any equipment configuration. The question is whether their team and their equipment can get them back out."

Like all equipment and dive planning philosophies, however, Doing It Right gets its fair share of flack. Among the many other deep cave diving projects underway, the Hogarthian rig is considered overly Spartan and anachronistic, and its primary proponent, George, is regarded as little more than a cantankerous dinosaur. Critics charge that WKPP's task-oriented style limits the range of data that can be collected and results in an anemic understanding of the speleological phenomena at work in the caves themselves.

"Most people are just jealous," WKPP archeologist Michael Wisenbaker retorts. "People in our culture often bristle when they are told things they have been taught are either dangerous or aren't correct. I say look at what others are doing and have accomplished and compare this to what the WKPP has done and judge for yourself who's most effective at achieving their goals."

Critics also claim the technology now exists to facilitate on a weekly basis the same penetrations WKPP manages three times a year. But the notion that anyone with sufficient funds can buy a ticket into a cave like Wakulla, makes George and Jarrod fearful. It means someone's going to die, jeopardizing WKPP's carefully negotiated permits with a dozen private landowners and state agencies. It's also, Jarrod explains, anathema to the very spirit of deep cave exploration these days. In the twenty-first century, discovery is no longer about opening up the frontiers for the masses; it's about getting the data necessary to keep them protected and wild.

Suddenly, without the ceremony one would expect to accompany a world record event, it's dive time. The push team's scooters and drive bottles have been lowered down into the sinkhole, and the last setup team is already back at the surface awaiting its escort duties. Three safety bottles and extra scooters have been stashed 6500 feet into Big Dismal's main passage. Once through the unexplored restriction, the push divers will rely on equipment caches that have been staged from the other end.

At the bottom of the ladders leading down to the water, George, Jarrod, and Ted Cole, who's diving in Brent Scarabin's place today, begin their setup procedures on a small floating dive platform. The air is eerily quiet as they slip into the water without their equipment and float free on the surface to test their dry suits, stay cool, and focus on breathing. Husked in four layers of thermal insulation, they can remain comfortably submerged in the spring's frigid waters for up to 20 hours. Finally, George breaks the meditation and reviews the dive plan one last time, "Let's get in, get out, and get what we can."

With the help of the support crew, the divers climb into their rebreathers and double-check all peripheral equipment with grandmotherly fuss. When everyone's finally ready, George, Jarrod, and Ted take one last gulp of fresh air, put their regulators in their mouths, and disappear into the opaque green filth of Big D's thermocline. In stark contrast to the aquanauts, I follow in my own recreational gear. After so many record explorations, there are no emotional good-byes.

After 20 feet, as if dropping out of the clouds, we clear the organic haze and enter the ethereal clarity of pure Florida groundwater. Fifty feet across the sinkhole, I can see in vivid detail the remains of a rusted pickup truck and old iron stove. The skeletons of fallen trees lie around the silty bottom, giving the spring the feel of a Pleistocene graveyard. Above us, the thermocline plugs the circumference of the sinkhole like a giant green cork.

At the mouth of the cave, just above the bottom, Jarrod, George, and Ted hover briefly to recheck their gauges and equipment one last time. In the still water of the basin, their scooters, stage bottles, and survey gear drift clumsily. I drop down beneath them into the gathering darkness and reach into the soft, sugary bottom. Instantly, the sediments explode up around me in a slow-motion mushroom cloud, reducing visibility to zero. I rise slowly out of the cloud to regain my bearings. When I refocus, Jarrod is right in front of me pointing in the cave and drawing his hand across his throat. In there, his eyes say, you'd be dead.

Finally, George gives one last thumbs-up, and as the scooters build momentum, the divers' equipment feathers into a trim of total hydrodynamic efficiency. Within seconds, they are gone, motoring into a cerebral silence only a dozen other people on earth have ever known. Jarrod describes it like driving down a highway late at night. You begin talking to yourself—first mentally, then verbally through the regulator itself—rehearsing simple, reassuring pneumonics like (T)he (G)ood (A)lert (D)iver (L)ives—Training, Guideline, Air, Depth, and Light. Soon, the complexities of extended physical presence fade into a primi-

George Irvine, Jarrod Jablonski, and Ted Cole depart from the graveyard at the bottom of Big Dismal on their way to a record traverse of more than 12,000 feet.

tive awareness of bedrock and breath. At its best, the experience is transcendental. At its worst, it's a black and brutal loneliness so deep, "it's like being on the moon."

Surfacing back into the sunshine, I find Jarrod's girlfriend, Rebecca, hovering over the dive platform as if waiting for someone to come out of surgery. Even after so many world record penetrations, she is clearly distraught.

"I've been in some of the caves and caverns," she says, "and I know what can go wrong. I know how capable Jarrod is . . . but I'll never get used to the wait."

After the support crew breaks down the setup gear, we reach the tiny karst window of Cheryl Sink with more than three hours to go before the push team is scheduled to surface at the first of 12 decompression stops. Two support teams are already in the water double-checking the deco bottles, food caches, and extra scooters that have been stashed from this end. A dozen other divers and support personnel are seated quietly around the rim checking their watches and watching for bubbles. Twenty feet behind me, cars fly by toward Tallahassee, their drivers completely oblivious to the wilderness beneath their wheels.

Three hours later, the first support team returns with the expected news. The push divers have made it through and are decompressing already. George is at 190 feet, feeling great and rising fast. The connection was clean and clear the whole way through. Total distance: 12,480 feet. Average depth: 290 feet.

After 70 more minutes, just past lunch, George hops from the water, exchanges a few brief congratulations, and towels off as if he'd just slipped out of a hot tub. By dinnertime, Jarrod and Ted have also exited, leaving only cleanup divers inside the cave to pull out the stage bottles and extra scooters.

At the surface, there is surprisingly little celebration among the divers. Between packing up the survey gear and milling around the sinkhole, they talk more about dinner and the long drive home than about world records and superiority. This is what the True Heart is all about, Jarrod explains—exploration in its purest form.

As for today's record, the Leon Sinks Cave System now totals almost 18 miles. But more important, one more isolated strand of the Woodville Karst Plain has been linked to the collective web. In the long run, WKPP's ultimate goal is the "Holy Grail" connection: physical proof that a contiguous open line between all the primary north-to-south cave systems of the Woodville Karst Plain—Leon Sinks, Chip's Hole, Indian Springs, Sally Ward, and Wakulla—actually exists. Currently, three of these connections loom tantalizingly close at less than a few hundred feet.

Given what George, Jarrod, and the rest of the WKPP divers have accomplished so far, it seems a safe assumption the Grail will eventually be theirs.

The great white shark—*Carcharodon carcharias*—Gansbaai, South Africa.

It's All Fun and Games Until Someone Gets Munched

An old man in Key West, Florida, once told me that every living thing has a friend, no matter how loathsome it might act or appear. I doubt, however, that this man had ever met *Carcharodon carcharias,* the great white shark. Mention the name within a mile of any ocean and the descriptions are invariably the same: "ravenous," "blood-thirsty," "vengeful," "monstrous." Venture further inland and the legend grows larger still. Thanks to movies like *Jaws,* in fact, the mere existence of the great white shark is the reason many people don't go in the water.

Like most paranoias, though, fear of *C. carcharias* arises from ignorance rather than fact. Throughout the world, the myths about the "Great White Death" are spoon-fed to a hype-hungry public, which, despite media objections to the contrary, loves a good mauling. Therefore, when real-life attacks do happen, they serve only to perpetuate the notion that "the only good shark is a dead shark," and that the modern world needs *C. carcharias* about as much as it needs AIDS and ethnic cleansing. Simply, tragically, the great white shark is the villainous monster we most love to hate.

Unfortunately, decades of kill-or-be-killed reactionism have taken a grievous toll on the species as a whole. Sportfishing and by-catch statistics indicate that worldwide, populations are plummeting. Scientific data and anecdotal observations reveal an extremely slow natural replacement rate and an unsettling absence of reproductively mature adults. For the world's few white shark researchers, the dilemma is predominantly one of establishing certainty. No one knows how big the problem really is. No one knows how many white sharks are out there now, how many there were in the "beginning," or how many are needed to maintain viable populations in the future. As a result, no one really knows how close the white shark is to extinction, what needs to be done to save it, or what the cascade effects of taking away the ocean's top predator might be. Moreover, given the prejudgments, few seem to care, which is the overriding

Walker's Bay, South Africa.

problem. Like many of the earth's great predators, the great white shark may be disappearing into oblivion far faster than the data needed to save the species is being accumulated. In a small town off the southern tip of South Africa, however, a feeding frenzy of research is attempting to change all that.

By most measures, Gansbaai is thoroughly unremarkable, no better or worse than any other quiet coastal town along the southwest Cape of South Africa. There are three stop signs, seven churches, and more than a dozen havens where a seaman can drown his sorrow over abysmal catch statistics. Two hours east of Cape Town and an hour west of Cape Agulhas, Africa's southernmost point, Gansbaai is defined by the brute forces of the ocean. For as far back as anyone can remember, locals have carved raw, rudimentary lives out of fishing, whaling, and abalone diving. Today, the town is a gristle-and-geriatric mix of salty fishermen and aging apartheid-era retirees. For all of Gansbaai's 5000 residents, life is simple and uneventful, and that's exactly how they like it.

It's in the blood. Craig Ferreira (left), at age eight, was the youngest person in the world to catch a great white. He is now one of the species' greatest champions. (*Photograph by Norma Ferreira.*)

Eleven kilometers offshore, however, in stomach-churning contrast to Gansbaai's downhome tranquility, a narrow slot of water called Shark Alley serves as homefield for a gastronomic orgy of flesh and aggression. It is here that great whites from all along the southwest coast of South Africa—and possibly further—congregate to feed, lured in by what white shark specialist Craig Ferreira calls the "hors d'oeuvres effect." Because of a unique convergence of topographical, hydrological, and biological factors, Shark Alley and its environs represent the most abundant and predictable epicenter of great white shark activity in the world. It is one of three places on the planet, along with the Farallon Islands off San Francisco and Dangerous Reef in southern Australia, where for brief, transcendent moments the great white mystery of a million years materializes into something scientifically observable and quantifiable.

Technically part of the Dyer Island group, Shark Alley is the negative oceanic space between two small islands and several shallow rock reefs. Dyer Island, the larger of the two, is a kilometer and a half long and 500 to 800 meters wide. Rising just a few meters out of the cold southern Atlantic, it is home to a small cluster of deserted buildings and one of the world's largest colonies of endangered African penguins (*Spheniscus demersus*). The other island, Geyser Rock, is little more than a pile of storm-ravaged rubble. What it lacks in aesthetics, however, it makes up for in biomass. Geyser Rock literally squirms with cape fur seals (*Arctocephalus pusillus*), over 36,000 of them at last count. Schooling throughout the reefs and kelp beds are also yellowtail, salmon, potato bass, and at least a dozen other local species of fish. Not surprisingly, the great white feeds on all of it.

"Dyer Island is a white shark supermarket," Craig explains, gesturing out at the kelp heads bobbing on the surface of the water to port and starboard. "The prey here is abundant and diverse year-round, and the conditions for stealth hunting are perfect. We've got sharks every month, especially now."

Insulated in two fleece jackets and a wool hat, Craig throttles his open catamaran through a narrow channel between the reefs and banks out at the far eastern end of Dyer Island, where a big blue mountain range rolls in from open water. To the east and west, the silver hills of South Africa's tumultuous coastline recede into a low front of storm clouds. Over 3000 kilometers to the south, across one of the meanest oceans on the planet, lies Antarctica. We drop anchor on the edge of deep water just outside Shark Alley, a hundred meters from a breaking wave set and 200 meters from a cluster of other boats. Like us, all have cages and divers aboard.

The cape fur seal—*Arctocephalus pusillus*. Dyer Island is a magnet for white sharks, thanks to what Craig Ferreira calls the "supermarket effect."

"Those are the other shark boats," Craig jibes, an old-timer's irritation rising in his voice. "These days, anyone can go down in a cage to see the white shark."

As few as 10 years ago, however, when Craig and his father, Theo, first discovered Shark Alley as part of their early population observations, few people even knew the white sharks were here. In Gansbaai, the Dyer Island group was regarded as little more than a navigational hazard, and among residents and fishermen who knew the white sharks roamed local waters, their presence was considered much more of a menace than a miracle. That the sharks might one day fuel the local economy as a commercially valuable and legally protected species was unbelievable. That someone might intentionally get in the water with them was simply considered suicidal.

"While everyone else was still killing the sharks, still afraid for their lives," Craig remembers, "we were getting in the water every day here and observing things about these animals no one had ever seen before. We would camp in the parking lot and stay on Dyer Island for weeks at a time and never see another boat. It was just ourselves and the sharks. . . . When you're doing things like that, you get the juice into your blood. You have a purpose. There's time to see behavior and time to get to know the shark."

Craig Ferreira and his team prepare the shark cage for a day of diving.

Today, in a rather cruel irony for the great white, Dyer Island plays host to a commercial cage-diving circus. In town, there are "Carcharias" gift shops, so-called educational centers, and shark-tooth trinkets suitable for every family member. On the water, every freewheeling cowboy with a ski boat, a blow torch, and gas money is now a self-proclaimed shark expert. In a word, the most ravenous predator at Dyer Island turns out not to be *C. carcharias,* but the shark operators and "scientists" themselves.

For old-timers like Craig, the most unfortunate result of the cage-diving fad is overcrowding. With eight boats regularly hooking up in Shark Alley and putting people in the water, the good ole' days are definitely over. Many researchers and conservation agencies, in fact, are now concerned that the sharks are getting conditioned to the human presence and will be more likely to associate humans with food in other places, possibly provoking an increase in attacks. From a wider ecological perspective, they worry that anchors, prop noise, and excessive chumming are disturbing the local

Who's watching whom? A great white comes in for a closer look at the shark cage and its contents.

marine ecosystem and that Dyer Island itself, once a predatory superhighway for transient great whites, is fast becoming an oceanic zoo.

Nevertheless, there is good news. For the first time in history, the white shark in South Africa is more valuable alive than dead. Due to the protected status of *C. carcharias* since 1991 and the growing popularity of shark-diving, tourists from around the world will now pay as much as $150 per person to view a live great white in the wild. For scientists as well, Shark Alley has proven equally magnetic. In the search for something quantifiable about a species that hides for 99 percent of its life, the Dyer Island ecosystem is a "Holy Grail" natural laboratory. Consequently, there are now a half-dozen white shark research projects based out of Gansbaai, and a dozen more in the oven. Despite the explosion in research and recent accumulations of data, however, the white shark is still very much a ghost, and among the general public, myth-induced fears still prevail over rational facts.

"White shark research is a baby," Craig laments, "amounting to about 10 years of research by a handful of people. There's not one shred of data from 90 percent of the white shark's range. All of the data that currently exists on the white shark comes from just three epicenters of activity [Dyer Island, the Farallon Islands, and Dangerous Reef] . . . The bottom line is that we don't know much more about the white shark now than we did in the beginning."

A quick look at the available literature confirms Craig's assertions. Applied research in California and south Australia consists of basic population, feeding, and behavioral studies. While in South Africa itself, researchers spend more time discrediting each other than demystifying the shark. What scientists do know with certainty—that white sharks have no fat; that they are almost totally disease-free; that they are one of only eight shark species to be warm-blooded—amounts to little more than intellectual drive-by gleanings from aquarium studies and autopsies on beached carcasses and commercial by-catch. With the giant squid and the blue whale as possible exceptions, the fact is no popularized oceanic species on the planet has slipped through the hands of science so thoroughly as the great white shark. Where any data does exist in the literature, it is often "insufficient" or "inconclusive," and even Craig, who has spent more time in the immediate presence of great whites than virtually anyone in the world, knows only where to find them and how they eat.

"The tip of the iceberg metaphor is an understatement here," he explains, talking about the potential of a site like Dyer Island. "If only everyone with a hand in the pot here could cooperate, we could make major strides forward, and South Africa could be the number-one white shark research area in the world. As it is, we still don't know

Incoming. Craig's assistant films from the shark cage.

**The king of the ocean
rises to take the bait.**

much about these animals. It's presumptuous, in fact, for anyone to say anything about
the white shark with certainty." The reality of sharks in general, however, is that we
don't know much about any of them—especially *C. carcharias*.

Sharks and their cartilaginous relatives, the skates and rays, represent one of the oldest, most mysterious, and most diverse families in all of evolution. Of the 340 identified
species currently catalogued, many appear as if they came from entirely different evolutionary trees. The smallest, the pigmy shark, reaches a length of barely 30 centimeters; the
largest, the whale shark, can grow to more than 20 meters. Some, like the newly discovered six-gill, never leave the darkness at the bottom of the sea; others, like the parochial
nurse shark, can remain on one reef for their entire lives. A few particularly vicious species,
the great white among them, can saw a blue whale into discrete bite-sized chunks. The
basking shark, by contrast, can grow to over five tons on a diet of microscopic plankton.

Evidence from the fossil record indicates that the earliest sharks appeared on the
planet during the Permian period, approximately 400 million years ago, and quickly
evolved into the ocean's most dominant and well-distributed taxonomic clique. Further
evidence suggests the ascendancy of the first *Carcharodon* species during the Jurassic
period. Befitting the age of the "thunder lizards," early Carcharodons exceeded lengths
of 50 feet.

As the current configuration of *C. carcharias* suggests, there have been few significant morphological upgrades since. According to some firsthand accounts, not substantiated, the modern great white can reach lengths of eight meters and weigh up to four tons. Except for *Homo sapiens,* it has no predators. Like a full-grown lion or polar bear on land, a mature white shark can do whatever it wants, wherever and whenever it pleases. Along with the white shark's near-total rule of the ocean, the species is also considered one of evolution's most remarkable success stories. While thousands of other species have come and gone through the turnstiles of natural selection, the white shark has, simply and quietly, endured.

Although little is known about the actual extent of their sensory acuity, white sharks also possess a kind of big-brother, "I'm-watching-and-you-don't-know-it" clairvoyance which scientists call the "seventh sense." Using specialized electromagnetic receptors in their snouts and an exposed "lateral line" running down both sides of their bodies, great whites can "smell" foreign compounds in the water column in concentrations as small as one part in 20 million and sense equally minute variations in voltage and magnetic fields, such as the escalation of a human heartbeat. Optically, they can amplify light and see clearly in the most turbid harbors, focus both in and out of the water, and according to some researchers, even see in color. Given the sensory omniscience of the shark family collectively, it's unlikely that any one of us enters an ocean anywhere on the planet without being detected.

"White sharks are like swimming computers," Craig says. "They're collecting data all the time, analyzing every piece, always in tune with everything that's going on around them. They'd make great scientists."

Technically speaking, great whites are *macro-predators*, which means simply that they'll eat almost anything that will eventually synthesize into nutritional fuel. Although they normally feed on pinnipeds, like seals and sea lions, they'll also scavenge blubber from a dead whale and root up trash from the bottom of the sea. True to the myths, great whites will also prey on *Homo sapiens*, which is why most of humanity is averse to any program that endeavors to protect them. *Jaws* notwithstanding, the statistical odds of getting attacked by a white shark are about as good as getting gored by a pig or killed by a falling coconut. In 1986 in South Africa, of the 160,000 people who

Taking the bait—a white shark gulps down the back half of a potato bass. Notice how the eye has retracted into the head for protection.

died, only one was killed by a white shark. More than a thousand were killed by venomous plants, 300 from bee stings, and many more from falling down stairs or being hit by lightning.

"White sharks are dangerous animals," Craig admits, "but they don't go after humans like people think. They don't crave our flesh. . . . Where most white sharks exist, they would never eat a man. There are just too many seals."

As for all the so-called attacks, Craig and other experts believe that the great majority of them are unjustified vilifications of perfectly natural *carcharias* behavior. Like any animal, great whites will respond defensively if their territory is threatened, which these days is happening just about everywhere they exist. Other attacks appear to be cases of mistaken identity. In the cold, opaque waters where white sharks often cruise, underwater shapes and signals can be misleading, even to the king of the ocean. Recent experiments have shown, for instance, that a paddling surfer is a dead ringer for a seal when viewed from underwater.

Most of all, however, white sharks relate to the physical world around them by using their mouth as a tensiometer and biting it. In the same way a chimpanzee will examine a foreign object by handling it, a great white indulges its curiosities by taking almost anything into its cavernous maw and teething on it, a process called *investigatory mouthing*. Most of the time, the object is inanimate, like garbage or a shark cage. Other times, unfortunately, it's a swimmer or surfer. Experiments by Craig and other researchers in California that studied specific predatory preferences have shown that white sharks will "test bite" just about anything: pool toys, floating buoys, seal cutouts, surfboards, wet suits, mannequins, and even a human hand.

Craig and most experts believe the low attack statistics ultimately confirm what most people simply don't want to believe, that contrary to the hype, great whites aren't committed to a blood-thirsty vendetta against the human race, and that there's really no reason to hate them.

As he talks, Craig directs his student team through the process of attracting the great whites, employing methods refined during his early years on the water here at Dyer Island. First, two students mix up a witches' brew of tuna blood, fish guts, and crushed sardines, ladling it into the water at set 30-second intervals to create a scent corridor and lure the sharks to the boat. Another student rigs up the back half of a potato bass to a floating bait line and buoy. Still another prepares a box of barbed oval marking tags, which will be implanted in the sharks just behind the dorsal fin. A fifth fills out a standard data sheet with the day's environmental parameters: air and water temperature, wind speed, cloud cover, visibility, current, and seal activity—

things that might eventually indicate correlations between daily shark activity and extrinsic environmental conditions.

Craig sits on the bow and attaches one of the marking tags to the end of a three-meter aluminum pole, a task he has performed hundreds of times before. For almost a decade, the distinguishing achievement of Craig's White Shark Research Institute is that it has conducted the longest and most extensive white shark tagging program in the world. Since January 1992, some 400 great whites have been marked, many of which have been resighted in other known epicenters, such as False Bay near Cape Town and Mossel Bay to the east. The farthest resighting so far was in Durban on South Africa's extreme northeast coast, almost 1300 kilometers from Dyer Island. Scientifically, the tagging program allows Craig to make baseline estimates on the size of the white shark population as a whole and to assess their distribution along the South African coast. Extrapolated over the long term, the data will also allow experts to determine if certain seasonal or temporal migration patterns exist that are attributable to prey or habitat considerations.

Like all white shark specialists, however, Craig yearns to get up close and personal with *C. carcharias* and to tackle the more difficult questions about genetics, reproduction, internal anatomy, and sociobiology. Although his population information is critical for conservation, it does little to demystify the dynamic ecology of the white shark itself. Are white sharks territorial, for instance? If so, why are they so gregarious at Dyer Island? How do they organize themselves in such group situations? Why do they show up around the boats together? Do they cooperate when they hunt? Where do they breed and birth their young?

As the questions suggest, Craig's agenda differs from the mainstream currents of South African white shark research, long dominated by the country's "Shark Board," in one principal way: it has very little to do with attacks. By observing the white shark as a complex species in a dynamic ecosystem, without the central focus on human safety, Craig stands as one of a small minority of people endeavoring to understand *C. carcharias* as a species rather than a killer. To answer his questions, Craig has expanded his inquiries in the past few years to include not only population monitoring but blood and tissue sampling as well, both of which require a much more dangerous hands-on technique.

"With the tissue samples," Craig explains, "we can build a population pyramid for the sharks on our coastline—a kind of family tree. We can begin to look at gene pools and population mixing and see who's related to whom." Collaborating with geneticist Dr. Leslie Noble of the University of Aberdeen in Scotland, as well as initiat-

Facing page:
Biting the hand that feeds it. A white shark attempts to "test bite" the hand of a WSRI assistant.

ing contacts with other white shark researchers in California and Australia, Craig is hoping the data will reveal whether white sharks migrate as one vast, genetically mixed global population or cluster in geographically isolated subpopulations.

In the past year, Craig has also taken blood from five great whites in the wild, the only person in the world to have done so. Working with icthyologist Dr. Richard Lundraville from the University of Akron in Ohio, he hopes the samples will shed light on some of the white shark's deeper internal secrets, such as how they maintain such high body temperatures without fat tissue and when they become sexually mature. More important, by measuring the relative levels of enzymes, hormones, and ions, the blood samples may give the clearest idea yet of general population health.

In the future, Craig hopes to expand his work even further to include multiparameter satellite tags, which have been used successfully on such other wide-ranging pelagic species as tuna and whales. Embedded subcutaneously and operating for up to a month, these high-tech transceivers can log constant measurements of temperature, speed, depth, and feeding frequency, yielding precedent insights into predatory and reproductive ecology. Emitting a trackable *ping,* they may also lead Craig to the white shark's breeding and pupping grounds along the southwestern part of the cape.

Quick and painless. As furtively as it went in, Craig Ferreira's tissue sample pole removes a small core of tissue from just aft of the shark's pectoral fin.

The *claspers* of a sexually mature male *C. carcharias*.

"These tags can tell us where the white sharks might be going," Craig explains. "And this is where money and technology come in. They can solve problems of access. They can change the kinds of questions we're capable of asking."

The problem for Craig, of course, is that getting intimate with a great white shark represents, without doubt, the most dangerous animal encounter on earth.

"To get blood samples, for instance, you've got to get the animal to the back of the boat and insert the syringe by hand so as not to contaminate the sample with seawater," says Craig. "That means I've got to lie on the swim platform with the white shark right underneath me. I've had to jump out of the way many times with the teeth right in my face. . . . To determine whether a male is sexually active, you have to feel the claspers, and that's even harder to do." The claspers are the external sexual organs of a male white shark, which hang beneath the belly just aft of the anal fins in much the same way as a human penis. Craig smiles at me wryly, "That area is strictly off-limits."

Today, two hours have already passed without so much as a fin sighting. From the west, the wind rises to 20 knots, and even in the lee of Dyer Island, the swell grows long and deep. Three of the students sleep on the port-side thwarts. One has already thrown up twice. Another continues to ladle the chum mixture into the water, a cup every 20 seconds now.

Suddenly, a cry goes up from the stern.

"SHARK!!"

Everyone jumps to the gunwales. Craig is immediately on red alert.

"A four-meter male," he announces after a few seconds, squinting hard into the low winter sun. The shark's silhouette floats just feet under the surface of the water like the shadow of a cloud and locks into a counterclockwise circle around the boat. Finally, one of the students grabs a clipboard and begins transcribing Craig's estimates of the shark's vital characteristics: size, sex, weight, notable scarring and markings, tag number, and distinct behavioral characteristics. Another tosses the chunk of potato bass into the shark's path in an attempt to lure it closer to the boat. On cue, Craig takes up a three-meter aluminum pole with a small hollow rod at the end and moves to the stern, waiting for a clear strike behind the shark's dorsal fin. If successfully implanted, the result will be a tiny core of tissue which will be immediately frozen and exported to Dr. Nobel. The great white, however, just rolls an eye and glides on by.

"The big ones don't fall for it," Craig explains, relaxing. "They don't make mistakes. This is why they've survived. This is why they're kings."

The ultimate predator. (*Photograph by Hendrik Krugel.*)

As the great white continues to circle, the bait is thrown again, and again there is no response. Seconds later, however, the shark pirouettes on his right pectoral fin, flicks his tail, and drifts back behind the boat, curious. He inspects the bait with cocktail-party nonchalance as it's pulled in toward us, finally opening his mouth in a somewhat diffident attempt to gulp it down. Barely six feet from the boat, we can see that his snout is slashed and scarred as if by barbed wire, the result, perhaps, of test-biting one too many shark cages or engine mounts. Inside his mouth, the roof and gums are bloody and raw, perhaps the entrails of his most recent victim.

Craig Ferreira with one of 12 tissue samples he has taken from live white sharks in the wild.

"Closer," Craig whispers, "just a little bit closer . . ."

Finally, as the shark turns broadside to the swim platform, Craig jabs the tissue pole into the water in a lightning-quick strike, removing the tissue core from behind the dorsal fin before the shark can even react. The process is not only efficient, it's painless. When he's finished sealing the tissue sample in a small plastic vial, Craig gestures to a pile of wet suits and scuba tanks in the front of the boat and invites me to suit up so I can see the tissue-sampling process up close this time, from inside the cage. He nods toward the red chum line. "When they come, they come in groups," he says. "They'll be back."

Designed by Craig and his dad to facilitate face-to-face observation and identification, the shark cage now ubiquitous at Dyer Island more closely resembles the foil wrapper on a burger "to go" than the maximum security prison one would hope for. Constructed out of a galvanized steel mesh barely thicker than chicken wire, it's based on what Craig calls the "bobbing for apples" principle. As opposed to actually withstanding the brute force of a shark bite, the circular cage is designed to roll away if attacked, much like a soccer ball from a puppy's mouth. In theory, Craig maintains, the logic is thoroughly tested, citing his own 1000 hours of internment. There have been many close shaves, however. Six times, Craig has had his air hose cut and almost been dragged to the bottom by great whites entangled in the tethering lines. Three times, he's been trapped in the cage and shaken like a martini by sharks tearing at the bars. Two cinematographers have actually had sharks panic upon contact with the steel mesh, thrust themselves through the camera ports, and thrash into the cage itself, an

Craig Ferreira's assistant documents *carcharias* behavior.

experience they likened to being locked in a coffin with a running chainsaw. Outside the cage, Craig's luck hasn't been much better. He's almost had his boat sunk twice, and has narrowly escaped being pulled into the water more times than he can remember. Given this history, it's a miracle no one's lost an appendage yet.

"We've had some pretty close calls," Craig assures me. "Between my dad and me, we have more experience with the white shark in the wild than anyone, and we're still careful. . . . Unfortunately, most people are treating the white shark like a circus animal now. They don't have the respect anymore. They don't understand they're dealing with the greatest predator in the world." He pauses and stares thoughtfully into the distance, reliving something he's unwilling to share. In silence, we watch the cage float 10 feet away from the boat, well beyond the point where anyone could do anything should a worse-case scenario develop.

"You can never screw around," Craig adds, breaking the silence. "A white shark can end it for you whenever it wants."

Yet, taking calculated risks inside the cage has also yielded great observational data. In just five years of diving, Craig has identified over 184 sharks by their individual fin markings and scarring patterns, amassed over 50 edited hours of video footage, and compiled detailed data sheets on more than 600 individual sharks. In the process, he has observed population and sociological phenomena in wild great whites which few ever thought existed, things like curiosity, game-playing, group migrations, and a hierarchical size-sorting when multiple sharks get together. He has seen great whites use boats and wake foam for hunting blinds, tread out of the water to scan for basking pinnipeds (a strategy called "spyhopping"), and leap up onto the beach to pull a seal down. Although considered anecdotal from a purely scientific standpoint, these observations represent the first accumulations of information where only myths existed before.

"To me, this is all meaningful data," Craig explains, alluding to criticisms in Gansbaai that he's just another shark operator posing in a scientist's lab coat. "It means there are results. These are the beginnings of a bigger picture about an animal that's a total ghost."

Contrary to the conventional wisdom of the "10-minute" shark experts, who claim white sharks are only out for flesh, Craig also has witnessed touching moments of grace and placidity.

"The great white feeding frenzy is a terrible myth," he asserts. "These are dignified and noble animals. They can tear you in two, but they are also refined and controlled. They are always moving with a purpose. That's part of the reason we get in the water with them so much: to show that they're not monsters, that they're just as curious about us as we are about them."

To show me just how confident he is, Craig gestures to a newly arrived silhouette off the stern and suggests we forgo the cage altogether and go free-diving.

On a death-flaunt continuum, intentionally free-diving with a great white shark would be the subaquatic equivalent of hopping out of a safari vehicle and strolling up to the nearest pride of hungry lions. From a behavioral viewpoint, though, it allows Craig to observe firsthand how white sharks regard the human presence without the physical and electromagnetic interference of the galvanized steel cage and to what extent they might truly consider *Homo sapiens* as prey. So far, Craig has yet to observe the first gesture of predatory intent. His video footage, in fact, reveals exactly the opposite: a calm, cool curiosity he'd bet his life on—and mine as well.

Since he first ventured out of the cage in July 1995, Craig has free-dived with the Dyer Island great whites five times, and for rather obvious reasons, was the first person to do so without any form of backup protection, such as a spear gun. Only a half dozen or so other people have tried it since. With so many sharks in the water and so much bait being thrown, however, it's only a matter of time before someone gets shipped back ashore unassembled.

Like a freighter out of the fog, an incoming great white emerges from the cerulean southern Atlantic.

The free-dive. Length: 12 minutes. Casualties: none.

"I have no desire to be eaten by a shark," Craig says candidly. "If conditions aren't right, or if you don't feel right, you just don't do it. If a white shark does bite me, I'm in serious shit. It's a big animal, and I have a family and a wife." He pauses and breaks into a sly, suicidal smile, "It's all fun and games until someone gets munched."

Craig is already in the water just aft of the boat as I finally slip off the swim platform with only a mask, fins, and snorkel. With so great a predator in the immediate vicinity, the ocean feels as if it's charged with a high-voltage current. I can hear my heart slamming into the front of my chest, flushed with adrenaline. Trying to keep control, I fumble quickly to adjust my mask and scan the 10-foot perimeter around me. All I see is Craig. His eyes are wide and electrified, and he nods as if to say, "He's out there. He can hear you." We move back to back like nervous birds and wait.

Suddenly, to my left, a shadow glides out of the haze like a freighter from the fog. He is a four-meter male, thick and hydrodynamically perfect, free of scarring and other territorial markings. On top, he is the color of a cumulonimbus storm cloud; underneath, he is "great white." Just aft of the anal fins, his claspers hang conspicuously like twin remoras. Keeping a safe distance at the limit of visibility, he circles silently with the slow certainty characteristic of all apex predators, as if aware he's already the quintessential evolutionary specimen. Craig films the approach from a safe distance just behind the swim platform, keeping the camera defensively between himself and the shark. Lacking a similar defensive aid, I keep Craig between me and the shark.

With each pass, the great white circles closer in an ever-narrowing pattern. He eyes us intently, listening to our heartbeats, "feeling" the voltage of fear. Elvis-like, his mouth hangs just barely agape, and from certain vantages, you would swear he was smiling. Craig hasn't taken his eye away from the camera. He wants it all on tape: the irrefutable repose, the curiosity, the cohabitation and mutually respectful communion between earth's two most dominant predators. Eyeing the bait floating just above me, all I can think about is what it would feel like to be killed by slow exsanguination, the white shark's preferred predatory tactic.

Soon, the shark is banking in tight at six feet, and Craig wields the video camera like a billy club to fend him away. On the next pass, he's so close I can see the serrations in his teeth and feel the invisible wake from his tail as he turns. We've been in the water for just over 12 minutes and the shark is no longer simply intrigued with humanity, he's ready to interact.

Then suddenly, a second shark appears out of the blue beneath the boat, heading straight for the bait above me. There is no time to react, and as he drifts within arm's

Two's a crowd. When the sharks come, they come in groups, occasionally gathering into schools of up to five at a time.

reach, I close my eyes and pray he'll just go away. Instinctively, Craig grabs my arm and pulls me behind the lower unit of the engine, letting the shark glide over my head in an eclipse of white. I reopen my eyes just in time to see him nudge the bait, smirk in mild dissatisfaction, and fin away into the distance, unimpressed with both humanity and our offerings. With two sharks now in the area, Craig throws me back aboard the boat and quickly follows.

"You never free-dive with two sharks," Craig gasps, crawling back from the swim platform between hyperventilations, "because there's always one that can hit you from behind." He pauses briefly, then adds with a grin, "I suppose you could call that cooperative hunting." Just aft of the stern, the sharks continue to loiter like streetcorner thugs. One surfaces and spyhops briefly, as if to say, "Come on back. We're ready to play now." But the stakes of the game have grown too high. That's as close as Craig has ever come to a great white in the wild without any form of protection.

By the time the cage and baits are back aboard and stowed, the sun is setting behind a tide of incoming storm clouds, the wind has kicked up to 30 knots out of the southwest, and the swell in the channel back to Gansbaai is steep and breaking. Craig invites us all to take a seat, turn backwards, and hold on for dear life. Out past the edge of Dyer Island, he turns the boat into the swell and pauses, timing the waves in the channel.

"People still think the white shark is a species we can't live with," Craig says, gunning the engine toward home, "but it's really a species we can't live without. The ocean just wouldn't be the same without its king."

The Ice Man Cometh

On November 5, 1996, the Vatnajskull glacier made geographic history. For a few hours that night, the glacial-fed Skeidarar River in southeastern Iceland became the second largest river, by volume, in the world, flowing out of the glacier's terminal snout at a rate of up to 50,000 cubic meters per second and carrying icebergs the size of skyscrapers more than 25 kilometers to the sea.

In itself, that regular *jskulhlaups*—literally translated, "floods of the glacier"—were peculiar to the volatile Vatnajskull ice sheet was old news. Smaller outbursts had occurred every five or ten years for as long as anyone could remember. On the other hand, that billions of gallons of meltwater could be stored and then drained internally through the glacier in a matter of hours with few noticeable effects on the surface was enough to set the whole world talking. The hydraulic mechanisms behind the phenomenon were almost entirely unknown to science.

Over 2000 kilometers south of Iceland, in the renowned ski towns of the Swiss Alps, autumn is the off-season. The streets of Gstaad and St. Moritz are empty, the chalets and ski lifts are closed, and the vacant hours until Christmas tick by with typical Swiss precision. Autumn in Zermatt is different, however. It is the one brief window of opportunity each year when scientists can look into the glaciological phenomena and processes that may have been for responsible for the cataclysm at Vatnajskull.

"We've been coming here each October for over 10 years now to work in the glacial caves," Italian physicist and caver Giovanni Badino tells me as we begin our trek

The tools of the trade. A measuring tape, waterproof notebook and pencil, and survey compass provide speleologists with the basic tools they need to map underground caves.

Facing page:
Towering 4482 meters above Zermatt, the Matterhorn or *Il Chervino*, as it is known in Italian, keeps a watchful eye over Gornergletscher.

231

out of town, "and every year we find something new. . . . For the kind of exploration and research we're doing, this is the best location on earth."

Given its legendary autumn beauty, Zermatt might seem an unlikely place for a theoretical physicist to be doing anything but sightseeing. To the north and west of town, the gnarled spine of the western Alps rises in a roiling storm of rock and ice. To the west looms the jagged geologic belfry of the Matterhorn (4482 m). Lower down, fall's final colors smolder against the foothills. Yet, Zermatt is also home to Gorner-gletscher, Europe's second largest glacier and, for a variety of reasons, one of the most studied pieces of ice on earth. Extending 10 kilometers down from the ragged peaks of Mount Rosa (4634 m) and Mount Liskamm (4527 m), Gorner is a textbook lesson in glacial geomorphology, and due to its close proximity to Zermatt, an ideal natural labo-ratory for glaciological research.

Like most of nature's superlative phenomena, Gorner is also the kind of place that changes lives. Academically speaking, Giovanni boasts Ph.D. credentials in the field of cosmic ray physics, a hair-pulling, largely theoretical realm of science that endeavors to predict the behavior of exotic neutrino particles and high-energy gas in interstellar space. Thanks, though, to what he has found inside the crushing internal structure of Gorner over the past decade, Giovanni's work these days is anything but theoretical. Based on recent data and discoveries, Europe's second largest glacier appears to be the most hyperkarstic (cave-filled) glacier for its size on earth.

"For years," Giovanni muses, pausing briefly along the trail to base camp and ges-turing up to the ivory tongue licking at the mountains ahead, "my life was nothing but neutrino physics, theoretical equations, and lots of time in front of the computer—modeling and guessing at things I couldn't see. Then someone showed me the inside of a glacier. . . . When I first saw that the ice had been carved by the water flow, that there were surface [caves], then I realized that there were galleries under water too. This opened my eyes and changed my life. . . . Now my life is glacial caving. Now I *know*."

The problem is that one can't just go leaping inside a glacier. Deep endoglacial caves—many of which descend over 150 meters into the ice itself—are cruel, indis-criminate killers, threatening explorers with all the dangers of technical caving and high-altitude mountaineering combined. Yet in addition to his expertise in the dynam-ics of fluid transport, Giovanni is also one of the planet's best cavers. Since his first penetration underground in 1972, Giovanni has served as president of the Italian Speleological Society and the Italian Cave Rescue Team; authored six books on the physics of the underground environment, advanced caving techniques, and body recovery operations; cofounded the elite La Venta Exploring Team, recipient of the

Facing page:
Down the hatch. Reflecting sunlight from above, the beads and fangs of moulin G8 glitter like dangling chandeliers.

prestigious Rolex Award for Enterprise in 1993; and pulled off a list of speleological firsts that few have repeated, including more than a dozen penetrations greater than 1000 vertical meters, a half dozen multiday "solos," and a single record-breaking push of over 120 consecutive hours underground alone.

"I believe there are three kinds of activities in life:" Giovanni tells me, attaching his crampons to his boots and beginning the ascent onto the glacier proper, "to not cave, to cave, and to cave alone. . . . Among most people, I am a 'Shiite' on this issue; I am the extremist. I began to cave alone in 1974, so now I am very confident in many types of caves and in many challenging circumstances. This is why I am one of the only ones who make descents alone, the only one who will always say 'Let's go,' and one of the [few] who will go inside there . . ." Giovanni looks up from his boots and points to a black hole 20 feet downslope from us where a swift meltwater stream running along the edge of the glacier gets swallowed up abruptly into the ice itself.

"Those are the *moulins,*" he says with deep reverence, stepping onto an ice bridge at the edge of the hole. "The ice shafts are the doors to the heart of Gorner's ice caves. . . . This is what our research is all about." I step up behind him and dig my crampons in just behind the moulin's baffled lip. Inches from my boots, the river roars by with enough velocity to sweep a grown man off his feet. Upriver, the current sluices

"Loco"—the crazy man. Riccardo Pozzo has spent almost every weekend for the past two years underground.

through a narrow blue chute; downriver, it leaps over the edge of the moulin and into the darkness with sacrificial abandon.

Giovanni can feel my apprehension and smiles reassuringly as we press on to camp in the fading light. "Tomorrow," he says, "you will see. . . . It is a world that changes every day—a world that nobody knows."

At the most basic level, glacial mechanics are a matter of simple arithmetic: glaciers form where net annual snowfall exceeds net annual melting, most often in the high mountainous areas of the temperate and polar latitudes. During winter, a glacier gains mass in its *zone of accumulation,* as a function of seasonal snowfall and what is called "overburdening" compression. In summer, lack of snow and sustained warming cause a glacier to lose mass in the *zone of ablation* by means of daily melting, evaporation, and calving. Coaxed by gravity and hydrologic lubrication, glaciers also crawl inexorably downhill, excavating the underlying bedrock and transporting 10-ton boulders like pocket change. Some glaciers flow for hundreds of kilometers at speeds of over three meters per day. Others, like those irrigating the high Himalayas and central Antarctica, can drag on for tens of thousands of years.

The "ghosts" of Gorner. Giovanni balances on a thin ice bridge to inspect another moulin that has formed along Gorner's primary river.

Despite the pioneering nature of Giovanni's endoglacial explorations, it is hardly a new revelation that glaciers are not solid sheets of ice. By the late nineteenth century, the first wave of European glaciologists had discovered obvious physical features in the supraglacial surface—like whirlpools and deep vertical shafts—which indicated clearly that the large ice masses did indeed possess some kind of internal anatomy. In 1898, Frenchman Joseph Vallot became the first person to find out how, descending into Mount Blanc's "Grand Moulin" to a depth of 60 meters before finally bailing out. His bold descent was the first visual confirmation that glaciers are "perforated" with temporary internal structures carved by meltwater. Later on in the 1920s, Italian Ugo Monterin, noticed that moulins seemed to appear in the same spot year after year, notwithstanding the movement of the ice downhill. He correctly concluded that the shafts formed in relation to constraining bedrock conditions and contributed brief, seasonal structures to the glacier itself, like whirlpools in a river.

That flowing water is a primary architect of glacial structure was certainly not a groundbreaking notion either. Long before the first penetration into a glacial moulin,

Giovanni descends the main rope into G17. The smooth, featureless walls result from immense "overburdening" pressures and the plastic collapse of the glacier itself.

physicists had learned to predict water's basic hydraulic behavior and geomorphic artistry. What scientists failed to do was put the two emerging bodies of knowledge together. Even as recently as 1996, leading glaciologists were still "[supposing that] glacial drainage systems are formed through crevasses."

"[After Monterin], speleologists forgot about caves in the ice," says Giovanni, "and glaciologists forgot they operated in a karst environment."

These days, however, thanks to Giovanni's inquiry into "the phenomenology of endoglacial drainage," conventional glaciological wisdom is fast unraveling. Using both physical simulation models and firsthand speleological data gathered from as deep as 150 meters inside the ice itself, Giovanni has shown that glaciers are inherently karstic in nature and drained by a complex web of interconnected conduit. By further modeling the dynamic physical processes which shape these internal networks, he has also begun to identify the universal boundary conditions which initiate glacial karst formation and catastrophic glaciological phenomena like the Vatnajskull outburst. In the process, Giovanni is changing the very way scientists look at glaciation and caves.

"The exploratory campaigns and the development of a simulation program have enabled us to outline the general characteristics of water flow inside the glacial mass,"

The "tube." Cave passages exhibiting phreatic (water-filled) morphological features, like a horizontal gradient and dimpling of the ice walls, are rare in any glacier.

Giovanni explains with a wry grin. "But glaciologists are only now waking up to what we are seeing and studying. They are not speleologists and physicists, and so they have a difficult time understanding why we are here. But I do not want to wake them up too soon. I want to have the results first."

By focusing on the one glaciological frontier which other scientists have so far avoided—the interior—Giovanni has also shown that theoretical physics can be life-threatening. Regardless of size or location, glaciers kill with cold geologic anonymity. On the slopes of Gorner alone, 20 lives have been swallowed up by avalanches and crevasses over the years and never found. On the high, glaciated peaks of North America, Antarctica, Patagonia, and the Himalayas, the collective death toll is well into the thousands. Yet, glacial caving is an unparalleled class of danger. Of primary concern are the perils that attend any act of technical speleology in the first place, like breaking an ankle in a crack a thousand meters from fresh air or getting buried by an underground landslide. Glacial caves also move; they can collapse catastrophically under overburdening pressure, flood in minutes with fluctuations in the water table, and sweep cavers to their deaths in torrents of meltwater flowing faster than 10 meters per second.

"The phreatic tunnels inside the glaciers are extremely unstable," Giovanni warns. "Once abandoned by water, they cave in; and the deeper they are, the more quickly they collapse. In practice, it is only possible to visit the superficial part [of the caves], where collapse times are much longer, but often these channels are fragmented by the forward movement of the glacier. Ironically, the 'stable,' submerged part [of the passage system] with an active flow of water is almost inaccessible."

Predictably, a decade of endoglacial explorations has handed Giovanni the worst glaciers have to offer: ice avalanches, free falls, full gallery floods, and the "seismic" collapse of the inner glacier itself, all while he was inside. Since no one was there to tell him what to look out for in the first place, Giovanni admits he's lucky to be alive.

"Our endeavors carry us to the limits of human knowledge and exploration," he explains, "but this also involves risk and the loss of human life. I hate danger. I minimize danger in every way I can. I accept it because it is a part of the job we must do . . . to go where no one else has gone before. The irony is that the only way these explorations become safer and we can refine the techniques is to continue to do them. My theory is to minimize the risks and go for it. You may have the hardware to be a caver, but you have to have the software to manage the risk."

On the upside, Giovanni has seen the best that glaciers have to offer as well. Glacial karst is God's quicksilver art, giving infinite physical form to the kinetic inter-

Going down? The main shaft of G8 drops for over 90 meters straight down
before collapsing into a chain of small rooms carved by three waterfalls.

play of ice and water. Unlike karst in limestone and dolomite, endoglacial caves operate on a largely human time clock. Some moulins and passages only exist for a single season, advancing quickly downhill and sinking into the ice as much as one meter every week until they are crushed at depth. Other galleries in places like Patagonia can open and collapse in a matter of weeks. Individual ice flutes, chutes, and tusks closer to the surface can disappear completely in just hours of heavy summer melting.

At work behind the glaciers' artistic wand is the dynamic interaction between pressure, temperature, and ice. Kinetically speaking, glacier karst is formed by a phenomenon called *viscous dissipation,* by which frictional "energy deposits" capable of doing work—i.e., digging holes and excavating caves—are generated by concentrated liquid flows. On top of the glacier itself, the process starts where meltwater begins to pool and circulate in small depressions and surface cracks, usually where tongues of ice meet or change speed over uneven surface topography. As the internal circulation of the pool generates heat and melts the ice, the depression eventually expands into a full-blown whirlpool. Assuming a sufficient volume of meltwater continues, that whirlpool will quickly bore down into the ice itself like a liquid drill bit and become a waterfall. It is here that vast amounts of potential energy become available for melting, karstic excavation, and the creation of an expanding phreatic cave system. As water circulates through the glacier under pressure, the ice walls literally melt away.

At depths beyond 30 meters, however, endoglacial ice also becomes harder and denser, ultimately compressing beneath overburdening pressure to the point that it behaves more like a liquid than a solid. Inside a water-filled glacial cave, the result is a hydraulic phenomenon called *ice plastic collapse,* in which glacial ice begins to cave in on itself as a function of ambient pressure, ultimately counterbalancing meltwater excavation. As water burrows deeper into the ice, its energy surplus is eventually offset by this internal pressure and cavity formation quite literally stops cold. At this point, conditions in the caves are said to be isostatic; water pressure is exactly equal to the compression of ice plastic collapse. In real-life glacial caves, though, conditions are rarely isostatic. Pressures vary with depth; stress bends energy sideways; meltwater fluctuates on daily, seasonal, and annual cycles; drainage systems sink overall; and the whole ice mass itself grinds inexorably forward.

"In this way," Giovanni explains, "we are not studying a permanent phenomenon; we are exploring an ephemeral process, a hole in the water. These glacial caves form in the same spot every year where energy deposits exist, and then collapse and disappear just as quickly. . . . The deep network also appears to be a structure that fluctuates around a pattern of equilibrium according to the seasons, and [literally] moves upstream as the glacier moves downhill. . . . The glacier caves are like ghosts."

Facing page:
Tullio Bernabei ascends from the bottom of a deep, blue shaft on the Tyndall glacier in Chile.

Given the spectral nature of the entire process, it's hard to not wonder what any of this has to do with the average person. What's the universal benefit of understanding glacial hydrology and ice plastic collapse when people are dying from starvation? And why would someone risk his life for these cold kingdoms of ice and stone?

The answer is power. Contrary to what current thirsts suggest, the world's supply of freshwater is finite. Available freshwater reserves amount to less than one half of one percent of all water on earth. Unfortunately, global consumption—primarily for industrial, technological, and agricultural use—is doubling every 20 years, more than twice the rate of human population growth, and widespread shortages are already taking their toll. In many regions of the world, like the Middle East and sub-Saharan Africa, tens of thousands die each day from draught, groundwater contamination, and diarrheal afflictions. Given the apocalyptic potential, freshwater in all its forms has become the petroleum of the new millennium, and its conservation is literally a matter of international security. This is exactly why Giovanni's data are so relevant.

Glacial ice represents one of the most untapped and uncontaminated reserves of freshwater left on the planet, and its value, both present and future, is inestimable. In certain regions of the world, like Norway's Svalbard Islands and northern Europe, glacial meltwater already comprises a vital source of potable freshwater and hydroelectric power for homes, farms, and industries. In many countries, however, the issue is less about local lifelines and more about national sovereignty. In all its sordid permutations, the rush for "blue gold" is on. In Patagonia and the Himalayas, neighboring countries have already assumed a military posture in their claims to heavily glaciated mountain regions. In the southwestern United States—an area entirely devoid of glacial ice, but crystal clear on the value of freshwater—big business and policymakers have jumped into the game with sizable bets of their own, including visions of a pipeline to carry meltwater from Alaska to the desert tongues of Arizona and southern California. Given the current retreat of glaciers worldwide and forecasts for further global warming, it is a power struggle that will no doubt come down to the last pint of "blood."

"Fifty years ago," Giovanni says, "people wondered why we were trying to split an atom. Now we know. . . . In this way, research with exotic particles and glaciers have very similar points of view. The things that are most unknown appear unimportant and useless to the rest. People have long believed that glaciers are just sliding ice, but now we know they are wrong. Now they are learning the value of ice."

When Giovanni and I finally arrive at base camp, a weak prewinter sun is setting behind the western edge of Gorner valley, cutting dark serrations across a cold, iron sky. Glowing in a small, snowy depression on the glacier's northern moraine, the warm

The civilized comforts of base camp—cold Chianti, salami, bread, and lard—
provide vital replenishment after a day under the ice.

lights of the expedition's tents stand out starkly in the darkness, like fishing boats heaving-to against an angry sea.

Huddled inside the main shelter over a jug of frozen Chianti is a diverse assemblage of scientists, cavers, and La Venta team members: Pasquale Suriano, Paolo Petrignani, Chiara Silvestro, Giuseppe Giovine, Riccardo "Loco" Pozzo, Giuseppe "Cagiu" Casagrande, Tiziano Piovesan, Giusiano Maöro, and Tullio Bernabei. In the subzero air, the hut soon fills with potent exhalations of garlic and pesto and an unbroken dialogue on "women, wine, and caves." That night, we fall asleep among five scattered tents under a rising wind, clearing skies, and a radiant full moon. Beneath us, the glacier crushes its way downslope, cracking and snapping throughout the night with sudden releases of internal pressure and filling Gorner valley with the endless artillery sounds of seismic collapse. By morning, we are three feet closer to town.

Dawn breaks just before seven, clear and cold. There has been no new snow overnight, and it will be at least another three hours before the sun rises from behind Mount Rosa to begin its work on Gorner's jacket of snow and firn (polycrystalline "crust"). The conditions for penetration today are good, but we don't have much time. At this time of year, the glacier's tenuous balance between sunshine, snowfall, melting, and collapse poses a lethal mix to cavers on even the shortest descent beneath the ice. With nightly snows and bright, sunny days, meltwater fluctuations can transform empty passages into surging pipelines in a matter of hours.

"Because of the recent snow," Giovanni warns, "the water table will be rising fast after just a few hours of sunshine. . . . Later this morning, caving may be very dangerous, may be canceled."

Based on recent weather reports, October's two-week penetration "window" may also slam shut sooner than expected. A barrage of harsh winter storms is forecast for the next two weeks, which will create conditions inside the ice that are not near suicidal. As winter then sets in for good, snow cover will build, crevasses and cave entrances will ice over, and the glacier's internal water table will begin to swell by as much as two meters per week. By December, many of the moulins here will be completely submerged and impenetrable.

In spite of the dangers, it is this very question of seasonality that brings Giovanni back to Gorner each year. Until now, virtually all theoretical models attempting to successfully predict the basic hydraulic processes at work inside the glacial drainage system have had as their primary prerequisite the assumption of a "steady state," that is, isostatic, or unchanging, boundary conditions. Yet, glacial caves are inherently unstable structures, perpetually reshaped in direct relation to short- and long-term fluctuations

The "ice man" cometh. A cave diver emerges from beneath the ice of a small glacial lake after looking for evidence of water storage phenomena.

in meltwater, temperature cycles, and the complex dynamics of overburdening stress. Change at every incremental level—by the day, month, or year—is their very essence. As such, repetitive annual data on the same moulins and caves allows Giovanni not only to predict how glacial karst forms in the first place but also to model the way endoglacial architecture is sculpted over time.

"By penetrating the glacial caves at regular intervals," he explains, "we are adding more and more real data to the theoretical models and defining in greater detail the true relationship between stress, meltwater, and glacial cave formation. . . . Ultimately, we are discovering how glaciers really work."

Giovanni suspects that the seasonal nature of endoglacial gallery formation may also explain what happened at Vatnajskull. His theory centers around the concept of water storage and recent computer simulations which predict the formation of hermetically sealed chambers inside the ice as a result of rapid winter impedance and passage collapse. According to the models, as tunnel excavation slacks off with decreasing meltwater, the deepest caves collapse catastrophically under the overburdening pressure of the ice, eventually sealing off the inner drainage system. With freezing and compacting over time, the chambers eventually stabilize into semipermanent structures that are pulled along inside the ice like internal organs. In the spring, as temperatures warm and meltwater increases, new moulins form and old ones reopen, ultimately giving birth to a new generation of shafts and storage chambers. Drawing from various data, Giovanni speculates that the regular collapse and reconnection of the overall glacial gallery system may ultimately be responsible for large-scale glaciological events such as *jskulhlaups*, glacial "surges" of up to 100 meters per day, and rapid surface "settling." The problem is proving it.

"We know [from the Vatnajskull outburst] that glaciers store large amounts of water," Giovanni explains, his frustration clearly evident, "but we don't know how or where. We know the caves well [until we reach] the water table, but we know nothing about the deep internal water. Yet, this is where the big energy is stored."

Scientifically speaking, the only way to confirm the models is to actually observe the water storage chambers before they collapse. The only way to do this is to scuba dive inside the glacier itself.

"Direct diving may give some clues about where these chambers are and how they form in relation to the endoglacial caves," Giovanni tells me casually. "Then we can say, 'Yes, we have seen them.' Only then can we attempt to model their construction."

Few human endeavors represent flirtation with death like high-altitude, endoglacial cave diving. In addition to the obvious dangers of hypothermia, gear failure, valve freezes, disorientation, embolisms, and decompression sickness, there are other, more insidious risks intrinsic to glacial karst itself. Phreatic caves wide enough to permit human passage to the glacier's deep drainage system are also the most volatile, flushed with the largest volumes of meltwater and compressed under the most intense overburdening pressures. What this means for endoglacial cave divers is the simultaneous risk of sudden meltwater surges and bone-crushing passage collapses. Not surprisingly, Giovanni has found only five people willing to attempt glacial cave diving. For this year's goal—a more technical, full-blown penetration into Gorner's innermost atriums—only two have volunteered.

"When you are on the cutting edge," Giovanni smiles, "you are always alone."

The plan for today is twofold. Team one, consisting of myself, Giovanni, Pasquale, loco, and Tiziano, will strike out for moulin G8 to assess its suitability for diving. Due to G8's massive size and recent snow conditions, it is our best chance for mounting an exploratory penetration before our window slams shut. The rest of the expedition members will continue the push into G17, a still-bottomless, downstepping cave which has so far displayed the most unique morphological features of any glacial cave in the world.

Given the dangers of getting in and out of a glacial cave alive at any time of year, preparations for today's penetrations are meticulous. Carabiners and ice screws are checked for fractures, ropes are inspected hand over hand for chafe, and packs are prepared with tapes, slates, cameras, and VHF radios. With appropriate emphasis, emer-

Mountain without mercy. Giovanni is dwarfed by the Matterhorn as he prepares ropes for the day.

Gambling with the slots. Giovanni descends from the surface through
a narrow slot canyon into the glacier itself.

gency plans for accidents and weather contingencies are also reviewed, and a safety officer is left at camp to coordinate rescue and evacuation should they be required.

By the time we depart base camp, the sun has been on the glacier for almost an hour, and most of the expedition members wear only T-shirts and sunglasses under their packs. Out on the glacier itself, the surface ice is covered in a film of water and perspiration. It gathers in small cracks and builds into rivulets, pools, and capturing streams, which, at least for now, seem to be going nowhere fast. Giovanni is attentive but unconcerned. He motions for me to join him on the edge of the moraine just south of camp to take in the full panorama of his study area.

Like water in all its forms, glaciers are geologic agents, and nowhere is their urgent industry more obvious than on Gorner itself. High on the flanks of Mounts Rosa and Liskamm, the glacier's three accumulation tongues flow over steps in the rugged surface topography like sinewy, white musculature. Where the summit splits into vertical faces, the ice sheers abruptly in menacing, 200-foot cross sections, offering a textbook lesson in glacial layering and compression. On less precipitous slopes, the glacier breaks like accordion folds into wide, water-filled crevasses. Lower down, Gorner's tongues converge into three parallel ice flows and begin the pulverizing journey down to Zermatt.

The most striking feature is the effluvial topography of the glacier itself. Exaggerated by exfoliation, Gorner's surface is a perfect model of arborescent, watershed drainage. In places where the ice is smooth and flat, the primary "trunk" runs downslope in a wide riparian valley, fed by thin, interconnecting drainage veins that trend transversely across the ice. In the tighter channels, the river coils into a gray, liquid blade that carves the ice as if it were nothing more than a cloud. Less than a kilometer downslope, the river bores into the glacier and disappears. In at least a dozen other places within five square kilometers of where we stand, significant meltwater streams disappear in like manner into the endoglacial system. What is remarkable from a geomorphological standpoint is the fact that such aggressive drainage exists here in the first place.

No room for error. Loco drives in an ice screw at the top of G8 to anchor the primary descent rope into the shaft.

High-volume streams like those characteristic of Gorner carry vast amounts of potential energy. Concentrated at the bottom of a 50-meter shaft and pressurized under the weight of the glacier, they can excavate ice like diesel machinery. High-volume glacial streams are less the result of water quantity, however, than they are a function of topographical gradient. In general, steep slopes mean more crevasses, and hence a more uniform absorption of meltwater. A horizontal surface gradient does just the opposite, promoting stream capture, big rivers, concentrated energy flow, and ultimately, deep, water-engorged moulins. On long, flat glaciers, like those in Patagonia and the Himalayas, big rivers and glacial karst are virtually endemic. In contrast, on most temperate glaciers, like these in the Alps, short lengths, steep gradients, and fast, dendritic drainage systems preclude the physical conditions for high-energy, kinetic water flows. Gorner, though, is not like other temperate glaciers.

"Here, the glacier is flowing flat over the top of a large [subglacial] lake," Giovanni elaborates, gesturing out over the broad ivory plain, "and this may explain why Gorner is so hyperkarstic. . . . The flattest area is also the most hyperkarstic because the water channels into big rivers and 'digs' instead of flowing as surface runoff."

Drawing on comparative data from similarly hyperkarstic glaciers around the world, Giovanni suspects that glacial karst formation is also governed by temperature. With average ice temperatures below zero (the global average is three to five Celsius degrees below zero), polar glaciers in Antarctica and the Arctic suppress karst formation by freezing meltwater on contact and limiting overall drainage. Glaciers with mean ice temperatures above zero are in a constant state of ablation and cannot support stable conduit structures in the first place. Not surprisingly, Gorner's average endoglacial temperature, almost zero, is as conducive to glacial karst development as its topography.

"Gorner is the ideal place for glacial caves," Giovanni tells me as we finally arrive at G8. "It is the best site for us to generate baseline models on glacial cave formation and refine the techniques and modalities of exploration and diving inside the water table itself. . . . You see, the gold really *is* in Switzerland."

Fighting the altitude and exhaustion, we drop our packs 20 feet back from the edge of the moulin on a flat, snowy plateau and begin rigging the shaft immediately. The sun is now directly overhead, burning through a dome of crystal blue sky as if through a magnifying glass. Up from the indigo darkness at the bottom of the moulin comes a deep, bestial roar.

Giovanni surveys the surface of the shaft intently, like a fisherman scrutinizing the sky for signs of incoming weather. He looks for distinct features in the ice below that might indicate how fast meltwater may be rising and for unstable structures dangling from the walls below. To the left of the waterfall, Loco prepares the anchor for the primary descent rope with an assortment of slings, carabiners, and ice screws, choosing

Antonino De Vivo, La Venta cofounder, rigs a waterfall on the Tyndall glacier in Chile.

the clearest line to the bottom of the shaft, which is over 24 stories below us. Pasquale assembles a small backpack with a waterproof notebook and pencil, a 40-meter measuring tape, a surveying compass, eye screws, and stainless steel tensioning wire for measuring relative rates of ice wall collapse. A few meters away, Tiziano double-checks his dive lights and scuba regulators. For the first time since I arrived on Gorner, there is no banter. Despite a bright, salubrious sun overhead, everyone is intently concerned with what's happening underneath us.

When the anchor is finally ready, Loco throws the rope into the hole and descends into the shaft. With little fanfare or concern, the others quickly follow. As the last to drop, I am left alone at the top to contemplate how serious the stakes have just become—that from here forward, simple decisions about where to place my boots and how to shift my weight could cost me my life. Glacial caving, as it turns out, is advanced almost entirely by leaps of faith: faith in one's equipment; faith in one's strength and technical skills; and most of all, faith in one's ability to accurately predict the behavior of ice and stress. Unfortunately, I have faith in none of these. What I do have is some basic common sense about death and heights. The further up you are on the rope, the further you will have to fall.

Low-tech tool, high-profile results. By pulling a compression wire tight between the gallery walls at the bottom of G8, Giovanni can quantify relative rates of passage collapse by measuring how much the wire slackens over time.

As I take my first tenuous steps over the edge of the waterfall, I sit back firmly in my harness and test the rope. To my left and right, the glacier twists into a mantel of looming translucent gargoyles and long, icy prongs. Over 80 meters below, the last rays of sunshine scatter onto hanging chandeliers of water and light. It is here, dangling above the roaring darkness below, that one begins to ponder essential questions about gravity itself. How fast can a human being actually fall? What does terminal velocity really feel like? Questions about the sanity of betting one's life on single pieces of manmade equipment come next. Is that a scratch on my rappel device, or a hairline stress fracture about to break? Compounding these technical doubts are sub-zero temperatures, frozen ropes, rushing torrents, increasing darkness, and deafening waterfalls.

"Just trust the rope and drop," Giovanni yells from below. "Caving is not like climbing; you must trust your equipment to support you." Finally, I release the cam on my rappel device and hit the sweet spot "going down."

At the bottom of the shaft, G8 collapses into a chain of downstepping rooms carved by three small waterfalls. Above us, the ice canyon walls twist up in perfect symmetry, like the tight-sheeted sails of a tall ship. Their surfaces are smooth and milky, holding the last breaths of daylight in a soft full moon glow. Embedded deep inside the ice are millions of tiny air bubbles. Each is a microscopic world unto itself, a sample of what atmospheric conditions were like decades ago, when the ice here was at the surface. At the bottom of the cave, meltwater flows swiftly over deformations in the conduit floor like liquid crystal.

By the time I detach from the descent line and clip into the first anchor, the rest of the team is already at work. In the second room, Giovanni has stretched a compression wire finger-tight between the walls and is busy jotting down the initial numbers. Assuming we are able to reenter the moulin over the next three days, we will be able to determine the rate at which the walls are collapsing by the amount the wire has sagged. Down in the third room, Pasquale and Loco are finishing their initial survey measurements and preparing the next set of ice anchors.

Beyond the last waterfall, the cave compresses into a narrow, hourglass crack barely a meter wide. At the bottom, the river accelerates between a series of leg-snapping folds and funnels into a tapering channel. Overhead, the ice walls loom up like skyscrapers of cold, gray glass. Pasquale volunteers to set up the passage by "pressing" his way through the gap to a small ice shelf five meters away. By any measure, the route is highly technical. If the ice splinters beneath Pasquale's boots, he will fall instantly into the freezing water.

"Very rare" is how Giovanni describes the chances of finding phreatic passages like this one inside of Gorner. "This is a world that no one knew existed until just 10 years ago," he says. "Now we know it as new frontier."

Nevertheless, with five fluid movements, Pasquale is halfway into the passage, where he stops to place another anchor. He kicks his crampons into the front wall, unclips a single eight-inch aluminum ice screw from the sling at his hip, and scrutinizes the face in front of him intently for the proper placement point. With over 80 meters of ice overhead, the slightest energy anomaly can trigger catastrophic releases of internal pressure. He finally chooses a spot to his right and begins to chisel warily at the ice for signs of imminent stress. So far, so good, says Giovanni quietly. With the first full turns of the ice screw, however, the wall explodes. Cracks splinter up the ice in a maddening fractal map, and the narrow passage reverberates like the inside of a cold steel drum. Giovanni freezes instantly and scans the passage for signs of extended collapse, but the tremors end as quickly as they began. He then turns to me and smiles.

"In places like Pakistan," he says, "this happens every day. You hear every kind of noise from every kind of stress, but you just get used to it. Nothing moves at first, but then the caves fill with enormous noise and vibrations, like the earth is bending and about to break. You then realize there is nothing to fear." After two more failed attempts lower down, Pasquale finally gets the ice screw to bite into the wall and take hold. With the full support of the rope, the entire team traverses the canyon in minutes.

Beyond the ice shelf, the cave tapers into a narrow tunnel approximately 20 meters long and a meter in diameter. Along the bottom, the meltwater gathers into slushy pools. On the walls, the ice warps into scalloped waves, briefly giving negative shape to the roaring torrent that created them. I put my hand to the cold surface, absorbing the deep, blue density of the ice itself. It's impossible not to feel the weight of the glacier above us, impossible to ignore the fact that we are being crushed.

"To find a phreatic tunnel like this is very rare in Gorner," Giovanni interrupts, stroking the curves of ice with loving delicacy. "It [represents] only maybe 5 percent of the karst here. Where the specific feature exists elsewhere in the glacier it is almost always submerged in meltwater and completely impenetrable." Giving the discovery its due importance, Giovanni takes detailed notes on the passage's dimensions and characteristics and sets up a series of illustrative photographs for presentations and journal articles before moving on.

"In the beginning," he jokes, waving his camera imperiously as he finishes, "they thought we were just jokers—just a bunch of cavers. Now, what will they think of this?"

Giovanni looks at his watch. We've been in the cave for almost two hours now, and time is getting tight. Meltwater velocities could peak at any time. Giovanni warns everyone to keep an eye out for signs of water table rise, like overflowing pools and "breathing" shafts. Darkness also will fall within the hour. Should we emerge from the cave into an unexpected snow squall, we'd have no choice but to bivouac for the night on the open ice. But given the discoveries thus far, the team is unanimously in favor of pressing on. Phreatic passage is formed as a direct result of full-submersion water flow. If Giovanni's reckoning proves correct, the permanent water table cannot be much farther away.

Following Pasquale's lead once again, we squirm on our hands and knees through the tunnel and emerge onto the lip of a wide cylindrical shaft. Somewhere in the darkness far below, the stream empties into a large pool of standing water, filling the gallery with the brittle echoes of shattering glass. By the time I arrive, Pasquale has already dropped over the edge to rig the wall. From below, his spotlight backlights the gallery into chambers of a great white heart. Giovanni looks at me brightly.

"This is it;" he says, "this is the water table. Now we will see if it is possible to dive." He loosens his grip on the rope, kicks back into the darkness, and turns his headlight on the water.

The news from the bottom of the shaft is not good, however. The water is 30 meters higher than it was just last week, and up 50 meters from its level two weeks ago. According to Pasquale, the chamber is also breathing. As Giovanni motions for silence, we hear a series of small gaseous eruptions rising up from the shaft. Using the fixed descent rope as a reference, it is clear that the water table is rising a few centimeters with each release.

"This is where we will find the proof of water storage," Giovanni says. "This is probably where the water table begins and connects to the rest of the passage system. . . . This is where we will need to dive."

Giovanni then pauses thoughtfully, calculating the risks of an immediate penetration with programmatic efficiency. As on so many other expeditions before this one, we have come to the crossroads of exploration. In one direction lies success and heroism; in the other lies the crowded gallery of jealousy and defeat. Yet, it is at precisely this point that life itself can rest on a single decision. Finally, Giovanni shakes his head. With today's coming melt, the water table will continue to rise another 10 meters over the next 24 hours. To mount the exploration dive now would put everyone's life in jeopardy. We all agree it is better to get out safely with the data we already have.

Back on the edge of the shaft, Giovanni sits back on his boots, disheartened but inspired. Although diving has proven impossible this year, he has identified where the water table begins, and has come one step closer to Gorner's heart. He has also pushed further into a moulin here than ever before. This alone is a reward he would be willing to die for.

"Now you know what our research is all about," Giovanni says sanguinely, "not just to see what no one else has seen or to do what no one else has done, but to understand why. How can we see such amazing things and know that they are important—that the forms and phenomena are part of the glacier—and not ask why? What is most important is not to succeed, but to pose the question in the first place."

Back outside in the lingering twilight, no words are exchanged among us, though I yearn to scream out loud—not just because of what I've seen and done, but because I've descended over 100 meters into a glacier and come back alive. Instead, we all agree with silent smiles that to put your hide on the line and pull it back at the last yawning moment is without doubt one of life's most electrifying rushes.

"You see," Giovanni says finally, "we are surrounded by mystery and unknowns, and we just don't know it." He then pauses and bows graciously toward the moulin.

"The bottom of the cave does not exist," he adds. "The bottom of the cave is you."

SOURCES

INTRODUCTION AND PART OPENERS

ARTICLES

Fisher, Ron: "Lewis and Clark," *National Geographic,* vol. 194, no. 4, October 1998.

"The Great Minds of the Century: Scientists and Thinkers," *Time,* vol. 153, no. 12, March 29, 1999.

Greenfield, Karl Taro: "Life on the Edge," *Time,* vol. 154, no. 10, September 6, 1999.

Junger, Sebastian: "The Lure of Danger," *Men's Journal,* vol. 7, no. 3, April 1998.

Marden, Luis: "Master of the Deep," *National Geographic,* vol. 193, no. 2, February 1998.

Parfit, Michael: "The Essential Element of Fire," *National Geographic,* vol. 190, no. 3, September 1996.

Webster, Dovovan: "Walking a Wildlife Highway from Yellowstone to the Yukon," *Smithsonian,* vol. 30. no. 8, November 1999.

"The Year in Science—1997," *Discover,* vol. 18, no. 1, January 1998.

"The Year in Science—1998," *Discover,* vol. 20, no. 1, January 1999.

BOOKS

Adams, Douglas, and Mark Carwardine: *Last Chance to See,* Ballantine Books, New York, 1990.

Cunningham, William P., and Barbara Woodworth Saigo, *Environmental Science: A Global Concern,* Wm. C. Brown, Dubuque, Iowa, 1990.

Elsom, Derek: *Earth: The Making, Shaping, and Workings of a Planet,* Macmillan, New York, 1992.

The Houghton Mifflin Dictionary of Geography, Houghton Mifflin, Boston, 1997.

The National Geographic Desk Reference, National Geographic Society, Washington, D.C., 1999.

Scientific American Science Desk Reference, John Wiley, New York, 1999.

Thurman, Harold V.: *Introductory Oceanography,* Merrill Publishing Company, Columbus, Ohio, 1988.

Wilson, Edward O.: *Consilience: The Unity of Knowledge,* Alfred A. Knopf, New York, 1998.

THE COMEBACK KING

ARTICLES

Alexander, Brian: "People of the Amazon Fight to Save the Flooded Forest," *Science,* vol. 265, no. 5172, July 29, 1994.

Brazaitis, Peter, Myrna F. Watanabe, and George Amato: "The Caiman Trade," *Scientific American,* March 1998.

"Community Involvement in Wetland Management: Lessons from the Field," in Gordon Claridge and Bernard O'Callaghan (eds.), *Proceedings of Workshop 3: Wetlands, Local People and Development, International Conference on Wetlands and Development,* Wetlands International, Kuala Lumpur, 1997.

da Silveira, Ronis, and John B. Thorbjarnarson: "Conservation Implications of Commercial Hunting of Black and Spectacled Caiman in the Mamiraua Sustainable Development Reserve, Brazil," *Biological Conservation,* vol. 88, 1999.

da Silveira, Ronis, William Ernest Magnusson, and Zilca Campos: "Monitoring the Distribution, Abundance, and Breeding Areas of *Caiman crocodilus crocodilus* and *Melanosuchus niger* in the Anavilhanas Archipelago, Central Amazonia, Brazil," *Journal of Herpetology,* vol. 31, no. 4, 1997.

da Silveira, Ronis, and John Thorbjarnarson: "Nesting Biology of Caiman in the Mamiraua Reserve," *Progress Report to the European Union,* January 1997.

Deeming, Charles, and Mark Ferguson: "In the Heat of the Nest," *New Scientist,* vol. 121, no. 1657, March 25, 1989.

Eveleigh, Robin: "Brazil's Mega-Reserve for the Millennium," *Geographical Magazine,* vol. 71, no. 4, April 1999.

Frey, Eberhard, Jurgen Riess, and Samuel F. Tarsitano: "The Evolution of the *Crocodilia:* A Conflict Between Morphological and Biochemical Data," *American Zoologist,* vol. 29, no. 3, Fall 1989.

Gans, Carl: "Crocodilians in Perspective," *American Zoologist,* vol. 29, no. 3, Fall 1989.

Gower, David J., and Erich Weber: "The Braincase of *Euparkeria,* and the Evolutionary Relationships of Birds and Crocodilians," *Biological Reviews of the Cambridge Philosophical Society,* November 1998.

Hamilton, Roger: "Man and Nature in a Flooded Forest," *IDBAMERICA,* July–August 1998.

Kotsilibas-Davis, James: "A Monster from the Briny Deep?" *Science Digest,* vol. 94, March 1986.

Sociedade Civil Mamiraua: "Sustainable Wildlife Utilization: Potential for the Subsistence and Commercial Utilization of Reptiles in the Brazilian Varzea," *Progress Report to the European Union,* August 1996.

Thorbjarnarson, John: "Crocodile Tears and Skins: International Trade, Economic Constraints, and Limits to the Sustainable Use of Crocodilians," *Conservation Biology,* vol. 13, no. 3, June 1999.

Thorbjarnarson, John: "The Hunt for Black Caiman," *International Wildlife,* July–August 1999.

Thorbjarnarson, John: "Inside Mamiraua's Flooded Forests," *Americas* (English ed.), vol. 49, no. 1, February 1997.

BOOKS

Crocodiles and Alligators, Putney, London: Merehurst Press, 1989.

THIS IS YOUR BRAIN . . . THIS IS YOUR BRAIN ON SULFUR

ARTICLES

Chandler, David L.: "Cave Dwellers," *Boston Globe* (city ed.), August 24, 1998.

Herberman, Ethan: "Cave of Goo!" *Current Science,* vol. 84, no. 5, November 6, 1998.

Hose, Louise D.: "Cave of the Sulfur Eaters," *Natural History,* vol. 108, no. 3, April 1999.

Hose, Louise D.: "Impact of Microbial Processes on Karst Development; A Modern Example in Southern Mexico," *Geological Society of America,* vol. 30, no. 7, 1998.

Hose, Louise D.: "Reconnaissance Investigations of an Active Sulfur Spring Cave, Cueva de Villa Luz," *Final Flag Report,* The Explorers Club, New York, 1998.

Hose, Louise D., and James A. Pisarowicz: "Cueva de Villa Luz, Tabasco, Mexico: Reconnaissance Study of an Active Sulfur Spring Cave and Ecosystem," *Journal of Cave and Karst Studies,* vol. 61, no. 1, April 1999.

Hose, Louise D., and James A. Pisarowicz: "Exploration and Mapping of Cueva de Villa Luz," *Journal of Cave and Karst Studies,* vol. 59, no. 3, 1997.

Hose, Louise D., and James A. Pisarowicz: "Geologic Setting of Cueva de Villa Luz: A Reconnaissance Study of an Active Sulfur Spring Cave," *Journal of Cave and Karst Studies,* vol. 59, no. 3. 1997.

"Living Walls," *Earth,* vol. 7, no. 3. June 1998.

Moore, George W.: "Creatures from the Black Lagoon," *Nature,* vol. 369, no. 6476, May 12, 1994.

Pain, Stephanie: "Acidhouse," *New Scientist,* vol. 158, no. 2137, June 6, 1998.

Palmer, Arthur N., and Margaret V. Palmer: "Geochemistry of Cueva de Villa Luz, Mexico," *National Speleological Society,* 1998 Annual Convention. 1998.

Pisarowicz, James A.: "Cueva de Villa Luz; An Active Case of H2S Speleogenesis," *Karst Waters Institute,* special publication no. 1, 1994.

Rivera, Rachel: "Snot-tites!" *Science World,* vol. 55, no. 1, September 7, 1998.

Taylor, Michael Ray: "A Trip to the Lighted House," *NSS News,* February 1997.

Wexler, Devra A.: "A Living Cave," *Geotimes,* vol. 43, no. 4, April 1998.

ARE YOU MY MOTHER?

ARTICLES

Anderson, Stanley H., and John R. Squires: "Changes in Trumpeter Swan (*Cygnus buccinator*) Activities from Winter to Spring in the Greater Yellowstone Area," *The American Midland Naturalist,* vol. 138, no. 1, July 1997.

Balcomb, Janissa R., Alan Burr, Donna C. Compton, James G. King, Madeleine H. Linck, and Harvey K. Nelson: "Trumpeter Swans—An Asset or a Liability?" *Proceedings and Papers of the Fourteenth Trumpeter Swan Society Conference,* The Trumpeter Swan Society, September 1994.

Baskin, Yvonne: "Trumpeter Swans Relearn Migration," *Bio-Science,* vol. 43, no. 2, February 1993.

Bliven, Naomi: "Aristocrats," *The New Yorker,* vol. 65, no. 45, December 25, 1989.

Burr, Alan, Donna C. Compton, Madeleine H. Linck, and Ruth Shea: "A Vision for the 21st Century," *Proceedings and Papers of the 15th Trumpeter Swan Society,* The Trumpeter Swan Society, August 1996.

Cooper, James A., Todd A. Grant, and Paul Henson: "Feeding Ecology of Trumpeter Swans Breeding in South-Central Alaska," *The Journal of Wildlife Management,* vol. 58, no. 4, October 1994.

Donahue, Bill: "A Sweeter Home for Swans," *Wildlife Conservation,* vol. 96, no. 3, May–June 1993.

Ross, Drew: "Gaining Ground: A Swan's Song," *National Parks,* vol. 72, nos. 3–4, March–April 1998.

Elliott, Laura: "Teaching Birds to Fly," *The Washingtonian.* October 1996.

Gillette, Laurence N., Timothy M. Dyhr, and Judy Dale: *A Guideline for Propagation of Captive Trumpeter Swans,* The Trumpeter Swan Society, March 1977.

Mills, Judy: "The Swan That Would Not Fly," *National Wildlife,* vol. 29, no. 6, October–November 1991.

Mitchell, Carl D.: "Trumpeter Swan (*Cygnus buccinator*)," *The Birds of North America,* no. 105, A. Poole and F. Gill (eds.), The Academy of Natural Sciences, Philadelphia, 1994.

Slayden, William J.: "Atlantic Population of Trumpeter Swans: Finding Their Way Home," *Waterfowl 2000,* vol. 11, no. 1, April 1998.

Smith, Dwight G.: "Come Blow Your Horn," *World and I,* vol. 14, no. 2, February 1999.

U.S. Dept. of Agriculture, Forest Service, Intermountain Region, "Trumpeter Swans: A Closer Look," leaflet no. 26.32.400, 1994.

SITTING ON TOP OF THE WORLD

ARTICLES

Bronaugh, Whit: "The Monarchy," *American Forests,* vol. 104, no. 1, Spring 1998.

Cockburn, Alexander: "The Headwaters Deal," *The Nation,* vol. 268, no. 11, March 22, 1999.

Cole, D. W., D. F. Jacobs, and J. R. McBride: "Fire History and Perpetuation of Natural Coast Redwood Ecosystems," *Journal of Forestry,* vol. 83, no. 8, August 1985.

Dawson, T. E.: "Fog in the California Redwood Forest: Ecosystem Inputs and Use by Plants," *Oecologia,* vol. 117, no. 4, 1998.

Komp, Ellen: "Image vs. Reality," *E,* vol. 10, no. 2, March 1999.

Langenheim, J. H., and J. L. Rollinger: "Geographic Survey of Fungal Endophyte Community Composition in Leaves of Coastal Redwood," *Mycologia,* vol. 85, no. 2, March–April 1993.

Lenihan, J. M.: "Forest Associations of Little Lost Man Creek, Humboldt County, California: Reference-Level in the Hierarchical Structure of Old-Growth Coastal Redwood Vegetation," *American Journal of Botany,* vol. 37, no. 2, April–June 1990.

"News from the World of Trees," *American Forests,* vol. 105, no. 3, Autumn 1999.

Ornduff, R.: "The *Sequoia sempervirens* (Coast Redwood) Forest of the Pacific Coast, USA," *Biological Resources Management Series,* Oxford University Press, New York, 1998.

Sillett, Stephen C.: "Canopy Epiphyte Studies in the Central Oregon Cascades: Implications for the Management of Douglas Fir Forests (*Lobaria oregana, Pseudocyphellaria rainierensis, Sphaerophorus globus*)," Ph.D. thesis, Oregon State University, 1995.

Sillett, Stephen C.: "Tree Crown Structure and Vascular Epiphyte Distribution in *Sequoia sempervirens* Rain Forest Canopies," *Selbyana,* vol. 20, no. 1, 1999.

Snyder, James Arthur: "The Ecology of *Sequoia sempervirens*: An Addendum to 'On the Edge: Nature's Last Stand for Coast Redwoods,' " master's thesis, San Jose State University, 1992.

BOOKS

Brown, Joseph E.: *Monarchs of the Mist,* Coastal Parks Association, Point Reyes, California, 1982.

Eifert, Larry: *The Distinctive Qualities of Redwoods,* Larry Eifert and FJN Corporation, Redcrest, California, 1991.

Jepson, Willis Linn: *Trees, Shrubs, and Flowers of the Redwood Region,* Save-the-Redwoods League, San Francisco, 1984.

Lowman, M. D., and N. M. Nadkarni: *Forest Canopies,* Academic Press, New York, 1995.

Lyons, Kathleen, and Mary Beth Cooney-Lazaneo: *Plants of the Coast Redwood Region,* The Looking Press, Boulder Creek, California, 1988.

Moffett, Mark W.: *The High Frontier,* Harvard University Press, Cambridge, Massachusetts, 1993.

Rasp, Richard A.: *Redwood: The Story Behind the Scenery,* KC Publications, Las Vegas, 1996.

Spring, Ira, Robert Spring, and Harvey Manning: *Redwood National Park and Jedidiah Smith Redwoods State Park, Del Norte Coast Redwoods State Park, Prairie Creek Redwoods State Park,* Superior Publishing Co., Seattle, 1975.

BRIDGE OVER TROUBLED WATERS

ARTICLES

Banasch, U., and G. L. Holroyd: "The Reintroduction of the Peregrine Falcon (*Falco peregrinus*) into Southern Canada," *Canadian Field Naturalist,* vol. 104, no. 2, April–June 1990.

Bell, D. A., and J. T. Wootton: "A Metapopulation Model of the Peregrine Falcon in California," *Ecological Applications,* vol. 2, no. 3, August 1992.

"Bird Man," *The New Yorker,* vol. 69, no. 16, June 7, 1993.

Bradley, Robin Johnstone, Gordon Court, and Tom Duncan: "Influence of Weather on Breeding Success of Peregrine Falcons in the Arctic," *The Auk,* vol. 114, no. 4, October 1997.

Burnham, William A.: "Peregrine Falcon Egg Variation, Incubation, and Population Recovery," Ph.D. thesis, Colorado State University, 1984.

Chavez-Ramirez, Felipe, Alan Tennant, and George P. Vose: "Spring and Fall Migration of Peregrine Falcons from Padre Island, Texas," *Wilson Bulletin,* vol. 106, no. 1, March 1994.

Clum, N. J.: "Effects of Aging and Mate Retention on Reproductive Success of Captive Female Peregrine Falcons," *American Zoologist,* vol. 35, no. 4, September 1995.

Henny, Charles J., and William S. Seegar: "DDE Decreases in Plasma of Spring Migrant Peregrine Falcons 1978–1994," *The Journal of Wildlife Management,* vol. 60, no. 2, April 1996.

Lavendel, Brian: "Too Soon for Peregrine Delisting?" *Wildlife Conservation,* vol. 102, no. 2, March–April 1999.

Line, Les: "Symbol of Hope?" *National Wildlife,* vol. 34, no. 6, October–November 1996.

Millsap, B. A., P. L. Kennedy, M. A. Byrd, G. Court, J. H. Enderson, and R. N. Rosenfield: "Review of the Proposal to Delist the American Peregrine Falcon," *Wildlife Society Bulletin,* vol. 26, no. 3, Fall 1998.

Moser, Don: "One More Chance at Survival for the Cloud Runners," *Smithsonian,* vol. 21, no. 1, April 1990.

Rowell, Galen: "Falcon Rescue," *National Geographic,* vol. 179, no. 4, April 1991.

Sherrod, Steve K.: "Behavior of Young Peregrine Falcons After Leaving the Nest," Ph.D. thesis, Cornell University, 1982.

Stap, Don: "Returning the Natives," *Audubon,* vol. 98, no. 54, November–December 1996.

Wexler, Mark: "A Case of Urban Renewal," *National Wildlife,* vol. 27, no. 4, June–July 1989.

White, Clayton M.: "Biosystematics of the North American Peregrine Falcons," Ph.D. thesis, University of Utah, 1968.

BOOKS

Cade, Tom J., James H. Enderson, and Janet Linthicum (eds.): *Guide to Management of Peregrine Falcons at the Eyrie,* The Peregrine Fund, Boise, Idaho, 1996.

Linthicum, Janet and Brian James Walton (eds.): *Peregrine Falcon Monitoring, Nest Management, Hack Site, and Cross-Fostering Efforts, 1992,* Santa Cruz Predatory Bird Group, Santa Cruz, California, 1992.

TOO HOT TO HANDLE

ARTICLES

Abrams, Michael, Jose Luis Macias, Johannes Obenholzner, and Claus Siebe: "Repeated Volcanic Disasters in Prehispanic Time and Popocatépetl, Central Mexico: Past Key to the Future?" *Geology,* vol. 24, no. 5, May 1996.

Calvin, Edward Masterton: "Geology, Petrology, and Geochemistry of the Southwestern Part of Pico de Orizaba, Mexico," master's thesis, University of New Mexico, 1989.

Cantagre, Jean Marie, and Armann Hoskuldsson: "Volcanic Hazards in the Surroundings of Pico de Orizaba, Eastern Mexico," *Natural Hazards,* vol. 10, no. 3, 1994.

Carrasco-Nunez, Gerardo, and William I. Rose: "Eruption of a Major Holocene Pyroclastic Flow at Citlaltépetl Volcano

(Pico de Orizaba), Mexico, 8.5–9.0 ka," *Journal of Volcanology and Geothermal Research,* vol. 69, nos. 3–4, 1995.

Carrasco-Nunez, Gerardo: "Structure, Eruptive History, and Some Major Hazardous Events of Citlaltépetl Volcano (Pico de Orizaba), Mexico," Ph.D. thesis, Michigan Technological University, 1993.

Carrasco-Nunez, Gerardo, William I. Rose, and James W. Vallance: "A Voluminous Avalanche-Induced Lahar from Citlaltépetl Volcano, Mexico: Implications for Hazard Assessment," *Journal of Volcanology and Geothermal Research,* vol. 59, nos. 1–2, 1993.

Conger, Lucy: "The Smoking Mountain Stirs," *U.S. News & World Report,* vol. 125, no. 10, September 14, 1998.

Crausaz, Winston: "A History of Geological Exploration in the Pico de Orizaba Region, Mexico," *The Geological Society of America 99th Annual Meeting,* vol. 18, no. 6, 1986.

De la Cruz-Reyna, Servando, and Claus Siebe: "The Giant Popocatépetl Stirs," *Nature,* vol. 388, no. 6639, July 17, 1997.

Goff, Fraser, Cathy J. Janik, Hugo Delgado, Cindy Werner, Dale Counce, James A. Stimac, Claus Siebe, S. P. Love, Stanley N. Williams, Tobias Fischer, and L. Johnson: "Geochemical Surveillance of Magmatic Volatiles at Popocatépetl Volcano, Mexico," *The Geological Society of America Bulletin,* vol. 110, no. 6, June 1998.

Granados, Hugo Delgado: "Los Peligros Volcanicos," *Correo del Maestro,* no. 28, September 1998.

Granados, Hugo Delgado: "Tectonica de Placas Tipos de Volcanes y Erupciones," *Correo del Maestro,* no. 27, August 1998.

Hoskuldsson, Armann, and Claude Robin: "Late Pleistocene to Holocene Eruptive Activity of Pico de Orizaba, Eastern Mexico," *Bulletin of Volcanology,* vol. 55, no. 8, 1993.

Joyce, Christopher: "Volcano Prediction Was Bang On," *New Scientist,* vol. 130, no. 1767, May 4, 1991.

Kerr, Richard A.: "Dancing with Death at Unzen Volcano," *Science,* vol. 253, no. 5017, July 19, 1991.

Love, S. P., F. Goff, D. Counce, C. Siebe, and H. Delgado: "Passive Infrared Spectroscopy of the Eruption Plume at Popocatépetl Volcano, Mexico," *Nature,* December 10, 1998.

McDowell, Bart: "Waiting for Popo . . . to Blow," *Insight on the News,* vol. 14, no. 36, September 28, 1998.

Monastersky, R.: "Nature Fouls Mexico City's Clean-Air Effort," *Science News,* vol. 155, no. 16, April 17, 1999.

Monastersky, Richard: "Volcano Dumps Ash on Mexico City," *Science News,* vol. 152, no. 4, July 26, 1997.

Plunket, Patricia, and Gabriela Urunuela: "Appeasing the Volcano Gods," *Archaeology,* vol. 51, no. 4, July–August 1998.

"A Volcano on the Verge of Collapse," *New Scientist,* vol. 117, no. 1603, March 10, 1988.

Williams, A. R., and Sarah Leen: "Popocatépetl: Mexico's Smoking Mountain," *National Geographic,* vol. 195, no. 1, January 1999.

BOOKS

Graydon, Don, and Kurt Hanson (eds.): *Mountaineering: The Freedom of the Hills,* The Mountaineers, Seattle, 1997.

Instituto de Geografia: *Volcanes de Mexico; Esperanza Yarza de De la Torre,* Universidad Nacional Autonoma de Mexico, Mexico City, 1992.

Lorenzo, Jose L.: *The Glaciers of Mexico,* Mexico City, 1958.

Newson, Lesley: *The Atlas of the World's Worst Natural Disasters,* Dorling Kindersley Limited, London, 1998.

Secor, R. J.: *Mexico's Volcanoes: A Climbing Guide,* The Mountaineers, Seattle, 1993.

ONE SMALL STEP FOR INNER SPACE

ARTICLES

am-Ende, Barbara Anne, William C. Stone, and Fred L. Wefer: "Automatic Underwater Surveying and Mapping," in Debbie Johnson (ed.), *National Speleological Society 1998 Annual Convention,* 1998.

am-Ende, Barbara Anne, William C. Stone, and Fred L. Wefer: "The Wakulla-2 Expedition," in Debbie Johnson (ed.), *National Speleological Society 1998 Annual Convention,* 1998.

Bullen, Thomas D., Tyler B. Coplen, J. Hal Davis, and Brian G. Katz: "Use of Chemical and Isotopic Tracers to Characterize the Interactions Between Ground Water and Surface Water in Mantled Karst," *Ground Water,* vol. 35, no. 6, 1997.

Cardozo, Yvette: "Diving the Bottomless Pit: The Small, Closed World of the Cave Diver," *Oceans,* vol. 17, March–April 1984.

Deloach, Ned, and Sheck Exley: "The World's Longest Underwater Cave," in *Proceedings of the Eighth International Con-*

gress of Speleology, *Journal of Spelean History,* vol. 15, nos. 3–4, 1981.

Jablonski, Jarrod: "Threat to Wakulla Averted," *Underwater Speleology,* vol. 22, no. 4, July–August 1995.

Kincaid, Dr. Todd R.: "Hydrology of Wakulla Cave," in "Morphologic and Fractal Characterizations of Saturated Karstic Caves," Ph.D. thesis, University of Wyoming. 1999.

Kincaid, Dr. Todd R.: "Three Dimensional Geometric Modeling and Visualization of Phreatic Karst Caves with Implications for Hydrologic and Geomorphic Studies," a special paper prepared for the Woodville Karst Plain Project and Global Underwater Explorers, 1998.

Lenihan, Daniel J.: "Raptures of the Deep," *Natural History,* vol. 105, no. 11, November 1996.

Martin, Dr. Harris: "Interpretation of Water Chemistry Data from Florida Underwater Cave for Determination of Possible Groundwater Pollution," a special report prepared for the Woodville Karst Plain Project, 1997.

Norman, Geoffrey: "Battle for the Black Lagoon," *National Geographic Adventure,* vol. 1, no. 2, Summer 1999.

Revels, Tracy Jean: "Watery Eden: A History of Wakulla Springs," Ph.D. thesis, Florida State University, 1990.

Ringle, Ken: "Unlocking the Labyrinth of North Florida Springs," *National Geographic,* vol. 195, no. 3, March 1999.

Rupert, Frank R.: "The Geology of Wakulla Springs," *Florida Geological Survey Open File Report #22,* 1988.

Rupert, Frank R.: "Karst Features of Northern Florida," in Stephen A. Kish (ed.), *Geologic Field Studies of the Coastal Plain in Alabama, Georgia, and Florida,* (Field Conference Guidebook), Southeastern Geological Society, Tallahassee, Florida, vol. 33, 1993.

Rupert, Frank R.: "The Wakulla Springs Mastodon," *Newsletter of the Florida Paleontological Society, Inc.,* vol. 8, no. 2, 1991.

Stone, Bill, and Barbara am Ende: "USDCT Produces First Full 3D Cave Map," *Deep Tech,* no. 13, 1998.

Taylor, Michael Ray: "Deep, Dark, and Deadly," *Sports Illustrated,* vol. 81, no. 14, October 3, 1994.

Werner, Christopher: "Hydrologic Constraints on Conduit Development within the Woodville Karst Plain, Florida," "Development of Preferential Flow Paths in Soluble Porous Media and Conduit System Evolution in Carbonates of the Woodville Karst Plain, Florida," master's thesis, Florida State University, Spring 2000.

Werner, Christopher: "The Hydrology of the Woodville Karst Plain," a special paper prepared for the Woodville Karst Plain Project and Global Underwater Explorers, 1998.

Werner, Christopher: "Overview of Theoretical Cave Development in Carbonates," *Underwater Speleology,* vol. 25, no. 1, January–February 1998.

Wisenbaker, Michael: "Unraveling the Mysteries of the Maze," a special paper prepared for the Woodville Karst Plain Project, 1997.

Wisenbaker, Michael: "The Woodville Karst Plain Project," *Conduit,* vol. 3, no. 2, Winter 1995.

Zuidema, H. P.: "Florida's Amazing Springs," *Earth Science,* vol. 32, no. 1, 1978.

BOOKS

Burgess, Robert F.: *The Cave Divers,* Dodd, Mead and Co., New York, 1976.

Stamm, Doug: *The Springs of Florida,* Pineapple Press, Inc., Sarasota, Florida, 1994.

Stone, Williams C. (ed.): *The Wakulla Springs Project,* The U.S. Deep Cave Diving Team, Gaithersburg, Maryland, 1993.

IT'S ALL FUN AND GAMES UNTIL SOMEBODY GETS MUNCHED

ARTICLES

Armstrong, Sue: "Great White Sharks Defy Hollywood Image," *New Scientist,* vol. 144, no. 1955, December 10, 1994.

Cliff, G., B. Davis, and S. F. J. Dudley: "Sharks Caught in the Protective Gill Nets of Natal, South Africa," *South African Journal of Marine Science,* vol. 8, 1989.

Compagno, Len J. V.: "Government Protection for the Great White Shark (*Carcharodon carcharias*) in South Africa," *South African Journal of Science,* vol. 87, no. 7, 1991.

Cunneff, Tom: "The Great White's Ways," *Sports Illustrated,* vol. 82, no. 19, May 15, 1995.

Ellis, R.: "The Great White Shark," *Underwater Naturalist,* vol. 16, no. 3, 1987.

Ellis, Richard, and John E. McCosker: "What Fate Awaits the Great White Shark?" *Audubon,* vol. 93, no. 5, September–October 1991.

Ferreira, Craig A., and Theo P. Ferreira: "Population Dynamics of White Sharks in South Africa," in Peter Klimley and David G. Ainley (eds.), *Great White Sharks: The Biology of Carcharodon carcharias,* Academic Press, San Diego, 1996.

Hewitt, J. C.: "The Great White Shark in Captivity: A History and Prognosis," *American Association of Zoological Parks and Aquariums (AAZPA) Annual Proceedings,* 1984.

Johnson, Ryan Lloyd: "Effects of the Shark Cage Diving Industry on the Ecology of Dyer Island," master's thesis proposal, University of Pretoria, Pretoria, South Africa, 1999.

Klimley, A. Peter: "The Predatory Behavior of the White Shark," *American Scientist,* vol. 82, no. 2, March–April 1994.

Martin, Glen: "The Great White's Ways," *Discover,* vol. 20, no. 6, June 1999.

McCosker, John E.: "Great White Shark," *Science,* vol. 81, no. 6, 1981.

Morrissey, John F.: "Shark Research at Sea," *Sea Frontiers,* vol. 33, July–August 1987.

Pinnock, Don: "Lords of the Deep," *Getaway,* vol. 10, no. 12, March 1999.

Sadie, Dion: "Growth of the South African Cave Diving Industry," a special report prepared for the University of Stellenbosch, 1999.

Smith, E. D., and G. J. J. Van der Merwe: "Ultrasonic Taxonomic Indicator of the Great White Shark," *South African Journal of Science,* vol. 84, no. 11, 1988.

"Speaking of Sharks . . . Two Experts Consider the Science and Lore of the Great White," *Oceans,* vol. 19, May–June 1986.

Taylor, Valerie: "Great White Shark," *Oceans,* vol. 12, no. 3, 1979.

Tennesen, Michael: "The Myth of the Monster," *National Wildlife,* vol. 27, no. 6, October–November 1989.

BOOKS

Ellis, R., and J. E. McCosker: *Great White Shark,* Harper Collins, in collaboration with Stanford University Press, New York, 1991.

Klimley, A. Peter, and David G. Ainley: *Great White Sharks: The Biology of Carcharodon carcharias,* Academic Press, San Diego, 1996.

South African Sharks Board, *The Great White Shark,* Underwater Special Edition No. 17, Durban, South Africa, 1992.

THE ICE MAN COMETH

ARTICLES

Badino, Giovanni: "L'estrema Thule: Penultimo o Ultimo Limite Della Speleologia?" *Speleologia,* vol. 32, 1995.

Badino, Giovanni: "Fisica dei Buchi Nell'Acqua," in *Proceedings of the First International Symposium of Glacial Caves and Karst in Polar Regions,* Madrid, Spain, 1990.

Badino, Giovanni: "Ice Shaft Genesis: A Simple Numerical Approach," in *Proceedings of the Second International Symposium of Glacial Caves and Karst in Polar Regions,* Silesian University, Sosnowiec, 1992.

Badino, Giovanni: "Phenomenology and First Numerical Simulations of the Phreatic Drainage Network Inside Glaciers," in *Proceedings of the Third International Symposium of Glacial Caves and Karst in Polar Regions,* Chamonix, France, 1994.

Eraso, Adolfo, Giovanni Badino, Marco Mecchia, Carlos J. Galivan, and Tullio Bernabei: "Results of the Main Directions of Subglacial Drainage Prediction Method Applied to Perito Moreno Glacier," in *Proceedings of the Fourth International Symposium of Glacial Caves and Cyrokarst in Polar and High Mountain Regions,* Salzburg, Austria, 1996.

Heacox, Kim: "Ice Phantoms: In the Belly of a Glacier Lies a Vanishing Crystal Palace. But First, You Have to Dare," *Backpacker,* vol. 15, November 1987.

Hooke, Roger L.: "On the Role of Mechanical Energy in Maintaining Subglacial Water Conduits at Atmospheric Pressure," *Journal of Glaciology,* vol. 30, no. 105, 1984.

Iken, Almut, Kristian Fabri, and Martin Funk: "Water Storage and Subglacial Drainage Conditions Inferred from Borehole Measurements on Gornergletscher, Valais, Switzerland," *Journal of Glaciology,* vol. 42, no. 141, 1996.

Lawson, Wendy J., Martin J. Sharp, and Michael J. Hambrey: "The Structural Geology of a Surge-Type Glacier," *Journal of Structural Geology,* vol. 16, no. 10, 1994.

Mavlyudov, Bulat R.: "Glacier Caves Origin," in *Proceedings of the Fourth International Symposium of Glacial Caves and Cyrokarst in Polar and High Mountain Regions,* Salzburg, Austria, 1996.

Mavlyudov, Bulat R.: "Problems of En- and Subglacial Drainage Origin," in *Proceedings of the Third International Symposium of Glacial Caves and Karst in Polar Regions,* Chamonix, France, 1994.

Nye, J. F.: "Water Flow in Glaciers: Jokulhlaups, Tunnels, and Veins," *Journal of Glaciology,* vol. 17, no. 76, 1976.

Rehak, J.: "New Information on the Interior Drainage of Subpolar Glaciers of Southwest Spitsbergen," in *Proceedings of the Third International Symposium of Glacial Caves and Karst in Polar Regions,* Chamonix, France, 1994.

Rothlisberger, Hans: "The Physics of Englacial and Subglacial Meltwater Drainage—Theory and Observations," in *Proceedings of the Fourth International Symposium of Glacial Caves and Cyrokarst in Polar and High Mountain Regions,* Salzburg, Austria, 1996.

Rothlisberger, Hans: "Water Pressure in Intra- and Subglacial Channels," *Journal of Glaciology,* vol. 11, no. 62, 1972.

Schreve, R. L.: "Movement of Water in Glaciers," *Journal of Glaciology,* vol. 11, no. 62, 1972.

Trimmel, Hubert: "Karst and Glaciers—Notes from the Past," in *Proceedings of the Fourth International Symposium of Glacial Caves and Cyrokarst in Polar and High Mountain Regions,* Salzburg, Austria, 1996.

Walder, Joseph S.: "Hydraulics of Subglacial Cavities," *Journal of Glaciology,* vol. 32, no. 112, 1986.

Wegner, Remy: "The Cold Heart of Glaciers," *Geographical Magazine,* vol. 65, no. 8, August 1993.

BOOKS

Graydon, Don, and Kurt Hanson (eds.): *Mountaineering: The Freedom of the Hills,* The Mountaineers, Seattle, 1993.

ABOUT THE AUTHOR

Peter Lane Taylor is a writer, photographer, filmmaker, and explorer based out of Philadelphia and the Adirondacks. Regularly focusing on extreme, "out-of-bounds" subject matter, Peter uses his skills as an offshore sailor, technical climber, caver, mixed gas scuba diver, and triathelete to bring science, nature, and exploration together with the fine arts of photography, filmmaking, and natural history writing. Peter works part of the year on location from his sailboat, *No Paine,* and travels nationally and internationally the rest of the year on editorial and expedition assignments. As the owner of Maximum Exposure Productions, Peter specializes in environmental, expedition, adventure, landscape, wildlife, underwater, travel, and aerial imagery.

In addition to photojournalism and film, Peter has established a proven track record of original conservation initiatives. With two partners in 1994, he co-created and edited the *Otter Creek Journal,* the first magazine of any kind printed this century on totally tree free paper. In 1997, he co-created a pioneering effort to purchase and protect one of the Caribbean's last, virgin private islands located in the Honduran Bay Islands. Since 1999, Peter has served as expedition photographer and American representative for the Italian Exploration Team, La Venta, recipient of the 1993 Rolex Award for Enterprise. He is an active member of the North American Nature Photographers Association, the Society of Environmental Journalists, the Explorers Club, and the Outdoor Writer's Association of America.

Peter's recent articles and images have appeared in *Outside, Cruising World, Islands, Fly Fishing in Saltwaters, Backpacker, Paddler, Sports Afield, Wild Earth, E: the Environmental Magazine, Sail, Southwinds, Sea, Aqua, PhotoMedia,* and *National Geographic Traveler.*

ABOUT THE SCIENTISTS

Giovanni Badino, Ph.D., is a cosmic ray physicist in the Departimento di Fisica Generale at the University of Torino in Italy. He specializes in the thermodynamics of underground fluid transport. He is president of the Italian Speleological Society and a committee member of the Italian National Alpine and Speleological Rescue Service. A caver for over 30 years, Badino has led expeditions to Nepal, Pakistan, Chile, Argentina, Antarctica, and Iceland.

Hugo Delgado Granados, Ph.D., is a volcanologist at the Institute of Geophysics at the National Autonomous University of Mexico (UNAM) in Mexico City. Currently, his primary research charge is to monitor Popocatépetl, the world's tallest active volcano. "Nature has always been my passion and main attraction," he says, "professional and for sport." For over 20 years, he has participated in precedent-setting Mexican mountaineering expeditions all over the world, including attempts at Alaska's Mount McKinley, K2 and Kangchenjunga in the Himalayas, and the Cordillera Blanca in the Peruvian Andes.

Craig Ferreira is a shark specialist living in Cape Town, South Africa. Craig was just eight when he caught his first "white"—with his father, Theo, then the world's most famous great white hunter. These days, his goal is to protect the species from extinction.

Louise Hose, Ph.D., is coordinator and professor of the Environmental Studies Department at Westminster College in Fulton, Missouri. She holds a master's degree from California State University in Los Angeles and a Ph.D. from Louisiana State University. With more than 25 years of experience in caves around the world, Louise estimates she has spent over a year of her life underground.

George Irvine (right) is project director for the Woodville Karst Plain Project. With Jarrod Jablonski, he holds the world record both for the longest cave penetration (18,000 feet) and the longest cave penetration at depth (18,000 feet). He lives in Fort Lauderdale, Florida. **Jarrod Jablonski** (left) is lead diver and hydrogeologist for the Woodville Karst Plain Project, president of Global Under Water Explorers, and CEO of Extreme Exposure. He holds bachelor's degrees in English and geology from the University of Florida at Gainesville and has over 10 years of experience in technical cave diving and graduate level groundwater research.

Brian Latta is a field biologist for the Santa Cruz Predatory Bird Group at the University of California at Santa Cruz, where he has been working hands-on with raptors for nearly 10 years. He holds a bachelor's degree in wildlife biology and is also a master falconer. "If my hip didn't give out," he jokes, "I'd still be rock climbing too." He lives with his wife, Janet, a peregrine named Tomas, and a great horned owl named Tim outside of Santa Cruz, California.

Gavin Shire holds degrees in genetics and zoology from the University of Sheffield in England. He spent two years as lead biologist on a project to rehabilitate the rare Mauritius Kestrel—at that point, the world's rarest bird—and has also banded northern saw whet owls and traveled by motorcycle across Africa. In 1994, he worked as biologist for the Hollywood movie *Fly Away Home,* and is now a licensed ultralight pilot and instructor.

Steve Sillett, Ph.D., is Assistant Professor of Botany at Humboldt State University in Arcata, California. He holds a master's degree in botany from the University of Florida at Gainesville and a Ph.D. from Oregon State University. He is one of the few scientists studying the coast redwood forest canopy, the world's highest biological frontier.

Ronis da Silveira is currently completing his Ph.D. at the Institute Nacional de Pesquisas de Amazonia, where he also received a master's degree in ecology. After living for two years on a floating houseboat in the middle of the Amazon to study the reproductive life cycle of the hemisphere's largest crocodilian, the black caiman, Ronis has finally moved back to Manaus with his wife Barbara and new daughter Bruna. "They want me to be a teacher now," he says.

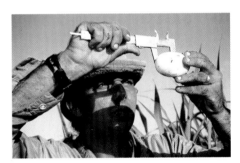